PEACE
IN
OUR
TIME

PEACE
IN
OUR
TIME

Matthew Melko

A PWPA BOOK

PARAGON HOUSE

New York

First edition, 1990

Published in the United States by

Paragon House
90 Fifth Avenue
New York, NY 10011

A Professors World Peace Academy Book

Library of Congress Cataloging-in-Publication Data

Melko, Matthew.
  Peace in our time.
  "A PWPA Book"
  Bibliography: p.
  1. History, Modern—1945–   2. Peace—
History—20th century. I. Title.
D842.M42 1990   909.82   88-32917
ISBN 1-55778-055-2

Manufactured in the United States of America

The paper used in this publication meets the minimum requirements of
American National Standard for Information Sciences—Permanence of Paper
for Printed Library Materials, ANSI Z39.48-1984.

"Things are getting better.
For Everyone.
Nothing disastrous has happened."

—Some of the dying words of
Donald Hope (1927–1969)—

DEDICATION

To my mother, who really cared about what happens to other people
and
To my granddaughter, Gwen, who will be in her seventieth year when the
guarantee runs out.

CONTENTS

ACKNOWLEDGMENTS

To Narasim Katary and Tom Koebernick, who helped socialize the manuscript in its formative years.

To Betty Snow, who put it on the word processor and made the changes as new information kept upsetting the old.

To Gaston Bouthoul, Rene Carrere and Bill Eckhardt, whose data proved to be amazingly rich in supporting, contradicting and elaborating the hypothesis.

To Bill Schwartz, Charles Derber and the Boston Nuclear Group, who proved to be somebody out there who saw things in a similar manner.

To Kenneth Boulding and Francis Beer who read the manuscript and provided so many fruitful suggestions.

To Diane Katz and Jack O'Gorman, who found the sources that supplied the data that made the tables.

To Mary Ridgway and John Ferrera, who transformed my primitive figures into works of art.

To Jill Thobe and Diane Bertke who made all those copies and did all that filing.

And to my wife Nelle, who has learned to live with a view of the world that (she says) contradicts the views of everybody else.

PEACE
IN
OUR
TIME

1

PEACE IN OUR TIME

The phrase has an ironic ring. It comes, of course, from Neville Chamberlain. On his return from Munich in the fall of 1938 he had brought, he said, peace in our time. As it turned out, Britain was at war with Germany within 11 months.

As often happens when one looks these things up, it turns out that this was not quite the phrase Chamberlain used. What he said from the window of Downing Street was: "This is the second time in our history that there has come back from Germany to Downing Street Peace with Honour: I believe it is peace for our time" (Palmer 1977, 39).

The previous time Chamberlain was referring to was when Benjamin Disraeli spoke from the same window in 1878 after the Congress of Berlin. Disraeli said he had brought "peace, I hope, with honor" (Stevenson 1967, 1472). Disraeli said nothing about peace in our time in that speech, but writing to Queen Victoria after the Congress, he did say that the settlement would "probably secure the peace of Europe for a long time. . ." (Bradford 1983, 353). And, except for the Boer War, Britain did have peace until 1914. So in that case "our time" meant a generation.

It would appear then that neither Chamberlain nor Disraeli actually used the often-quoted phrase "peace in our time." The change in preposition may have added a dimension. Perhaps it is less selfish. Perhaps it places us more comfortably inside. However that may be, and whether used ironically or hopefully, that is the phrase most students learned in school, or at least thought they heard.

Even in Disraeli's sense, peace did not mean the "lion and lamb" kind of peace, a peace pervading all mankind and accompanied by love, justice and a number of other positive qualities that resemble some mythic concepts of Heaven. In Disraeli's sense, peace meant the absence of a major, all-consuming war, such as the European world had known in Napoleonic times and was to know again in the World Wars period. It could incorporate a Boer War, serious enough in South Africa, but not itself threatening to world peace or European peace or even African peace.

1

The different areas in which peace occurs cause reflection on the pronoun "our." To whom does this refer? For Disraeli and Chamberlain it meant their own nation, the United Kingdom, and the European world with which it was associated. There would be no European war.

The phrase is resurrected as a title because, in Disraeli's and Chamberlain's sense, there *is* peace in our time. The peace, in this case, has not been brought by a statesman; it already exists and has existed for some time. It is not perfect peace, but it compares favorably with previously peaceful periods in our history. It covers a wider area, and already has lasted longer than Disraeli's peace and promises to last much longer.

The "our" in "our time" refers to the Western world at least, and possibly to much more of the world than that. The Western world would include Europe, North America, Australia and New Zealand. There is a good chance that the peace may also include Russia and East Asia. It is possible that South America may be experiencing a concurrent peace. The peace has not so far embraced Central America, the Middle East, Africa or South Asia, and it does not seem likely that it will in the next few decades.

The "time" involved if modern history is used as a guide, would be 10 to 15 decades, of which we have had four. So the peace would last until 2050, and possibly until 2100.

This book is about this peace: its origins, delineation, characteristics and prospects.

PEACE, IMPERFECT PEACE

The peace that is occurring in our time is limited in three ways. It is finite in time; it will not last forever. It covers a great area of the northern hemisphere, but not the whole world. It is not total, even within the limits of time and space acknowledged. It does not necessarily carry with it other positive qualities such as love, justice, mercy or even well-being. The limitation of definition (peace) will be discussed here, that of space (our) in the next section, and that of duration (time) at the end of this chapter.

Peace, as conceived here, means the absence of physical violence. There is rarely total peace for any substantial area for any great period of time. There may be total peace on the block, but one of the kids across the street may have sustained a bruise or two after being shoved by a playmate. The town is peaceful, but somewhere there has been family abuse and on the football field there will be a rugged practice this afternoon.

For larger areas, peace is relative. The peace that was obtained after World War II was obvious in Europe with the war damage as a backdrop. But there still was domestic assault, in peaceful Sweden rather a lot, and armed robbery and an occasional homicide. In the 1960s there were student and racial rebellions in Europe and America, but the rate of fatalities was much lower than even the very low European homicide rate. Intelligent individuals would disagree on the level of violence that would be acceptable in a period called peaceful. An attempt to quantify the relative peacefulness in the areas considered will be found in chapters two and four.

The definition of peace as an absence of physical violence, when applied and elaborated, has proved to be so controversial, that often discussion is not able to get beyond the definition. It has been called obscene, a definition worthy of the RAND Corporation (Leitenberg 1975). When I have occasion to speak about peace in history, I usually wait for question time to explain how I define peace, because once I answer that one, it is likely that nothing else will be discussed.

What is controversial? Perhaps the most controversial aspect is the idea that peaceful societies may be ruled by governments that are carrying on wars elsewhere. It is perceived as immoral to call England a peaceful society when its soldiers and sailors are out conquering the world. How can we call the United States "peaceful" when its government and soldiers are devastating Vietnam or attacking Grenada or Libya?

This perception, it seems to me, contains two elements. First, that military forces are fighting elsewhere and second, that their cause is dubious, unjust, immoral. If we are just considering fighting elsewhere, the term *pax* has been used to describe both the Roman Empire and nineteenth century Europe. The interior of the Roman Empire was peaceful, though Roman troops were fighting in Dacia or against the Parthians. And during the *Pax Britannica,* Europe was at peace, though Europeans were developing empires in South Asia and Africa. Certainly Europe and the Roman Empire were at least relatively peaceful in these eras, compared to the Napoleonic period or the decades before Actium.

The second perception concerns morality. The British were selfish imperialists. The Americans in Vietnam were brutal bullies. By contrast it would not be so bad to say that peace was preserved in the United States by the boys who died fighting the evil forces of Hitler. Insofar as they fought for their mothers and sisters, they were successful. Those mothers and sisters were not bombed, shot, beaten or raped by invading forces.

During a war, however, it is easier to look forward to peace. After World War II, there would be peace. But would there still be homicide, suicide, violent accidents? Would there be cheating and lying and stealing? Yes, but there would be "Bluebirds over the White Cliffs of Dover." Compared to the period of war, the period in the future would be better, for all its imperfections.

And it is. It is an imperfect peace. Not only does it contain the physical violence of crime in the streets and the even more deadly violence in the home, but it is full of anger and hate, unkindness and disloyalty, mental anguish, psychic and institutional violence. These are all part of peace.

It would appear, then, that there is considerable emotional hostility both to the idea that we live in normal times and to the concept of imperfect peace. It would not be surprising, then, if the suggestion that we live in a normal period of imperfect peace were received with less than unbridled enthusiasm.

It has been suggested that some other term be substituted for peace. One could refer to the present "remission of violence," recognizing that violence is normal but that for the time being it has subsided. Recently there has been increasing use of the term "negative peace" to describe the mere absence of physical violence. It is perceived that peace should be a positive term, not just an absence of something.

The study of war, however, does not labor under such restrictions. There are thousands of studies of wars without the slightest requirement that these wars be restricted to those that are evil, hate filled, unjust, psychotic or malevolent. It is possible to study just wars: wars in which military leaders ardently desired peace, wars fought under gentlemanly rules, wars fought abroad even though there was no war at home.

Let us take the same liberty for peace, understanding that there is never perfect peace any more than there is war that is literally total (though a major nuclear war may come close), that some periods of peace are preferable to others just as one might prefer to live in certain periods of war rather than others, that war and peace may be seen to be on a continuum and not all of us would agree on the point on this line at which one would say: here we are no longer at war and peace has begun.

So let us settle for imperfect peace. We perceive Victorian Europe as relatively peaceful, though it may have been interrupted now and again by a war of legitimacy or a six-week Franco-Prussian War that inflicted a considerable number of fatalities. But in the Europe of that time, as in the Europe of today, most people were not worried about invading forces coming their way, not expecting to spend the evening in the cellar fearing a bomb's direct hit. They had plenty of other problems, they may not have been happy or felt safe, but the prospect of political and social violence did not seem imminent.

Imperfection is essential in our world. It challenges us to do better. Our love is imperfect, and we try to become more loving. Peace, like love, exists; and, like love, it is imperfect.

PEACE FOR WHOM?

The word peace, as Richard Coudenhove-Kalergi (1959) has pointed out, is presented in the singular in most languages. It is, he says, perceived as the firmament in which the stars of war occasionally flare.

But why must peace be limitless? Why can there not be peace for a limited space and time? If Europe can have a Hundred Years' War, why cannot Europe have a hundred years' peace? And that, of course, is approximately what the *Pax Britannica* was.

So, if peace can be imperfect, it can also be limited. There can be a plurality of peaces.

The present peace, the peace of our time, is not perceived to be limitless. It seems more likely to prevail in some places than others. It may seem self-serving to see the prospects of peace as more likely to continue for "us" than for others. It so happens that there is one area of the world that, on the basis of past history, is likely to have a longer period of peace than we have had, unless that peace is destroyed by the termination of our peace. The focus of this book, however, is on "our" peace, the peace of the West since World War II that derives from Western history. Chapter four is devoted to a brief consideration of the varied prospects for peace in the rest of the world, although each section of that chapter would require a book in itself.

The Western world includes Europe and the areas colonized by Europe: North America, Australia and New Zealand. South Africa and Latin America were also colonized by Europeans, but they each have other problems.

The factors that bring peace to the West, the international settlement, could also bring peace to Russia. Russia was centrally involved in World War II and came out a winner. It achieved many traditional objectives, including a forward position of influence in Eastern Europe. But Russia failed to dominate Korea and Japan and, more importantly failed to acquire influence in the Mediterranean. These objectives, however, had never been achieved by Russia, and perhaps are not as vital to Russia as they are to the West.

In order to reinforce our historical perspective, let us use the term "Russia" to describe the country that currently calls itself "the Soviet Union" in the sense that we use "France" for the country that might be called "the Fifth Republic," "China" for the country that calls itself "the People's Republic," or "America" for the entity that was known to Europeans since the fifteenth century by that name, acquiring its preferred title, "the United States" after an eighteenth-century revolution.

The Soviet Union at its core is really Byzantine Russia, with a hierarchal structure and a cumbersome bureaucracy, a country of harsh leaders like Ivan IV and Stalin and occasionally innovative ones like Peter I, Khrushchev and possibly Gorbachev. This Russia has been invaded six times by Western nations and is understandably wary of danger from that direction. Four of these invasions, however, came in the times of crisis discussed in the next section. During the present period, there is virtually no danger of a land invasion, while an air attack would end peace for everyone.

Russia's problem, however, has been recurrent internal revolution.

These have occurred century after century both in the area of the capital and in the provinces. Now that these provinces include so many non-Russian areas, and the effectiveness of guerrilla warfare against great powers has been repeatedly demonstrated, it is difficult to expect that over several decades such internal conflict is not likely to recur in Russia. If it does, it may not be widespread and it may not be devastating. But there does not seem to be any reason to believe that such outbreaks are unlikely.

For East Asia, on the other hand, the chances for a long period of peace may be even better than those of the West. In the past two millennia, a united China under indigenous dynasties has maintained peace for periods of two to three centuries at a time. And China once again appears to be strongly reunited. A united Japan, also, has at least three times maintained internal peace for long periods. Korea also has a good peace record over the past two millennia (Melko 1973), and peace in that country has been affected by and coincided with that of China. Therefore it could be that the greatest danger to East Asian peace would be the violence of the ending of the Western peace, the "peace of our time."

For South Asia, the picture is less promising. Southeast Asia and Pakistan have already had major conflicts. India often has been divided in past history. Unity in recent centuries has been due to the Mughal and British Raj. Now that these have been withdrawn, the possibility of a violent division of India remains.

Africa, despite the creation of a number of new nations, has proved relatively free of international conflict, though internal dissension has been frequent, notably exploding in the Nigerian Civil War. South Africa remains a powder keg. The pre-Western historical situation in Africa has been normal for state systems: war was intermittent. It may be again.

Latin America is similar: prone to internal conflict but except for the dreadful War of The Triple Alliance in the nineteenth century, relatively free of serious wars between states. Such wars may have been discouraged by the possibility of intervention by the United States. The continent has the best record of any for peace in the past two centuries (Table 4.6). It is also argued, however, that Latin American conflict has been encouraged by the great northern power. There have been, moreover, power and population changes that could lead to violence in the coming decades.

The Middle East has been a tinder box for some time. It is difficult to see why this should change in the next several decades.

So the peace is for Western civilization, and possibly for Russia, with a good chance that East Asia will enjoy a separate and possibly longer peace. If other parts of the world also remain at peace, it would be for reasons not germane to this analysis.

THE RHYTHMS OF MODERN HISTORY

Let us consider modern history from the standpoint of its ages and crises, or its normal and transitional phases. Modern history is widely perceived to have begun in the latter half of the fifteenth century, which saw the rise of modern monarchies in France (1461), England (1485) and Spain (1479); the beginnings of the modern international system with the invasion of Italy by Charles VIII of France (1494) and the introduction of the use of artillery at Fornova (1495); and, of course, the beginnings of exploration of the world's rimlands (as seen from the West) with the voyages of Columbus and da Gama (1492, 1498).

Within this modern period, historians perceive longish periods of a century or more, which usually come to be called "ages," that are separated by periods of intense, widespread, high-casualty wars. Looking back, these ages tend to be categorized with generalized names—names not used by contemporaries but applied later by historians. Taking 1485 as an approximate beginning date for the modern period, Table 1.1 indicates the durations of recent ages and intervening periods of warfare.

TABLE 1.1
DURATIONS OF AGES AND CRISES

The Age of the Reformation	1485–1618	13 decades
The Thirty Years' War	1618–1648	3 decades
The Age of the Baroque	1648–1789	14 decades
The Napoleonic Wars	1789–1815	3 decades
The Victorian Age	1815–1914	10 decades
The World Wars	1914–1945	3 decades
The Present Age	1945–	4 decades so far

The periods of war are crisis periods involving major adjustments for Western civilization. They are exceptional, abnormal periods, when the survival of the system is threatened. The threat is widely perceived, occupies the energies of the elite, and causes a great deal of suffering for the general population.

In modern Western history, the first three crises have been surmounted, and the system has been maintained. In other civilizations, such crises sometimes have led to a change in the system, usually the establishment of an imperial system that marks a decline in the vitality of the society (Toynbee 1954, VII: 1–380; Quigley 1961, 158–159).

If the war periods are abnormal, then the periods we designate ages are normal. Each crisis has terminated in a resolution that has enabled various nations to function under recognized codes of international law and diplomacy. Such periods are a bustle of many ideas and activities, and it is usually the historians who search for their dominant themes or accomplishments who also name them. Thus the Age of the Reformation has been perceived as a period in which modern nation-states were being created and in which religious unity was undergoing challenge and modification. The Thirty Years' War (and the English Civil War) marked the end of this period, and set the stage for a purely secular period of monarchal government that followed. This was the Age of the Baroque, a 140-year period that terminated in the French Revolution. That revolution, of course, was concerned with the redistribution of class power in line with changes in the economic structure of the world. A new structure, involving middle-class power, the rise of the working class and the development of constitutional government was worked out during a hundred year period we have come to call the Victorian Age. Once again the political and economic structures became disjointed, the World Wars followed, and a resolution took place that involved a new distribution of political power, the rise of the "organization" and the decline of the entrepreneur and the emergence of a general framework for resolving widely perceived problems of economic distribution.

This normal period, this fourth "age" in modern Western history, does not yet have a name. Who would have known in the 1850s (four decades after the end of the Napoleonic Wars) that the unprepossessing queen of England would give her name to an age? Since our own period does not yet have a name, let us call it the Present Age, understanding that this title could have been given and probably was given to the Age of Reformation when Henry VIII was king of England, Francis I ruled in France, and Charles V had become emperor; or to the Age of the Baroque four decades after the end of the Thirty Years' War when Louis XIV was approaching the height of his reign, the Restoration was in full swing in England and the Dutch were in the autumn of their glorious century; or to the Europe of Louis Napoleon, Cavour, Lord Palmerston and Nicholas I.

The dating of the Present Age is tentative. Table 1.1 shows it clearly beginning in 1945, certainly a watershed year: the end of the era of World Wars, of a united Germany, of European predominance, of fascism and the beginning of the Atomic Age (Lukacs 1978). Just as the Victorian Age begins with 1815, so should the Present Age begin with 1945. But in terms of settlements like those of Westphalia or the Congress of Vienna, it could be argued that the settlement period of the World Wars took as long as ten years, and was not fully completed until the Geneva Conference of 1955. So to compromise, 1950 will mark the beginning of the Present Age, a date that also has advantages in terms of tidiness.

No one knows, of course, how long the Present Age will last. But each of the preceding ages has begun out of a resolution of international conflict that provided a basis for a century or more of relative stability. If we are living in a comparable age, perhaps the resolution of the World Wars crisis has provided us with a comparable period of relative stability.

NORMAL TIMES

"The most dangerous people of all are those who would have us believe that everything is *normal*," E. P. Thompson, 1985.

There are many astute people who believe that we are on the edge of catastrophe (e.g., Heilbroner 1980; Kaldor, Sinai and Ellul, 1978; Postel and Willard 1984). If we are not destroyed by nuclear warfare, there are difficult economic problems, including catastrophe through overpopulation or the exhaustion of resources, particularly sources of energy. These are perceived to be insoluble because we have already passed the point at which recovery might have been possible or because the nature of our political and social organization is such that we are incapable of responding.

Beyond these structural problems, some scholars see the danger of a moral or spiritual collapse that comes about as the result of social and technological processes. A general moral recovery, however, would exacerbate the economic and technological catastrophe, since the latter would become a secondary priority.

There are, on the other hand, also notes of optimism to be heard. Various scholars have seen on the horizon prospects for a new era in which man will achieve what he has never achieved before: universal prosperity, an end to physical misery, infinitely greater knowledge and understanding, truly richer and more caring social relationships—a really better world (e.g., Stavrianos 1976; Rifkin 1981; Kahn 1982; Cornish and Willard 1984).

My view is rather prosaic by contrast. I think the developed countries of the world are well into a period of relative peace and stability. We are neither on the brink of catastrophe nor on the launching pad of unimaginable attainment, but well into what might be called a normal period of history comparable to the Baroque or Victorian Ages. It is an age one can live in, imperfect but probably as good or better than any we have had previously. It is an age when the problem of violence is present but not overwhelming.

The international system has been redefined about as firmly as it was after Westphalia or the Congress of Vienna. The industrial system is functioning imperfectly, but probably more effectively than it did in Victorian times and not in a manner that suggests its imminent demise. Patterns of government are clear, with rather more franchise than has existed before in many countries. Important social problems are being confronted, as they were in Victorian times.

There is a widespread perception that we are experiencing incredible change. In my view, the great social, political and economic changes were made immediately before and during the world crisis of 1914–1945, and the rate of social and institutional change has been somewhat slower in the past three decades. It is possible to make projections over the next several decades with reasonable confidence, because what we can see already is what we are likely to have.

Social systems tend to reach periods of maximum efficiency, then to become more inefficient as institutionalization takes place, that is to say, as the institutions within the system become more concerned with their own maintenance than with performing the functions for which they are created (Quigley 1961).

As the institutions fail to perform, the necessity for adjustment arises, and the social system experiences considerable disturbance until the institutions are once again reconstituted or else replaced by other institutions more capable of solving the prevailing problems. Once the basic readjustments have been made, there may be a period of shaking down, when the reformed and new institutions are reacting and adjusting to each other.

Borrowing both from Pitirim Sorokin (1957) and Thomas Kuhn (1962), let us call the longer phases of relative integration "normal" and the shorter crisis phases of breakdown and reconstitution "transitional." During a normal period, a social system reaches a relatively high degree of harmony. The states within the system are at least reconciled to the existing situation. The economic system works fairly well and there are mechanisms for working out secondary difficulties. Attitudes are consonant with the situation, most people being content to work within the system, most not expecting rapid or radical change. Where change does take place, it is accompanied by dialogue, most of it rational in tone and content. There may be considerable dissent and decentralization, but this takes place within the context of the system.

Within all systems, change is going on continuously. Even when a system appears to be relatively stable, as a normal system does, many local changes are taking place as parts adjust to the whole. It is not always easy to tell whether a particular disturbance or series of disturbances represents an adjustment of a part of the system, or whether it is a sign of social change that is to transform the whole system.

The World Wars were the climax of a transition period between two normal phases, each of which had its own political forms, economy and outlook. The system then settled into a normal phase with various patterns reinforcing one another to increase integration and limit the possibilities for change.

Kenneth Boulding (1985) has been writing recently about what he calls "regions of time." In a given region parameters are fairly stable. But when you cross into a new region, the immediate past becomes a poor guide to the future. Just so. In the 1950s, the past was a poor guide to the future, but as we near the end of the century, because a normal period would be what

Boulding refers to as a region of time, the immediate past becomes more reliable.

During a normal phase, international peace fosters the reemergence of effective patterns of international law and diplomacy. The bureaucratic, committee-oriented structures of government and the economy work effectively to solve basic problems. Younger men coming into committee structures at lower levels begin to influence group decisions in more relevant ways, and the information coming to government leaders and upper management begins to change.

Various subsystems begin to coordinate better with one another. The organizational system is operated by men and women who were not strongly indoctrinated with the ideology that made entrepreneurs. The elites of government and business are in sympathy with each other's objectives. Social problems become the concern as well as the by-product of the organization.

The psychic world both responds to and affects the physical world. Artists and writers are responding to a changed situation. Their styles and subject matter are likely to be widely varied. To some extent they create models to meet problems, and to some extent the models they create will shape future problems.

Change can be accommodated where change is part of the pattern. "The status quo is change," Khruschev said to Walter Lippmann (Lippmann 1961). The same kind of changes occur everywhere because each state is facing the same kind of problems. Each has to transform its educational system to meet the changing economic needs of a "normal phase" in industrial society and each is free to borrow and modify the solutions of its neighbors.

But after a few decades, the rate of change slows down. The educational system is once again in harmony with the society. The graduates of the educational system come into positions of power and influence. Artists and writers have dealt with the major changes and now are more concerned with nuances. There are fewer surprises. The impression that we live in a world of exceptional change, however, persists. After all, it must be exceptional. We live in it.

PERIODS AND PHASES

It may be useful, at this point, to put our time in a longer ranged context. The spans of time we have been referring to as "ages," e.g., the "Victorian Age" may be seen as part of longer periods which, in turn, are part of our civilization histories.

Modern history, in turn, can be put in civilizational perspective. A common view shared by Spengler (1932), Toynbee (1934–61), A. L.

Kroeber (1944), Carroll Quigley (1961) and others is that civilizations go through a series of predictable periods. While these civilizationists have differed in terminology, Figure 1.1 shows a rough area of agreement among them as to the terminal period of classical civilization and the history so far of Western civilization.

There seem to have been three kinds of political relationships dominating these civilizations: feudal, interstate and imperial. Each of these periods can last a long time, but inevitably evolve into the next period. There is nothing mysterious about this. Empires become unwieldy and unmanageable, and in such periods, people look for more workable local forms that turn out to be variations of feudal relationships. These last a long time and contribute to a revival of economy and a transformation of outlook that is ultimately served better by the development of centralized states that interrelate in a decentralized interstate system. We live in such a system now. From time to time states within these systems engage in general conflicts. If such a conflict results in one state conquering the others, the system enters an imperial period. An empire may continue for a long time, but ultimately the disadvantages of centralization lead to its demise (Melko 1969, 47–57).

The time frames here are fairly long. Classical civilization lasted about 2,500 years and Western civilization, so far, has lasted between 900 and 1,300 years, depending on where you calculate its beginning.

Each civilization, probably, has an overarching outlook, as described by Spengler and more recently by David Richardson (Melko and Scott 1987, 29–31), who prefers the term worldview. Within these civilizations, each period also has a dominant worldview, though the coincidence of outlook and phase may not be exact, or sometimes even close. But still we recognize Mycenaean-Minoan, Hellenic-Hellenistic and Roman-Byzantine as being very different kinds of periods in classical history.

The phases in which one period is coming to an end and another beginning are likely to be crisis phases. But there will be other crises in which problems are resolved without tranformation from one sort of period to another.

Figure 1.2 picks up the period 1500–2000 from Figure 1.1 and indicates the relationship between the crises and ages of the Western interstate period along with corresponding transformations of outlook. The developmental outlook is subdivided into the "worldviews" discerned by Warren Wagar (1977). The Renaissance outlook could also be so divided if we were studying it here, but it is probably too early to subdivide the outlook of the Present Age, as it would have been for a Victorian of the 1850s to distinguish between romanticism and positivism. (For reasons discussed later in this chapter, I shall call this outlook "relational.")

It may be that crises between periods are deeper and longer than those between phases, as the Hundred Years' War preceding the Age of Refor-

Figure 1.1

Civilizational Periods

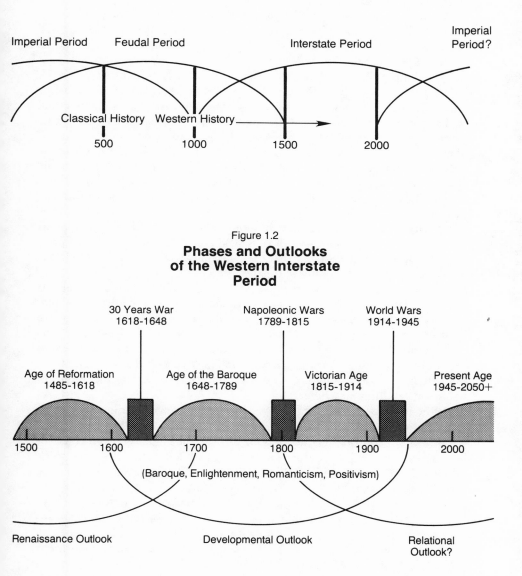

Figure 1.2
Phases and Outlooks
of the Western Interstate
Period

mation, or as a nuclear war dividing Western interstate and imperial phases might be.

When all this has been written and diagrammed, is it persuasive? Even if there were three periods of relative peace that lasted ten to fifteen decades, is that any reason to believe there will be a fourth?

We have the example of Norman Angell's *The Great Illusion,* published in 1912. In that book, Angell was perceived to have argued that war had become impossible. Could *Peace in Our Time* be another such mistaken attempt to project the future? Well, to be fair to Angell, he neither said that war was impossible nor projected the past into the future (Angell 1933, 267–270). But what was thought about Angell could be applied to this book. The perception that we shall have peace for decades to come could be as bad as the prediction falsely attributed to Angell, as bad as the assessment by Chamberlain from which the book takes its title. And if next month or next year we are all killed in a nuclear war, there is nothing much we can do about it. On the other hand, if there is a reasonable chance that there may be a time of peace, even several decades, then possibilities open up for acting, and even for thinking or just living. The possibility that we may perish in a holocaust is all too obvious. The possibility that we may not perish should also be considered. Of course, we do consider it in the way we live, but to many this is just denial. Let us remain open to the possibility that there are more positive aspects in living today as if we shall be living tomorrow.

If, on the other hand, we acknowledge the possibility that such periods and phases exist, how do we explain them? It is not surprising that physical systems, even very large ones like galaxies, should behave in recurrent patterns. Nor are we surprised that particular species like ants or termites behave in recurrent and predictable ways. Then it does not seem out of the question that *Homo sapiens* also behaves in predictable long-term patterns though, because of the culture factor, the range of behavior variation may be greater.

If the interstate system can be perceived as a period within the civilization, and crisis and normal phases can be discerned within that period, why do they recur as they do? Civilizationists like Toynbee and Kroeber have given a great deal of attention to these problems (e.g., Toynbee 1934, III:301–304; Quigley 1979, 127–166; Melko 1969, 47–53), and it is not possible to summarize or present an alternate version of their work here. But we can assume the following about crises within an interstate period:

1. They always involve challenges to the political order. There is always a strong desire for political reorganization.

2. There will be outlook changes occurring as well, and usually these precede political challenges. The political challenge is not independent from other aspects of the system.

So it would appear that a normal period comes about as the result of political resolution, and with this resolution there comes some consistent accommodation of outlook. It is difficult to say why this accommodation lasts several decades, or why it does not last longer.

Interstate systems tend to be unstable and periodically enter crisis phases that will be terminated either by a reversion to normality or the formation of an imperial system. The length of the normal phase depends on the inherent stability of a particular balance of power, the opportunities for new powers to emerge, the given capacities of leadership at the time, and possibly the power of the outlook of the time. All of these are very difficult to assess because historians make their judgments within the confines of the situation they are considering.

Stabilities of balances are judged partly from the situation. For instance, the present balance might be judged as being exceptionally stable by future historians, but it is the reason for that stability that we are here trying to assess. The only immediate challenger visible is Japan, which at present seems to be an unaggressive nation with moderate leadership. Is this because of the present situation, past memories of still living people, or just that so far an aggressive, charasmatic leader has not appeared? In 1858 one would not have guessed that Prussia would be the next challenger to European stability or that Bismarck was already on hand to create the German state. The outlook, the way of seeing of the period, may provide a bond of commitment to the civilization and its interstate system, which may affect the goals of leaders and their perceptions of the will of others to resist substantial political change. But is this readily broken when a nation challenges the system, or does the nation challenge the system because the outlook has lost its hold?

All that can be said is that in normal periods peace can be maintained for a number of decades by normal means. There comes a time, finally, when these means no longer work. It is difficult to say whether the primary cause of this is a cumulative political maladjustment, as new sources of power emerge, or whether changes in outlook accumulating over time make the normal political processes less effective. In a social system, these factors are interrelated.

This is not an adequate explanation. The outlook of our own time leads to holistic approaches, and these are never quite satisfactory, at least to someone who has been socialized in a Victorian educational system. It is not an adequate explanation, but it will have to do. All that is necessary at this point is to accept the possibility that such periods and phases occur, and that possibly we live in a normal phase, whether the underlying reasons are satisfactory or not.

If these normal phases do recur, and we do live in one, then what? What perceptions, what possibilities, does that open up?

If, on the other hand, it becomes clear that such phases do not occur, that this is in fact a reincarnation of the misperception of Norman Angell, then there is no point in reading further. One would be better occupied in eating, drinking and merriment, or in coming to terms with the condition of one's immortal soul.

THE RELATIONAL OUTLOOK

I have described the view presented here as prosaic, in contrast to many models that envision millennial transformations. But the term prosaic is inadequate to describe the unique characteristic of the period, a particular outlook, born of transformations that also precipitated the most recent world crisis, but most fully absorbed by the generation born late enough to miss experiencing the effects of the world crisis. This outlook is so basic and different that it has created an obvious communication problem between generations, and it seems to be of central importance in shaping the character of the age.

Thomas Kuhn (1962) argues that science develops through the adoption of a series of paradigms that serve to provide a common focus for research. In the sixteenth century, for instance, the possibilities of the Ptolemaic system were about exhausted and scientists were beginning to feel a need for an alternative basic theory that would be helpful in furthering explanations of particular phenomena. After a period of hesitation and opposition, the Copernican theory was accepted as providing a better basis for research. In Kuhn's terms, the acceptance of the Copernican theory by seventeenth century astronomers inaugurated another period of "normal" science, when there is lots of work for everyone who wants to lend a hand, and little desire for new all-encompassing theories.

Every so often a paradigm becomes exhausted or loses its power for some other reason and a new paradigm is sought. This period of discovery is a transformative one. When the new paradigm is found, a new "normal" period of creative development takes place. The paradigm is likely to affect much more than the scientific world, because all the best minds of an epoch will be attuned to the same cultural situation.

The most recent Western paradigm to be adopted came into being around the turn of the century. It included a series of ideas having to do with relativism and indeterminacy associated with Einstein and Planck, but of course there was a whole climate out of which these ideas emerged. Burckhardt foreshadowed it in his emphasis on the separate identity and value of each society, which anticipated the development of the relativistic science of anthropology. Freud reenforced it by introducing theories of personality that featured immensely complex variables, inversions, displacements and symbolic substitutes in which almost nothing was what it appeared to be. What all these approaches had in common was that no element was seen as an absolute, but always in relation to other elements; and as perspectives change, the elements changed.

Let us call this way of seeing the "relational outlook."

Even the term "element" is inadequate to describe what is related. The systems theorist, Downing Bowler, once described a system as a relationship of entities. But the entities themselves turn out to be relationships of other entities. In other words, the entities composing systems are systems themselves. There is no basic entity; everything breaks down to energy.

Thus we perceive systems of systems: the changing relations of those systems forming one aspect of reality, but our perceptions of those changes forming another aspect of reality. The most reenforcement we get from these ambiguous and fluctuating perceptions is that others, at least for a time, share them too.

Let us contrast this outlook briefly with the way of seeing that it is now replacing. This earlier outlook developed in the time of Newton and reached its culmination in Darwin. In other fields it may be exemplified in Gibbon, Adam Smith, Kant and in Victorian architecture. This outlook is concerned with the reality of things, with a set of absolutes or basics from which development took place. The development was important, even more important than the things: man had the capacity to utilize his knowledge and make things better. It is in Newton, Smith and Kant that we think of solid reasoning from the particular and in Gibbon, Darwin and Victorian architecture that we are thinking of the idea that things are better than they were, that development takes place everywhere, that progress is essentially additive.

Let us call this older way of seeing the "developmental outlook."

When Trollope writes a sequence of novels, the Palliser series for instance, he takes them in sequence. Each carries the story forward in time sequence, and we see change and progress in the society. The story is told from different viewpoints, but by the end of each novel we know what has happened. The omniscient author steps in once in a while to set things straight.

When Lawrence Durrell writes a series of novels, such as the *Alexandria Quartet,* you could hardly call it a sequence, since there are overlaps of time. When you finish the first novel, you don't even know who is telling the story. When you finish the second, you find that there was a very different view of what was happening, and your perception of the first novel is altered. Then the omniscient author steps in to narrate the third novel, but there is no reason to believe that Durrell has a better view than Darcy or Balthazzar. He has enriched, provided other perspectives. The final novel gives us resolution of a sort, but no progress.

The twentieth-century novel also has a device called the flashback, though the name is developmental (Victorian) because the "flash" can go in any direction in time. What it does is juxtapose events according to relationships instead of sequence, even though writing is a sequential device, better fitted to the Victorian than the relational writer. That, probably, is one reason for the popularity of television, film and visual aids.

It takes several decades for a major new paradigm to win general acceptance. The period of the main discoveries connected with the relational paradigm involved principally the two decades preceding World War I, but there was a breeding period before that, and a period of modification and refinement between the wars.

There is also a time lapse between the adoption of a new paradigm by those who are most intelligent and perceptive in a society and the rest of us who for the most part teach what is known. We first of all have to be persuaded that the new approaches have sufficient merit to warrant even partial displacement of the "tried and true" which, furthermore, we have taken considerable trouble to learn. Then, if we are persuaded, we have to learn the new, and this is hard because it involves a way of seeing that cuts across the grain of the way we have already learned to see. And even after we learn, and even if we are intellectually persuaded that the new way is better, most never develop a feel for the new. We always have to fight our earlier orientations, and when under stress we often retreat to developmental approaches. These retreats are stemmed, however, by the fact that developmental methods are no longer adequate.

The younger generation, let us say roughly those who entered the public school systems after World War II, have an easier time with the relational outlook than their teachers. They follow and employ relational ideas readily. It follows that as they become teachers they are likely to have fewer problems using relational methods. What fails and what succeeds comes to be understood, and when they are under stress or when they fail, they switch to other relational methods. Similarly they employ relational ideas in business and government, with the result that there is developing a considerable transformation in the methods and objectives employed in our regulatory and productive institutions, and this in turn is having a considerable effect on our society.

Changes in general ways of thinking after the acceptance of a new scientific paradigm are long-term recurrent events in the history of Western civilization. The last such occurrence, as we have indicated, followed the development of Newtonian physics and gave rise to what we have subsequently come to call the Age of Enlightenment. Changes in outlook following a period of crisis are also long-term recurrent events, the last being that which followed the Napoleonic Wars and gave rise first to the revolutions of 1830 and 1848 and more enduringly to the establishment of constitutional government and humanitarian social reforms. I think our own times can be more completely understood if they are seen in terms of a transformation of outlook that results both from a return to normal times and the widening acceptance of a new scientific way of seeing.

Obviously, people continue to deal with things in a sequential manner, as have people in all cultures at all times. But in Victorian times, this was central to reality. During the period of transition between outlooks, when the relational outlook was gaining followers as it opened up a new set of problems, there was also a major political crisis. The resolution of the political crisis can be dated to a single year. The acceptance of the relational outlook took decades longer, as those taught in the new way reached adulthood and came to power, and those steeped in the earlier outlook retired and died.

One unfortunate characteristic of the relational outlook, perhaps, has been the reduction in interest in history, which, being structurally sequential, has more appeal to the developmental mind. It is not surprising when people encounter a return to the normal after several decades of crisis, and that normal period is dominated by a major change in outlook, that the uniqueness of change will be exaggerated. And when this tendency to exaggerate is accompanied by a declining interest in history, the uniqueness and extent of change may be perceived as virtually incomparable, or comparable only to the transformation that resulted in the emergence of civilization from primitive societies or at least to the emergence of a new civilization (e.g., Toffler's *Third Wave*, 1980).

The transformation is unique, in the sense that each age is unique, but there are parallels that are useful in giving us perspective. There have been three previous normal periods in modern history. And while the relational outlook is unique in Western history, parallel outlooks may be found elsewhere, especially in East Asian civilization.

DO THE OUTLOOKS CORRESPOND WITH THE AGES?

Figure 1.2, drawing from Warren Wagar, assigns the developmental outlook to both periods. But there certainly was a major change from the rationality of the enlightenment to the emotionalism of romanticism. If you consider the transformation from Haydn to Beethoven by way of Mozart, it seems tremendous.

Looked at from a Victorian standpoint, then, there is an immense change from the Englightenment to the romantic outlooks. Romanticism seemed to turn everything upside down, stressing feelings where intellect had reigned supreme. Looked at from the relational viewpoint, however, romanticism can be perceived as a necessary expansion of pattern, the introduction of the intuitive means to hypotheses, after which positivism could continue to work out developmental problems, as the Enlightenment had been doing a century before.

THE DECLINE OF GENERATIONAL CONFLICT

The much discussed gap between generations is exceptional in terms of our lifetime experience, but probably normal in the early phase of any normal period. It comes about because the younger generation lacks the crisis experience of the older generation and because the older generation lacks the relational outlook of the younger.

Generations always disagree, as Lewis Feuer pointed out, but the problem in the first generation after the crisis is most severe, because the older generation grew up in the crisis, and regards the crisis as normal. Therefore, it does not have the relevant experience to pass on to the younger generation, which is probably why Feuer was moved to write on the subject in the 1960s (1969). The younger generation, for example, could not see Munich in Vietnam, for indeed it was not there. But how could the older generation convey its perception of a powerful, ideologically united enemy? "It is often true, in history," says E. P. Thompson (1985), "that the 'normality' of one time turns out—a few decades later—to have been absurd."

The younger generation is no longer young. It might include some persons born as early as 1925 since such a person would be only 20 at the end of World War II and might not have participated very actively in it, but might have been sensitive to emerging relational approaches. The older generation might include anyone born as late as 1935, since a person of 15 might have had his political attitudes indelibly formed by the Cold War as it was in 1950, and by the intensity of emotions evoked there, while being insulated from relational attitudes.

So for our purposes, let us think of the younger generation entering the 1990s as including people from childhood to late middle age, people who dominate the middle echelons of industry and government and are making policy decisions. The older generation would include people in their fifties and older, people who are parents and grandparents, who are in middle and top echelons, whose past decisions still dominate present law and policy, and who still can effectively block or stall the policy changes proposed by the younger generation.

We are aware that people can be mixed, and have attitudes that are inconsistent. It is certainly possible for members of the older generation to be steeped in the relational outlook, which, after all, has its roots in the science of the turn of the century. It is equally possible for young people, those who are docile and who have been taught to believe in the truth of whatever their teachers tell them, to assimilate the outlook of the World Wars' generation.

The crisis experience of the older generation often leads to overreaction. If something goes wrong, members of the older generation want to do something about it. They call out the national guard, send in the marines, build bomb shelters, write detailed laws explicitly providing or forbidding. When members of the younger generation protest that such responses are inappropriate or irrelevant, members of the older generation have tended to reply:

"Wait until you have experienced what we have experienced. Then you will understand why we do what we do."

But members of the younger generation never will have such experiences, never will "understand," and as they come to power, they respond differently to crises and the problems that cause them.

This propensity to do something derives from what Herbert Marcuse (1964) calls the "performance principle." Working from Freud's theory that as we mature we are able to resist a gut pleasure principle in favor of a reality principle that is consonant with a mature view of the world, Marcuse points out that there may be more than one reality principle as the world changes. "Performance" happened to be the reality principle of the Victorian Age, and you could argue that, as indeed Max Weber does (1961), it has been the dominant principle since the Reformation.

The relational outlook suggests a different reality principle. If systems are more real than things, then nominalism may have passed its peak, and with that materialism. If systems involve an understanding of the whole in relation to its parts, the younger generation may be more interested in understanding the meaning of a crisis before reacting to it, the more so if a crisis does not represent an immediate and overwhelming threat. In other words, if relationships rather than performance become the dominating reality principle, then understanding may become more important than acting.

Table 1.2 is a not awfully successful attempt to quantify the change in outlook. Supposing that the Victorian outlook is to be found in people born before 1940, and the relational outlook begins to appear in people born after 1920, the table shows the ratio of people who could be carriers of the relational outlook compared to people who could be carriers of the Victorian outlook. It is evident that in 1950, in most if not all countries, the majority of the population would be carriers of the Victorian, while by 1970, in most if not all countries, the majority would be likely to possess the relational outlook. By 1980 the relational outlook would have become dominant. It should be said, of course, that no matter how firm, despite

TABLE 1.2

RATIO OF POPULATION BORN AFTER 1920
TO POPULATION BORN BEFORE 1940

YEAR	1950–51	1960–61	1970–71	1980–81
Poland	42–58	54–46		
Italy	37–63	48–52	62–38	
U.K.	35–65	42–58	56–44	64–36
U.S.		51–49	61–39	70–30

(*European Historical Statistics* 1975; *Annual Abstract of Statistics* 1984; *Statistical Abstracts of the United States* 1983).

gaps, the table may look, it is quantifying the unquantifiable. If the ratios were given as percentages, they would total more than 100, since everyone born between 1920 and 1940 could be possessors of both outlooks. It is, of course, a mere coincidence that the author, born in 1930, is perfectly poised to understand both outlooks.

Anyway, insofar as these outlooks can be apprehended and verified, the relational outlook would have been making an impact by 1950. But in the 1950s the older generation outlook dominated while an increasingly baffled younger generation was scornfully dubbed the "silent generation." In the 1960s this generation gained its maturity and became more articulate in powerless protest against what appeared to them to be absurd institutions and decisions protected and made by the older generation. At the beginning of the 1970s a humorless older generation leader, unconscious of the irony, acknowledged the transformation by claiming the adjective "silent" for a diminishing older generation majority.

By the 1980s the majority, both in numbers and power, belonged to the younger generation. Outlook and reality were again more in consonance. As this was happening, concern about the generation gap correspondingly declined.

THE COMPREHENSION OF CHANGE AND COMPLEXITY

It seems sometimes that the modern world is incomprehensible to the layman. New inventions and ideas burst forth with such rapidity that no one can keep up with them. Moreover computers, electronics, Keynesian economics, relativity theory and the like are too complicated for those of us who are pinned down by housework and commuting.

Yet very large cultures can have a great deal changing within them without changing all that much themselves. Victorians might be impressed or distressed by freeways, nuclear weapons or the waning of colonialism, but they would recognize the system that has emerged from the World Wars' crisis: the international system, parliamentary government, air pollution, the family system, public education, the establishment. So even in a crisis period, though many examples of change may be given, the effect of all these changes may not be overwhelming.

In normal periods, once structures have been revised, the rate of change is slower still, even though there may be a great deal of motion and activity. The things that change are more likely to be variations of changes already familiar: families move more often, but the nature of the moves is similar; methods of computation are changing everywhere but the kinds of changes in method have limited patterns; modern communications make it possible to speak today with people almost anywhere in the world within a few minutes, but you will still be able to do it tomorrow, and the messages delivered may be trivial. Even the idea that things are changing rapidly is old, commonplace, almost comfortable and reassuring.

In underdeveloped countries the situation is the opposite. Many of the countries are small, and materials and ideas are being introduced into them in a quantity and at a speed that is greater than they can absorb. The effect of the change is indeed overwhelming. The mixture of fear, exasperation, disappointment and hope generated by what must seem to be total unpredictability and instability may be unbearable. You can do today what you could not do yesterday and you cannot do today what you could do yesterday.

Thus, in rate of change, as in so many other ways, the two parts of the world are undergoing entirely different experiences.

As for the complexity of the age, it is hard to see why general principles involved should be harder to grasp than they were in earlier periods. Perhaps it is only a kind of egoistic indulgence to imagine that our world is so much more difficult to cope with than other worlds have seen. The primitive men facing the creation of an entirely new social form at the dawn of civilization met problems much more difficult than those that confront us.

The problem of complexity is an old one. Whenever the aspects of any problem become too complex to grasp, we respond by looking for means by which we can simplify. Generally we simplify by concentrating on essentials, on what is really important. We find that a structure of seeming endless complexity is full of recurring patterns, that the problems that are being met are relatively few, some of them unique, but most of them the same old problems.

Alvin Toffler's *Future Shock* (1970) has been widely perceived as representing a scientific study of a world dilemma. While Toffler's observations are interesting, cases of future shock are hard to find. Most of us do not, in our daily lives, worry about having a test-tube baby, changing our skin color to end discrimination, freezing our bodies in order to return in a future age, or having outselves cloned for the benefit of mankind. We have stresses of various kinds, but no worse than those of the past: farmers wiped out by locusts, pioneers leaving families forever to face the ultimate in nuclear family isolation, city dwellers facing decimation by plague, husbands losing wives to childbirth or tuberculosis.

Loneliness, alienation and unhappiness are problems throughout history. They are not worse in the twentieth century, and in the Relational Age probably not as general or ubiquitous as they have been in earlier times and may be again in a more distant future. Awareness of alienation, on the other hand, is likely to be high because of the relational outlook.

Perhaps we can all derive some gratification from picturing ourselves coping with all this change, but what change are we talking about? The most common response concerns the revolution in transportation and communications. The world has become small. You can reach anyone (or at least their answering service) by dialing, you can fly any place in the world overnight, and beyond that we have reached the moon. But with the exception of the moon shot, those changes came about during the last crisis period. Telephones became common then, and Lindbergh made his flight in 1927. By the time the crisis was over, it was possible to fly anywhere. Flying times have gotten somewhat briefer since then, but the change has not been all that great. Lindbergh's flight (Lindbergh!) meant that we could someday fly to Paris. Paris! Armstrong's flight (Armstrong?) meant we could someday fly to the moon. The moon?

Once the pathbreaking voyage is made, others know it can be done. They may make faster voyages or longer voyages, but they will not receive the fame of the first voyager. Despite television, Armstrong does not share Lindbergh's fame. Why? Because his voyage was perceived as a corporate adventure or because the moon flight was not perceived as the same kind of thing as the Atlantic flight? In the twenty-first century will Armstrong share the obscurity of John Cabot or of Clyde Pangborn and Hugh Herndon, Jr., who made the first nonstop flight across the Pacific, from Sabishiro, Japan to Wenatchee, Washington on October 5, 1931?

Other incredible changes also belong to the past. The organizational world described by William Whyte and John Kenneth Galbraith is pretty well established. It changed a great deal during the crisis, but its form is set. So, correspondingly, is that of suburbia, shopping centers, television, health care programs, economic theories. The main changes have been made, and implementation is the problem of the day. The changes of the next several decades may include considerable readapting to the old: coal furnaces, bicycles, public transportation, lower protein diets. The computer revolution? So far a filing revolution. How or whether computers will transform society is not yet apparent.

The Victorian Age was a period of working out. The industrial revolution was in progress. The processes of urbanization and industrialization had been established. The concomitant problems of adjusting forms of government appropriate to changes in class and outlook were being worked out, sometimes with disruptions like the revolutions of 1848 and the American Civil War. Universal male suffrage was introduced by Disraeli's Conservative government, while Bismarck was a pioneer of welfare and health programs. These were important first steps to the resolution of important and difficult problems that, nevertheless, did not constitute world crises.

"Our time," then, is no more complex or unintelligible than any other time. There is an impression of complexity partly because people generally think their own times are more complex; partly because coming into normal times gives a vision of a wider range of problems than were visible during the crisis; partly because the relational outlook dims the historical vision; partly because the relational outlook causes people to seek out complexity.

THE MORASS OF CONTEMPORARY EXPLANATIONS

The facts never speak for themselves. We must attempt to explain the relationships between isolated facts or the world would appear as utter chaos. This is difficult to do, even on a small scale. There are a number of conflicting theories (Henslin and Light 1983) explaining the existence of relatively concrete, contained, recurrent phenomena we call ghettos. Revisionist historians continually provide new explanations for events that occurred centuries ago, even when they have discovered no new facts. It is obviously difficult to come up with an explanation for the general state of the world in one's own time. There are likely to be many explanations.

Encountering so many explanations may seem to be a discouraging experience. How is one to sort them out? Some must be contradictory: If one is right, the other must be wrong. But in the Relational Age we can also perceive that many are alternative explanations that do not contradict so much as focus on different relationships. One writer may be concerned with spirit, another with economics. Since, given the relational paradigm, neither is likely to insist that his area of focus is the cause of everything else, two such theories may complement rather than contradict one another. So it is quite possible that many explanations will stand up.

The theory that the present is a period of peace and stability, however, is not one that can last forever. If really serious conflicts dominate the developed countries, and if these persist for any length of time, theories presuming general stability will be forgotten. If, on the other hand, the period of peace persists, older generation theories based on the common assumption of overwhelming crisis will become tiresome. They will be replaced by theories that attempt to deal with the situation that exists in the contemporary world. In either case, the rejected theories will not be disproved so much as discarded.

If, as of course I suppose to be the case, peace and stability continue in developed countries, the range of acceptable explanations will narrow. The paradigm will focus on relational studies of normal times. There will be so much to do here that there will be little time for studies that seek to analyze and solve the problem of overwhelming totalitarianism when no one is aware of any overwhelming totalitarianism. Instead, if a study of totalitarianism is to be taken seriously, it must focus on the phenomenon as a recurrent historical anomaly that tends to occur under certain circumstances.

It is also likely that the astute theories about disaster or utopia, referred to earlier in this chapter, are likely to lose their audience. Impending disaster doesn't play forever if the disaster doesn't occur. And long-term progress gets forgotten when you are in the valley of daily, specific striving for social or personal improvement.

It seems probable that the early part of a normal period is most susceptible to a multiplicity of explanations. The early part of a transitional period is rapidly perceived, and soon everyone is trying to cope with the general crisis. But the onset of a normal period occurs more gradually and, as the realization that the crisis has been resolved begins to spread, various problems emerge, some long deferred by the crisis, some arising from novelties in the contemporary period that had not existed in the previous normal period. Thus, after the Napoleonic Wars, governments had to resume coping with public services problems that already had been the preoccupation of enlightened despots, but they also had to deal with novel franchise and welfare problems that were the result of the industrial revolution. After the World Wars, governments had to resume dealing with egalitarian and ecological problems that arose from philosophical and economic transformations in the nineteenth century, but they also had to face novel problems arising from the more recent development of air power, nuclear energy, and concepts of economic planning.

The perception that we live in the first half of a normal phase with a particular outlook is subject to the same laws as other perceptions. It does not explain everything and it is not the underlying explanation. But it has limited and specific uses, not the least of which is serving as a device for coping with the morass of contemporary explanations.

The explanation presented here for the probability of continued peace is one in the morass. In my opinion, of course, it is the true explanation. But for the majority of people one would expect it would be just another of many.

It is understandable that there would be skepticism. Historical comparisons are rarely satisfactory because there are different contexts and different events. The present is always unique. Nuclear weapons proliferation, geometrically multiplying population, and rapid depletion of physical resources have no real parallel in the past. Yet imagine if an editor of an American journal in 1860 (45 years after the ending of the Napoleonic Wars) had received a contribution from an historian (there would not have been a sociologist) who contended that the Present Age (he would hardly call it "Victorian") is not a crisis, but "normal." As the editor returned the article, he might well remark that the author had ignored such present-day phenomena as the proliferation of the industrial revolution, the desperate condition of slaves and proletariat, and the widespread demand for participation in government, all of which had no real parallel in the past, not to mention the violent revolutions of 1848–1849, the recent catastrophic Crimean War, and the possibility of serious conflict in America.

The response to the idea of normal times has often been a good deal stronger than skeptical. It has been downright hostile. Manuscript readers and audience members alike have been very angry at the idea. Partly, as we shall see, this may relate to a threat to activities that have to do with personal identity. But for those with older generation perceptions, there may be another problem.

For the older generation, possibly, the problem is one of having been trained for crisis. It is a wonderful feeling to see oneself surviving crisis after crisis, and it is an excuse for not doing more. Merely to survive is an accomplishment. It may be scary then to be told that now choices are open that were not open before, it is now possible to leave your job or your family, and to do what you always wanted to do. Like the characters in O'Neill's *The Iceman Cometh,* we find that illusions have become essential to our lives.

For the younger generation, the only model is the day-to-day conflict one reads about, hears about and learns in school from the older generation. All other times are distant and pale. Few young people are versed in history. Not many ever were, but in a time of many kinds of media they are probably weaker in this area than were their predecessors of 1860. As some are becoming the teachers, however, and they have lived through the same kind of world they are teaching about, perspectives are being restored and the gap in outlook and moral perception between generations is narrowing.

Normal times, once perceived, provide a rich set of alternatives. We can focus on aesthetics, economics, politics, society. It is not necessary for everyone to devote themselves to the cause of survival. It is not irresponsible if they do not. They may survive for many decades without trying. And the route to long-term solutions may be found through a diversity of activity, because the more obvious routes seem impossible. Men are no longer bound by moral obligation to rid the world of threat or fear. They are not bound to do what cannot be done either. On the other hand, if it is understood that there is quite a reasonable possibility that destruction is not imminent, that the four decades of peace to date could continue for another half or full century, it gives us some breathing space. It puts problems in a different context. People can be free. But a basic requisite of freedom is an awareness of one's situation.

THE DURATION OF OUR TIME

This normal period in which we live will not last forever.

How long will it last? On the basis of past experience, we can assume it will probably last more than a century, but less than two. European history doesn't give us much to go by. The three normal ages in modern history have lasted from 10 to 14 decades (see Table 1.1). We have already struggled with the explanation for this. Social systems, like other systems, undergo periods of relative crystalization when the physical and psychic worlds are relatively in harmony and working fairly well. But after a period of time, social change, which is constantly taking place, begins to have a cumulative effect. Political institutions that worked well enough at one point no longer are relevant to new social problems for which they were not constructed. Not only that, but the political institutions, like other institutions, have been undergoing a long process of institutionalization that makes them cumbersome, less able to adapt to new situations. The inability to solve problems leads to the development of new ideologies, men become more willing to take extreme measures. The old institutions disintegrate or they are circumvented by *ad hoc* groups trying innovative, possibly violent, methods that get around the system. Piecemeal reforms may work for a while, but not for a long period, and finally the social system—which involves the political, economic, social and ideological systems of the individual states, the interrelating systems, and the world system itself—becomes so convulsed at so many points that the system simply breaks down and a period of violence and disorder follows.

In the most recent crisis, ideological commitments became more important than life itself, and use of gas, machine guns, blockbusters or any other weapon was considered justified in defense of a cause.

Atomic bombs were considered justified.

With the onset of the next crisis, whatever precautions may have been taken during the normal period, nuclear capabilities would still exist. The social proscriptions that prevented nuclear weapons from being used would break down, and sooner or later, and probably on several separate occasions, major and minor nuclear conflicts would occur. Peace itself would work to foment these conflicts, as it worked to bring on the First World War. For then, as in the future, responsible people had never experienced a major war. There is no question that many were stimulated by the prospect of a major war and that many others were not sufficiently fearful of the consequences.

Must peace come to an end when the present conditions no longer prevail? That depends on whether, in the decades remaining of the present peace, we are able to solve several difficult problems.

The nuclear dilemma itself must be solved. Increasing armaments does not provide security so much as it adds to the fear of potential adversaries. Building defense is threatening and life constricting. Arms freezes and reductions also can be frightening, because know-how remains, and an even more destabilizing arms race could recur when crises begin to mount.

The energy dilemma also must be solved, either through the development of safer sources of nuclear energy, or some combination of other energies that are not yet technologically feasible.

The problem of peace as a cause of war must be anticipated. Some method of passing on the consciousness of those who experienced the World Wars crisis must be found.

Are these problems soluble? Something might be learned from the problems that confronted the Victorians and their successes and failures: e.g., slavery, the widening of franchise, and the providing of support and aid for the socially oppressed: the children, the poor, the aged.

These are not problems I wish to dodge, but at the same time, I do not have plausible solutions for them. They would each be the subjects of books themselves. After considering the present peace, I shall at least try to consider the dimensions of the problems to be solved.

But for the next several chapters, we shall be concerned with the present, and with the beginnings of the next crisis, this present will end. Imagine, once again, our European writer considering his own times in 1860. The Crimean War has taken an immense toll in lives. The revolutions of 1848 are a recent memory. Heavy clouds of potential conflict hang over the raw and wild American nation. the Taiping Rebellion is devastating China. Yet he could see a continuity in the period in which he lives, and that it has been coherent and peaceful in the preceding decades as compared to the violent times of Napoleon. He can see prospects for peaceful decades in the future. We can see from our vantage point that the period he was trying to grasp was that between 1815 and 1914, but of course he would not know that.

That European world has expanded, and an American writer today sees himself as part of what has come to be called Western civilization. There is no Crimean War in sight, but for an American, Vietnam is still a painful memory. Heavy clouds of potential conflict hang over the Middle East and Central America. Yet the American can see a continuity in the period in which he lives, and coherence and peace in the decades since World War II and in decades to come. Scholars in the twenty-second century will be able to see that the period he was trying to grasp had a name, and that it lasted from the middle of the twentieth century to the middle of the twenty-first, or to the end, or if something not now visible has occurred (or not occurred) it may be continuing still. These scholars will have a name for that period. They might call it, for instance, the Relational Age.

But our American, writing at the end of the A.D. 1980s (as Toynbee liked to describe his own time), lacking clairvoyance, can only refer to "our time."

2

THE MYTH OF NUCLEAR DETERRENCE

WHY THE REMISSION?

In chapter one it was suggested that we may be living in a normal period, similar to the Victorian Age. But how can we tell whether the relative absence of violence of the past few decades is attributable to this or to the existence of nuclear weapons? Might the Victorians have fought some minor wars that we cannot chance today because of nuclear weapons? Might the Russian interventions in Hungary or Czechoslovakia have been directly challenged if it had not been for nuclear weapons? Would the Suez Crisis or the Yom Kippur Wars have ended as soon as they did? Would the Soviets have backed off in the Cuban Missile Crisis? Or might not all of these have developed into skirmishes involving major powers making limited commitments, as they did in Victorian and Baroque times?

In normal times, nuclear war seems totally inappropriate to any goal anyone might have. We envision it as occurring by accident or at the whim of some fanatical Third World leader whose goals are unintelligible to us.

But we know that in crisis times, the stakes do change. We know that in World War II we did not hesitate to kill civilians by the hundreds of thousands to win a war that seemed to us to involve survival. We know that Germany continued to fight long after there was no chance of winning the war. We know that in ancient and medieval times, whole populations were destroyed, sometimes choosing destruction over surrender. Their losses were personal, because the destruction of Plataea involved the loss of all the known citizens of that city, a much more meaningful and personal loss than the so far incomprehensible idea of the destruction of humankind. We know, then, that circumstances can change, that situations can arise in which we are willing to die for others, or for a cause that we regard as more important than life itself. These circumstances have occurred in the past and we have no way of knowing that they cannot occur again. It is probable that they will occur again. In such circumstances, there is no way of knowing whether collective perceptions of nuclear war, transmitted perhaps through several generations, would cause people to act differently than they had in crises of the past.

But if these are normal times, and we are for the time being less fanatical, has the presence of nuclear weapons contributed to the remission of violence? We don't know, of course, but it does seem possible that in one or more of those cases, major powers involved would have been less cautious. If you consider the Victorian period, however, it is very hard to see how nuclear weapons could have made any difference. There were several minor wars of legitimacy in which the great powers were in concert against small powers. Since they were in concert, they were not threatening one another.

But the conflicts that caused the most fatalities were the revolutions of 1848 and the Crimean War. Revolutions don't lend themselves to nuclear intervention. Even our relatively minor riots of the 1960s had nothing to do with nuclear weapons. What would the great powers of Europe have done: annihilate themselves to destroy the revolution?

The Crimean War, on the other hand, resembled more the wars we have had in the Third World. The war was fought at the very edge of the developed world, and its casualties were greatly increased by disease. The great powers confronted one another as they had in the Age of the Baroque and were doing elsewhere in the Victorian in the Western Hemisphere, South Asia and Africa. Such wars in our own period have been responsible for more than 10 million fatalities (see chapter four).

The Franco-Prussian War occurred later in the Victorian Age, and that seems to be the one that most likely would have been prevented. Though if West Germany had cause to invade France today, the United States would probably come to the aid of France without using nucler weapons. So Germany would be deterred by superior American power, not nuclear weapons.

After the Franco-Prussian War, there were three more decades of peace that were comparable with the present peace. The yearly fatality rate was only 1 per 100,000, though nuclear weapons had not yet been invented.

It would appear that the present peace may not owe its existence to the presence of nuclear weapons. It may be that nuclear weapons neither preserve peace nor cause war, because the times are already peaceful. It may be that peace is not due to nuclear deterrence; rather that nuclear weapons are not used because this is a peaceful period.

THE MUNICH EFFECT

For many people who lived through the 1930s, the Munich agreement among the great powers had a traumatic effect. It was felt then, and subsequent events justified the feeling, that Britain and France had made a serious mistake in failing to oppose Hitler. By allowing Germany to gain the German-speaking sections of Czechoslovakia, the Western powers made the defense of that country impossible, so it was an easy matter the following year for the Nazis to complete their occupation. Not only that, but the Russians, excluded from these negotiations, became convinced that the Western powers were trying to turn the Germans eastward, and this led to the Molotov-Ribbentrop Pact, which assured the conquest and repartitioning of Poland.

The moral of this story was obvious. Nations who wish to maintain the status quo should, at an early stage, vigorously oppose nations who wish to change it, so that the latter have no opportunity to build their strength or improve their position.

This moral was applied in 1950 when the Americans and numerous allies went to the defense of South Korea when it was invaded by countrymen from the north. It was assumed that Russia was behind the invasion, and the Russian dictator, Joseph Stalin, was to be stopped immediately, as Hitler was not.

Unfortunately, there is no analogy between Munich and various postwar crises. Moreover, there is evidence that the moral was incorrectly drawn in the first place. If the moral is correct, Hitler should have been stopped when he recovered the Rhineland in 1935. The French should have driven him out. But suppose they had? Should they then have invaded Germany and made the Germans depose him? Could this not have started a major war anyway, and would such a war have had any support?

If the moral is correct, the European powers should have snuffed out Napoleon as soon as he came to power. But they tried to snuff out the French Revolution earlier than that, and they were beaten. The Medes should have snuffed out the Persians before Cyrus got started, the Greeks should have united to put down Philip of Macedon before Alexander was born. It is obvious that it is not always possible to do these things, and further, it is not always possible to tell which leaders are going to be Hitlers and which are only John Foster Dulleses, given much to bluff but little to action. It would be an unhappy world if nations were to ally to put down any potential threat. The British recognized this when, after the Napoleonic Wars, they refused to join the other great powers in attempting to uphold the principle of legitimacy, i.e., that every holder of every throne was entitled to keep it. This led to several Mediterranean interventions by continental powers in the 1820s, but could not prevent the revolutions of 1830 and 1848.

There is something of an analogy between the legitimacy wars of the 1820s and the attempts of the British and Nationalist Chinese to preserve Vietnam for the French after World War II, or even the American intervention to preserve the *ad hoc* government of South Korea. And as the legitimacy concept faded after the 1820s, so did it fade in the 1950s for the continental powers and in the 1960s for the rimland powers.

For the postwar period is not producing world-conquering Napoleons or Hitlers, it is producing Louis Napoleons and Helmut Kohls. It is not possible to stamp out the world conqueror at an early stage—for he does not exist.

Be this as it may, governments still contain ministers with older generation outlooks who believe the primary problem in the world is aggression and the principle cause of aggression is instability and weakness on the part of potential victims. The prescription that follows this analysis is to oppose aggression wherever it is encountered, and to inculcate stability wherever it is lacking.

Unfortunately this analysis is erroneous and the prescription irrelevant and impossible.

Fortunately the Munich effect is fast losing its meaning for the same reason that the principle of legitimacy disappeared. A new generation has come to power and to this generation Munich means no more than legitimacy meant to the postwar generation of leaders in the 1850s.

THE COLD WAR

The Cold War represented a kind of reversal of Clausewitz in the eyes of diplomats, the press and the public. Diplomacy was perceived as an extension of war by other means. But, if peace is defined as an absence of violent conflict, the Cold War was actually the beginning of peace and might better have been called the Cold Peace (see "Cold Peace" 1984).

In retrospect, it is not surprising that the Cold War was perceived as a continuation of war. There had been war for 30 years, and there had been no peace treaty signed by all the participants. There were a series of short-term crises that could have led to resumption of war, and who could have seen that the Berlin Airlift Crisis or the Suez Crisis was any different from interwar episodes such as the Manchurian Incident or Munich itself? But there was one difference: the episodes of the late 1940s, 1950s and early 1960s involved resolutions rather than changes. Whereas Manchuria and Munich resulted in gains for an expanding power, the Berlin Airlift and Suez episodes resulted in maintenance of the status quo and resolutions that defined the future.

There was to be a great deal of unpleasant, threatening rhetoric. Americans were direct, righteous, and lacking subtlety. The Russians tended to be rude and boorish. There were exceptions like Adlai Stevenson and Anatol Dobrynin, but they never reached positions of real power. It was also the beginning of the period of television, and there was often a disparity between the vehemence of oratory in the General Assembly and private horse trading in the embassies. Or even when horse trading was absent, a Bulganin or a Dulles could appear to be threatening nuclear bombing or massive retaliation without ever actually doing anything. Both of the newly recognized great powers were engaging in what Hans Morgenthau called a policy of making faces. They were reflecting their own inexperience and fear, compounded by an absence of experience in European diplomacy on the part of the Americans and a Byzantine brutality combined with Marxist rhetoric on the part of the Russians. But in the years following World War II, it was not easy to recognize that the situation had changed.

It is Morgenthau, also, who writes about errors that are made in foreign policy when countries mistake the motives of other countries (1973). The Russians and the Americans in the 1930s had been involved in "appeasement," the mistaking of an expansionist policy for one of maintaining the status quo. So the Russians and the Americans had misunderstood Hitler, had rationalized that he would be satisfied if finite demands were met, because they did not wish to resume the World War.

Having made that mistake, it is not surprising that they made the opposite mistake in the 1950s, perceiving policies of the status quo as expansionist policies. And they had good reason. The Russians had installed puppets in the East European countries, most egregiously in Czechoslovakia. How much further would they come? The Americans, at the time clear leaders in atomic power, had invaded Korea, a country that shared a border with the Soviet Union.

There were domestic developments that reenforced the tenseness of the times. The McCarthy reaction swept the United States in the 1950s. Those who would appear to be sympathetic with the Russians, or who had even been sympathetic 20 years earlier, were purged, removed from positions of authority, forbidden to publish or make films. It was, from a Russian viewpoint, a mild purge to be sure. But there was the trial and execution of the Rosenbergs who, the Russians would have known, had little or nothing to do with their development of nuclear weapons. The great secret had been revealed on August 6, 1945.

As for the Russians, they were in the last paranoid days of Stalin, recovering from the incredible tribulations of World War II. Then came the death of Stalin and the appearance of a brilliant and perceptive leader. But the ebullient Khrushchev was scary to Westerners, and as it turned out, scary to the Politburo as well.

So the 1940s and 1950s, a period of incredible recovery for Europe, Russia and Japan, the period of the now-revered Harry Truman (what if he had played his role opposite Khrushchev?) and the revisionistically resurrected Dwight Eisenhower, not to mention Willie Mays and Mickey Mantle, seemed at the time to be a brief respite before the onslaught of the already named World War III.

Looking back, then, we can see that the Cold War was not a war, not a prelude to war. It was the first 15 years of the present peace. The World Wars had ended, for the developed world, in 1945 with Potsdam and

Nagasaki, just as definitely as the Napoleonic Wars had ended with Waterloo and the Congress of Vienna.

THE MYTH OF NUCLEAR DETERRENCE

The *Pax Atomica* does not owe its existence to the atomic bomb. It exists *despite* the atomic bomb.

Nuclear warfare may be unthinkable, certainly, but that does not make it impossible. What qualities would it have that would make it impossible? Certainly it would be terrible. But there have been terrible wars before: the Thirty Years' War, the Taiping Rebellion, World War I.

Nuclear warfare, however, would have unprecedented magnitude. Tens and hundreds of millions of people could be killed. Nuclear weapons are blind and impersonal. They kill the old and the young, the civilian as well as the soldier. They are cruel. They cause lingering, painful death. They are thorough. Chances of escaping pain and death would be much smaller than they would be in the case of invasion. Their effects are long lasting. They can affect the reproductive powers of men for generations to come. We might be thrown back to a feudal period in which small groups of hunters, gatherers and subsistence farmers would band together under some bully or despot to defend themselves against other such boorish and pitiful groups. Moreover, the ecological plundering of the earth might leave our posterity in a situation in which it could hope to recover no more than an agrarian civilization, a metal age civilization of immense social inequality, peasant oppression, and lives that are brutal and short. The effects on environment might be such that temperatures are raised or lowered a bit, or ozone and other components of the atmosphere so affected, that the earth would be for centuries or millennia a less hospitable place than it was during the several millennia in which civilization first developed. Beyond that our species might be wiped out altogether, which, as Toynbee (1948) remarked, would leave us with a record of dominating the earth for a million years or so, with nothing accomplished, whereas the great armoured fish dominated for 50 million years, and used the time constructively to develop the lower jawbone.

For all these reasons then, nuclear war would be unique. Once this is understood, we can expect a unique response. It is certainly clear that nuclear war is simply impossible.

The answers to these arguments have a family resemblance: they all attempt to demonstrate that the qualities of nuclear war are not greatly different from other kinds of warfare. The magnitude of war, for instance, has not prevented it from taking place. Forty million were killed in World War II. Seven million Russians died who need not have (unless they were Jews) if they had surrendered to Hitler. The impersonality of nuclear war is one reason why it is more likely to take place. In World War II it was easier to kill many people by dropping a bomb on them than it was to kill one man with a bayonet. It is probably also somewhat easier to be killed in that way. The cruelty of war is as old as war itself, and it was very bad indeed in days when wonder drugs did not exist, infection was the great killer, and surgery was practiced without anesthetics. As for the thoroughness of nucler weapons, they can be no more thorough than the victor in the siege of a town or castle. The rules there often were that if there was resistance the men would be killed, the women raped, and the children carried off into slavery. Yet people resisted anyway, even if the cause was hopeless. As for the effects on progeny, we are still more concerned about ourselves than the unborn, the more so because we live in an age in which it is not important to have heirs for property, business or money.

Perhaps then nuclear war is not impossible. But it is then argued that it is prevented by rational policies of deterrence. No great power will use nuclear weapons against any other because it knows that attack will bring overwhelming counterattack in a useless cause. If nation A attacks nation R, nation R will retaliate, both nations will sustain immense destruction, and neither will gain anything. Knowing this, nation A does not attack.

There are so many answers to this it is difficult to decide in which order they should be presented. But briefly, nations do not behave rationally, technostructures often make decisions that would differ from those of a chess player, nations can have values higher than survival, wars can come from rational miscalculation. You can say, probably, that the history of warfare is full of examples of irrational decision compounded by rational miscalculation. It was irrational for the Arab leaders to initiate yet another hopeless war against Israel, for Tsar Nicholas and his advisors to enter a war for which they were not prepared, for Louis Napoleon to fight a war against Prussia that he was sure he would lose, but each government was driven by price, by situation, and by the system in which it operated. Egoists like Napoleon and Hitler are ready to take risks that are not in the interests of their countries, but they are allowed to come to power by rational elites. Governments easily misjudge the vital interests, the capacity and the national morale of other nations. The Americans did not realize their economic policies would provoke Pearl Harbor. The Japanese underestimated the will and capacity of the Americans to mobilize (Melko, 1971).

There are times when a government might consider a defense of its honor or of a religion more important than existence itself. In such times we cannot expect that rational considerations would prevent the use of all means available to achieve the supreme objective. But the period of *Pax Atomica* is not one of these times. This is a secular period. This is a period in which commitment to nationalism has considerably receded. There are no major economic problems that would give rise to radical new ideologies. This is a normal period in the development of Western civilization in which there are not likely to be differences of a magnitude that would require recourse to the use, by major powers, of all the force they command.

When Harold Brown was secretary of defense under President Carter, he told a Senate committee that it wasn't credible to a Soviet planner that America would launch an all-out attack if the Russians were to take out a single missile site. Senator John Glenn replied that it might give the planner more pause than if we said "we will respond by taking out a railhead or something like that."

Brown said the point was that you had to have a range of possible responses in order to maintain credibility. "I get lost," Glenn responded, "in what is credible and not credible. This whole thing gets so incredible. . . ."

"That," replied Brown, "is why we sound a little crazy when we talk about it" (Zuckerman 1984, 180).

What you have here is two older generation political leaders sensing the change in our time, realizing that the crisis logic no longer works. And one of them happened to be the man who in the 1960s had been chosen to make the nation's first space orbit partly because his spirit and personality were perceived to be the qualities expected in an American hero.

The assumption that deterrence is what prevents war makes people uncomfortable. Perhaps even the term "mutually assured destruction" was intended to be more comforting. President Reagan, for instance, believes it has prevented war for several decades. But, as he remarked in 1983, to rely "on mutual threat is a sad commentary on the human condition." The longing for the good old days came out in 1982 Senate testimony by Strategic Air Command General Bennie Davis, who declared we are no longer relying on deterrence but on "counterforce," which he translated as ". . . war fighting. The two are synomymous." (Zuckerman 1984, 205–207). Oh, General Davis, for the days when we could solve our problems by war fighting, the good old days of World Wars and Depression.

More often than not, governments are rational and do calculate correctly. But in the case of nuclear war, more often than not is hardly good enough. The existence of nuclear weapons poses a continuous and frightening threat. If we must rest our hopes on their capacity to deter, it would seem likely that a major nuclear war in the not-too-distant future is a probability.

But we do not depend on the capacity to deter. The concept of deterrence is a myth of normal times, created to explain the absence of nuclear war. Despite the cases one can bring forth to show that deterrence would not have worked in the past, the concept appeals to our presumption of rational mutual interest, a presumption that has considerable validity in normal times. Nevertheless, the bomb does not preserve the peace; the peace deters the use of the bomb.

PROLIFERATION

In the 1960s, we thought of this problem as a threat. More and more nations would become nuclear powers, the chances of a conflict between two of them would increase geometrically: only one combination if there were two, three if there were three, ten if there were four, and a horrific number if there were more.

Not only that, but the whole principle of deterrence was based on the idea that if you were bombed, you would know who to retaliate against. In a world of 15 nuclear powers you might not know, and the credibility of deterrence would be much reduced, hence the greater likelihood of nuclear war.

It seems probable that newer nations will try to acquire nuclear weapons either by producing them or by purchasing them (Evan and Hilgartner 1987, 19–24). It also seems possible that where nationalism remains strong, where the preservation of a way of life seems vital, the chances of nuclear weapons being used by one such power against another are considerable.

The use of nuclear weapons anywhere would be a terrible thing. But the use of such weapons by newer Third World nations, if it were to take place, would not result in the indiscriminate use of nuclear devices by every other nation that possesses them. Rather it would be a disaster, like the 1988 earthquake in Armenia, that would call into effect all the lifegiving and lifesaving capacities the developed world has accumulated. It would create fear all right, but the counter use of nuclear weapons by other nations would be extremely unlikely. The nation that used them would find its friends censuring it as well as its foes and the objectives it sought would certainly be lost. It would hardly be surprising if a demand for Nuremburg Trials emerged, and if these were restricted, an investigation and domestic trial would be likely to occur. This would involve no setting up of a special UN political commission. It would be the consequence of the climate as it is now.

Proliferation is probably more of an evil than otherwise, but it is doubtful that it can be prevented. The history of war indicates that superior techniques tend to be assimilated in time by all nations within a configuration. It is interesting that, in a great deal of discussion about the possibilities involved in the Strategic Arms Limitation Talks between Russia and the United States, there has been scarcely any comment on the fact that the agreements would include only two nations. Clearly proliferation is not a major preoccupation of the arms control specialists.

There may be some advantages for the peace, however, if proliferation cannot be prevented. Small nations will have the defense of a scorpion's sting, and this should give them a little more confidence in attempting to free themselves from some of the restrictions of great nations. In the crunch, however, nuclear weapons probably are not as effective for a small nation as the development of a believable capacity for guerrilla warfare. The presence of such a capacity enabled Yugoslavia to resist Russia. The Czechs and Hungarians were not able to resist Russia, and the presence of nuclear weapons would not have helped. What would they have done with them? Bomb Moscow and reap return bombs on all their major cities? Use them for tactical defense and foul up their own country in a losing cause?

What about the acquisition of neutron or other "clean" bombs? It doesn't seem likely, if these are developed, that a small power is going to have them. And if big powers have not used dirty bombs in losing causes like Vietnam, why would they use clean bombs? The advantage is difficult to perceive, but the disadvantage (e.g., the inconvenience of your government falling or losing the next election) is obvious.

There also has been some concern about terrorists making or acquiring bombs (e.g., O'Heffernan and Lovins 1983). But this would not change the proliferation problem. What would be the difference between a terrorist acquiring such a bomb, and an Idi Amin or a Qaddafi acquiring it? Irrational use of a nuclear weapon by a small power or by an individual would not change the situation.

The fact is that more lethal weapons have been available throughout the twentieth century. At the beginning of the century, anarchists used bombs. Between the wars, organized crime used machine guns. Juvenile delinquents have caused more fatalities through greater use of handguns— good ones, not just Saturday night specials. Terrorism could return to the United States, and if the belief were strong enough, a modern explosive device might kill hundreds of thousands of people. There are many clever people and many true believers. There is no defense against this kind of catastrophe. But because we are in a rational period, we will probably respond rationally when the catastrophe occurs. No amount of disarmament, no amount of security, can do much to reduce the possibility of such events occurring. When a particular type of problem arises, we can often take action to deal with it, as we have with airplane hijacking. But no amount of foresight can eliminate the possibility of catastrophe wrought by small groups of irrational fanatics, dedicated believers, megalomaniacs, psychotics, or cynical thugs.

Nations or groups may acquire nuclear weapons, but that does not mean they will use them. If, very occasionally, they are used, say once or twice in the next several decades, these will be individual disasters and treated as such.

THE SUPERIORITY OF DEFENSE

Through most of the history of war defense has been superior to offense. This situation has been masked by attention given to great conquerors like Alexander III of Macedon or Chandra Gupta II of India. But in most instances, the attacking state has been at a disadvantage. It has had to operate in the territory of the defending state, and even as it succeeds it moves further from its source of supply and becomes weaker. Its soldiers are subject to homesickness and the corruption of an alien culture. Since the attacker is at such a disadvantage, most of the time states do not attack one another. But history does not record nonevents, hence we get a disproportionate picture of exceptions.

Attacks do succeed under exceptional leadership or when the situation has changed so that one state is considerably strengthened or weakened in relation to its neighbor because of the development of a new technique or because of internal revolution. When an attack is successful, a new balance of power is created and the defeated state accepts loss of territory. If a new technique has caused a disruption, it is adopted by other states. If rebellion has caused weakness, it must be resolved either by overwhelming defeat of the rebels, or by concessions to their demands. Once the problem is resolved, our attention is turned to some other exception.

It would therefore seem to be anomalous that in the present world situation, the nuclear powers appear to possess long-standing offensive superiority. Each can attack other powers, nuclear or nonnuclear, and it is doubtful that such attacks can be prevented. Each can inflict incredible damage on others, but none can defend itself against attack.

Since peace has coincided with the superiority of defense in the past, it might be supposed that there would be considerable concern about the present situation. Quite the opposite is the case. Concern is manifested, rather, over the possibility that defense might be restored. If one country were able to defend itself against land invasion, it would apparently acquire an overwhelming superiority over all other powers. It is therefore interpreted as a threat if a country tries to develop a civilian defense program, an antiballistic missile system (Warnke 1978), or a Strategic Defense Initiative (SDI), the "Star Wars" project of the Reagan administration. Much of the debate about SDI has to do with its feasibility (e.g., Brower 1988; Kounosu 1987). If such a debate were won by the proponents, that could be perceived as dangerous. But how can it be won without testing? It even has been argued that actually employing a civilian defense system and someday ordering the population to disperse to the country to enter a system of underground shelters, would be the equivalent of the mobilization before World War I. It would not be an act of war, but it would be an act preparatory to war.

The fallacy in this view is already demonstrated by the increasing independence of small powers. The nuclear power sometimes refrains from attacking the small power because of the defensive superiority of the latter, expressed through the use of guerrilla warfare or passive resistance. It can, of course, destroy the small power through nuclear attack. The government of Russia could have destroyed Yugoslavia and the government of the United States could have destroyed Cuba. They did not do so because such action would be irrational and this is a period of relative rationality.

There are still situations in which attacks take place. In the past two decades, Russia attacked Czechoslovakia and Afghanistan; El Salvador attacked Honduras; the United States attacked Vietnam, and Thailand attacked Cambodia; Israel has engaged in cross-border conflicts with Egypt, Syria and Jordan; Iraq attacked Iran. But there must be 600 borders that have not been violated in the past decade. Border crossings have been less common than internal rebellions.

Defense against nuclear attack is not taken seriously because the difficulty would be so formidable and the rewards so improbable. While governments are less concerned with shelters and even stockpiling, there are still serious people concerned with survival in terms of homesteading, retreat groups planning a tribal existence, and proposals for education on living in radioactive environments (e.g., Clayton 1977), methods of minimizing contamination in gardens. But these movements are private, small and usually related to other ecological interests that will bring returns even if total nuclear catastrophe does not occur. Such knowledge, for instance, might have been comforting to residents of the Harrisburg, Pennsylvania area in 1979, or Chernobyl in 1986.

If defense is not considered seriously, then neither is first strike. To be sure, there is plenty of discussion about whether a particular weapon, such as MX, is suitable for anything but first strike, but it does not follow that anyone is planning a strategy that assumes the other side has only first strike weapons and therefore is incapable of retaliation. But when plans for riding MX missiles around the country on trains are considered (Zirkle 1988), it is questionable whether the real issue is whether this makes MX a more believable defense weapon or whether the missile may pass our town in the middle of the night without our knowing it. Of course the trains could be labeled "MX Missiles: Thank You for Not Smoking" but then a new set of problems arises: could these missiles be hijacked by terrorists? And, do we want to experience the negative feelings associated with reminders of the nuclear dilemma? We are genuinely concerned about nuclear weapons being near us without our knowing and about unnecessary reminders, but the question of whether a weapon is of first or second strike calibre is of little importance when neither kind of strike is anticipated. Rather there is a general assumption that if there were a first strike there would be a second, in a game in which two strikes are out.

In general, then, the superiority of the defense continues in nonnuclear situations, as it has in other normal periods. And nonnuclear situations are the only kind there have been since 1945. States cannot easily gain rational objectives by attacking other states.

Would the development of some sort of umbrella defense, like the Strategic Defense Initiative, transform the situation? It is hard to see how. When systems are developed, they usually have flaws that need to be tested. How is the Strategic Defense Initiative to be tested? And if it were not, how much faith could governments and people have in it? Would it be threatening to the powers that did not possess it? Yes, in the same way that a system of civilian defense would be threatening. And for that reason it is likely that governments that could develop such a defense would refrain from doing so. If they were to develop such a system, it could be a sign that the rational period of normal times was passing, and the next period of danger was approaching. But more likely, both great powers would, at great expense and inconvenience, develop such systems and neither would attack the other, any more than they do now when one or the other thinks it has achieved a temporary superiority in some area of the arms race (cf. Schwartz and Derber 1986; Evan Hilgartner 1987, 84–104).

THE PEAKING OF THE ARMS RACE

As the younger generation comes to power, and fear of conventional attack declines, the arms race is coming to a halt. The measurement here should be in terms of military defense as a percentage of gross national product. If the defense budget of a country remains in proportion to other elements in the budget, that country cannot be said to be in an arms race.

Arms control negotiations are likely to reflect this stabilization. When an arms control agreement like SALT or INF is achieved, it is likely to involve a reduction of arms in situations in which both sides see no change in security.

As Table 2.1 indicates, in the most recent decade for which figures are available, there has been a modest increase in military expenditures as a percentage of gross national product all around the world, in developed countries as in underdeveloped countries, in the East as in the West among the developed countries. Even in the bellicose early years of the Reagan administration, the increase in defense expenditures was moderate. This probably represents the peaking of the arms race.

Certainly there have been vested interests in maintaining high levels of military expenditure. This has resulted in competition in contracts in the American automobile and aerospace industries, a tendency to build increasingly costly and vulnerable weapons, and a follow-on system where new weapons are designed that are geared to counter the weapons it is anticipated will be created by the Russians to counter the weapons we are

TABLE 2.1
WORLDWIDE MILITARY EXPENDITURES 1973 AND 1983
(As a Percentage of GNP)

	U.S.	U.S.S.R.	NATO Countries	Warsaw Pact	Developed Countries	Developing Countries
1973	5.7	13.7	4.7	11.4	5.8	5.4
1983	6.1	14.0	5.2	11.7	6.2	5.8

(From *Statistical Abstract of the United States* 1987)

now producing. Whether this process is caused by the Russian threat or whether the Russian threat is caused by the process is an interesting question (Kaldor 1981; Mok and Duvall 1988).

Those who for decades have been caught up in this process, live a nightmare of checks and counterchecks, in conventional as well as nuclear war. We are warned that we must dominate in long-range, unmanned precision weapons so our pilots won't be captured and tortured; we are reminded that though we usually are leaders in military research, we often lag behind the Soviet Union in deployment; we must keep up with the development of weapons that avoid radar, and respond to the effects that instant central intelligence will have on future battles. "We have no choice whether to run this marathon" (Cohen 1987).

But as decades go by, and new generations come to power, and nuclear war must be kept alive by television reproductions, it becomes more difficult to justify maintaining such an expensive level of production, especially when other very successful countries like Japan and West Germany do not seem compelled to maintain such levels. Military production, moreover, is highly inflationary, since it produces goods that cannot be consumed. Moreover, as new weapons become more complicated, they seem less likely to work and, like the MX or Trident as compared to the Minuteman or Polaris, more vulnerable to attack. It seems difficult to believe that increased armaments expenditure can maintain support.

There will remain in existence large quantities of nuclear weapons, and these will be improved and replaced continuously. This will involve a large amount of expenditure that from the point of view of the international relations specialist or the conservationist or the sociologist will seem to be unnecessary, although the economist and the manager might disagree.

In the 1960s and 1970s there were at least 20 international arms control agreements, half of them between Russia and the United States. These involved limitations on strategic nuclear weapons, both antiballistic and strategic offensive categories; nuclear test limitations in atmosphere, outer space, underwater and some restrictions underground; measures to prevent the spread of knowledge of raw materials for, and manufacture of nuclear weapons; and, measures to prevent deployment of nuclear weapons in certain areas such as Antarctica, outer space, Latin America, the ocean floor and, most recently, Europe (Caldwell 1984; Watson 1987).

There were also prohibitions against the development, production and stockpiling of bacteriological and toxic weapons, which updated the Geneva Protocol of 1925 that had forbidden development of asphyxiating gases and bacteriological weapons. There were agreements to protect the environment from nuclear contamination and other means of altering the environment for military purposes as well as crisis management agreements improving communications between American and Russian leaders, with particular reference to crises that might escalate in other countries and the possibility of warning in the event of an accidental firing (U.S. Arms Control and Disarmament Agency 1984).

Of these, only the prohibitions against development of bacteriological weapons (The Biological Weapons Convention of 1972) involved actual disarmament, getting rid of existing arms and agreeing not to develop or produce any more. The others involved either arms control—the limiting of arms production, or placement, or testing—or the management of problems arising from arms production. Arms control agreements do not necessarily reduce arms. During one 13-year period (1959–1971) there were 13 arms control agreements negotiated while world arms appropriations were more than doubling (Epstein 1973).

Consider the "zero option," which dominated negotiations over European disarmament from 1982 to 1987. At the center of the argument was how the United States would respond if the Soviet Union invaded Europe. Would there be intermediate-range weapons close enough for a regional rather than total response? There would be, it was thought, if each side kept a few nuclear intermediate range weapons near the edges of the continent. But then, verification would be much more difficult than it would be if there were no such missiles. Very much mixed-up with this were political considerations, such as how the European antinuclear movement would respond if the United States did not accept the zero option it had proposed at the end of the 1970s and how the Japanese would respond to the idea of a limited intermediate Soviet force defended only by a symbolic American force in Alaska (Krauthammer 1987).

But what underlies these discussions, perhaps, is a decline of concern about any of these problems. If neither the Europeans nor the Americans think the Russians are going to invade Europe, the problem of verification loses its intensity. A Russian sea invasion of Japan is even less likely. Of course, if American weapons are removed from Europe and Japan, the countries in those territories don't have to worry that the Russians will attack them to take out their missiles. But that involves some pretty improbable scenarios, a lot more improbable than a major nuclear war that would be overwhelmingly catastrophic to Europe and Japan anyway.

One advantage of the removal of nuclear weapons would be the removal of symbols of the presence of nuclear weapons in the world. That is why, perhaps, it is so unpleasant to come upon the coolers of a nuclear power plant. It isn't that visitors are worried about coming into an area that could become contaminated. But whether one is having a lovely day or an awful day, no one wants to be reminded of the eternal, unremovable presence of the nuclear threat. The coolers are too massive to ignore and seem impossible to oppose.

It is, therefore, precisely because of the realization of the secondary importance of arms negotiations, because the safety of Europe and Japan is little changed, because the world is hardly less dangerous than it was before, because the symbolic nature of the agreements is generally recognized, that feelings of pleasure or apprehension about such agreements is ephemeral, and the stock market flutters no more than it does at the resignation of a chairman of the Federal Reserve Board, or the discovery of a gene linked to a fatal disease.

Further arms control agreements, unilateral freezes, and simple refusal to support new projects are not likely to affect the military situation. The political balance and atmosphere are such that no problem is likely to arise that would require a nuclear solution. What will be given up in agreements, or not funded in the first place, will be those weapons that seem most expensive and vulnerable, those that seem least likely to work, and those backed by the least effective vested interests. If the reduction comes about through arms control agreements, that may give us all a nicer glow, but the effect of refusal to fund would be the same in terms of the decline of military expenditures. In fact, the refusal to fund may have one advantage in that it does not lend itself to future anguish about the possibility that the other side may not live up to its agreements, an anguish that may be greater for the sometimes paranoid Russians than for the negotiation-oriented Americans.

The growing antinuclear movement in Europe, North America and Japan (Price 1982) is a further indication of the growing awareness of a normal period and the rise to dominance of the younger generation. The threat of war cannot be maintained on an everyday basis when war has not been known for four decades and the majority of the living population cannot remember a previous war.

More widespread than the antinuclear movement is the "civil defense conspiracy." What conspiracy? The widespread conspiracy of national and local leaders not to develop a civil defense industry, an industry that could do for the housing industry what weapons systems have done for the automobile industry. Who is responsible for the conspiracy? All of us. From top to bottom, no one believes in civil defense. The Carter administration, projecting two billion dollars as necessary to develop a "crisis relocation," as the euphemism goes, met with so much ridicule that it eventually asked for a paltry $100 million (Zuckerman 1984). I recently heard the local disaster director of a midwestern city describe to a high school audience the measures that were being taken to evacuate the city in the event of a nuclear threat. We would ask the Russians to give us eight days notice. Odd-numbered license plates would leave on one day, even-numbered the next. The incredulity and laughter of the students was shared by the director himself. But this refusal to alter our lives with supplies of safe drinking water and escape routes, even more than the antinuclear movement, reflects the general appraisal that we do not really live in a crisis situation.

Could it be that this is a matter of denial? Is it possible that people feel the situation is hopeless so they just try not to think about it? Certainly it is possible. The trouble with the idea of psychic blocking, as expressed, for instance, by Robert Lifton in his book on Hiroshima survivors (1967), is that any time a person does not seem to be bothered by a past terrible experience or the threat of one in the future, it is too easy to say he or she is blocking. In Chapter Six I shall present a study that suggests that people are not blocking; they are just not worried. Admittedly, this is not easy to demonstrate either way.

Whether or not further arms control or reduction is achieved, however, will not make much difference to security. In the last decade of the twentieth century both dominant powers were considering the military use of space. This issue provides an opportunity for each to wait on the other. The commitment of resources to a space-based missile defense system would be immensely expensive without increasing security. Each could wait to see what the other does. "He who hesitates is sometimes saved" (Thurber 1945).

But short-term predictions are more difficult to make than assessments of the long-term situation. Declining to pursue missile defense in space would be consistent with the outlook of the younger generation, but the development of such a program, though an egregious waste, would not affect the present peace.

If the space systems were not developed, and if arms control followed by arms reduction were achieved, that would save resources that could be used for better purposes. But it would add little to security. After all, know-how cannot be lost, and in the future secondary crises might be magnified by the fear that excessive arms control had limited the capacity of one's own government to act and the suspicion that other governments might, in response to the crisis, begin reconstruction of their military technostructure. That could lead to an arms race, or even the threat of an arms race, that would greatly magnify the crisis.

On the other hand, it is possible to live with military power. We have done so for more than 40 years, and the governments of Europe did so in the nineteenth century. If the economic forces that profit from military expenditure continue to be effective, perhaps because of indifference in the general population, the arms race could continue indefinitely. So long as each great power perceives that the other power can retaliate to an unacceptable extent, it is extremely unlikely that either would consider the use of nuclear weapons as a rational choice. It does not matter whether either can destroy the other five or twenty times over or whether either thinks it has the advantage or is at a disadvantage. One authority who thinks the Russians had an advantage in the 1980s also thinks this might be good for world stability, since it would make them more confident (Kahn 1982). From this perspective Gorbachev could be seen, not as the first dominant power leader of the younger generation, but as the beneficiary of a perception of Russian superiority. Perhaps he is both.

From time to time, concern is expressed about the effects of restrictions on testing, such as a military flight test ban that would restrict tests on missile flight capacity. But what effect would this have? Suppose we deploy untested missiles? Who knows how much less reliable they are than tested missiles? Who would act differently in a crisis, knowing the missiles aimed at him are untested? Who, held up in a grocery store, asks whether the robber's pistol is tested or even whether he knows how to aim it?

It is difficult to imagine any country developing a defensive weapons system it would be eager to test. It also seems likely that if one side believed the other side might have developed a successful defense, it would be prudent to leave the matter untested. And in a normal period, prudence is likely to prevail. A recent study of the Cuban Missile Crisis and the Yom Kippur War shows that government decisions seem to have been made with almost no regard for current nuclear power distributions between the great powers (Schwartz and Derber 1986; cf. Kaplan 1983).

Through most of history, military power has tended to increase as technology accumulated, but the incidence of war and peace has fluctuated. Sorokin's attempt to measure the incidence of war and internal disturbance in the West and Classical Civilization indicated a confusing fluctuation of casualties with no evident long-term direction. A study of mine on societies that had managed long periods of peace indicated that they have turned up pretty much at random through several millennia. Naroll and Bullough found little correlation between defensive superiority or inferiority, and frequency of war. Wallace finds a correlation between arms races and war, but cannot say whether the arms races are causes of war or responses to changing political situation. (Sorokin 1957, 540–547; Melko 1973, 28–41; Naroll, Bullough and Naroll 1974; Wallace 1981).

Peace can exist in societies in which military expenditures are increasing. But the likelihood is that peace will make military expenditures less competitive compared to other perceived needs, and that over time such expenditures will tend to decline.

ACCIDENT

Armaments are not the cause of war. Still, one would feel safer living next to a cemetery than an explosives factory.

And what an explosives factory! More than 50,000 warheads, "most smaller than suitcases," a few of which can kill millions of people and destroy the environment for decades; long-range "strategic" weapons, land-based missiles, submarine-launched missiles, strategic bombers; battlefield, tactical, theater, intermediate and sea controlled nuclear weapons, all of them "nonstrategic" and capable of carrying nuclear, conventional or chemical warheads. They are located in many countries including Britain, France, China, Eastern Europe, South Korea, Vietnam and Guam.

They each have their charms. Land-based missiles, once launched, can't be recalled. Submarines can be contacted, but if you do, you give away their locations. Bombers can be called back, but of course they are vulnerable. So the dominant powers have a good supply of all three kinds of strategic weapons. Intermediate missiles are disconcerting because they must be deployed nearer their targets, e.g., the U. S. Pershing II's in Western Europe or the Russian SS 20's in Eastern Europe. Long-ranged sea-launched missiles are carried by surface ships, and they may or may not have nuclear warheads. Tactical bombs are for battlefield use (how?) and the United States has these in Western Europe and the Far East, Russia in Eastern Europe and Vietnam. Battlefield missiles, including nuclear artillery shells, also are carried by vehicles (Arkin and Fieldhouse 1987, 70–80).

It would seem that the more of these weapons there are, and the more they are under the control of subordinates, the greater the chance of accident or subordinate misjudgment. And certainly, if the perception develops that these weapons have little to do with increasing security, there would seem to be considerable motivation to see what can be done about reducing their numbers, and the number of people who control their release.

But what applies to proliferation applies, in part, to the possibility of accident. If a single episode occurs in which a submarine commander mistakenly or irrationally fires, or if a single missile is somehow released, there could be a terrible catastrophe. A single such episode could result in the deaths of millions of people if the target were a large city.

That would be a disaster. In terms of fatalities it could match or surpass the Biafran War or the total casualties of the war in Vietnam. There would be no event to match it in normal times in the developed world of the past 250 years, the worse previous experience in normal times having been the Crimean War. But still it would be an event distinguishable in magnitude of catastrophe from the Napoleonic Wars or the World Wars. It would not be an occasion for rejoicing, but it would be something different from a multiple exchange between the two superpowers.

The release of a single missile, understood to be an accident, would be a calamity that would draw world response and sympathy, sympathy of the sort that has come to the city of Hiroshima. Given the deployment of nuclear weapons, a deployment that is not likely to change, such an accident could occur in the Present Age. Yet the age could still be seen historically, as we see the Victorian Age today, as a period of relative peace.

No foreseeable reduction in armaments, whether it comes unilaterally or through some series of agreements, is likely to reduce the chance of such an accident. All that can be improved are the systems for assessing threats and delaying responses and perhaps a sensitivity to what is needlessly provocative (Arkin and Fieldhouse 1987). One suspects, for instance, that Russian and American diplomats may have discussed the 1984 American naval operations carried out within 15 miles of Vladivostok (Mack 1988, 65) and, perhaps with the Russians musing about the possibility of future operations carried out within 15 miles of San Diego, agreed that in the future perhaps a 200-mile limit would be more prudent. As is the case with arms reduction, such improvements are likely to take place quietly and unilaterally, rather than by negotiated agreement (Jamgotch and Finley 1988, 64). They are likely to occur because of a recognition that in normal times catastrophe is more likely to take place by accident than by design. Agreement is not likely to have much effect, since governments are reluctant to admit there is any danger of accident, and in any event they are not willing to discuss arrangements made to prevent it.

A catastrophe of different magnitude would be an accidental multiple exchange between the great powers. Much has been written about episodes in which instruments indicated a major attack was on the way and a counter response was ordered. Then it was discovered that the detected attack was an error caused by computer malfunction, sunspots, the aurora borealis or an amateur computer operator and the counter response was cancelled fifteen or ten or two minutes before it would have been too late to stop the launching of missiles. Some well-informed people have insisted that such episodes have not occurred, or that the orders that were given had to do with higher stages of alertness or readiness and came nowhere near commanding the launching of missiles. On the evidence of the record of authority in other areas, such as denying dangers of nuclear radiation from fallout or reactors, I am inclined to belive that such episodes have taken place.

A multiple exchange is also more likely to take place by accident rather than design, but unlike the accidental single missile, it is also more preventable. As security increases and governments think intentional attack less probable, they are likely to be more concerned about preventing an accidental multiple attack, first of all by taking measures to reduce the possibility. While they will always publicly deny the possibility, privately they will be more concerned about reducing the chances of its occurrence. And since the multiple attack is centrally controlled, it should be possible to take some steps in this direction.

There even may be private conversations among diplomats on the problem, and suggestions privately exchanged. These are not likely to occur in any "Conference for Prevention of Accidental Nuclear Exchange." The only way such a conference might occur is if the means of prevention had already been worked out, and the governments wished to take public credit for it. In other words, the advent of such a conference probably would be a sign that progress already had been attained.

It is possible that such private discussions already have taken place or are now taking place through normal diplomatic channels. There is no way of knowing. But it certainly would seem logical to share with your adversary any means that you have developed that will prevent him from accidentally obliterating you. Publicly such exchanges have taken place, but probably without serious intent (Gordon 1986).

The problem of accidental nuclear warfare is not to be discounted or minimized. The chances of an accidental, single mistake seem likely over a period of time, just as the chances of having an appendectomy are high over a lifetime but low in any given year. If such an event were to occur it would be horrible, but the peace could be preserved. The multiple exchange, while more preventable, would end the peace catastrophically.

The possibility of accident is a great worry that will never be relieved. But the chances against a multiple exchange occurring may be reduced as the Present Age continues.

WORLD WAR III? NEVER

The war has its name before it has been fought. We worried about it a great deal in the 1950s, but it has not come along, and we are now more inclined to be preoccupied with more manageable, more immediate problems.

The decline of fear of nuclear war has been a concern to many. Scenarios are endlessly evolved in which nuclear war is suddenly upon us, usually with a vividly rendered description of the process. "All now hinged on the President of the United States, who had an awful and solitary responsibility" (Bidwell 1978). It seems irresponsible for people to live in such a dangerous situation and not do anything about it. They should be writing letters to Congressmen supporting the latest weapons system, or marching against the latest weapons system, or at least stocking up on aluminum foil to preserve the genitals of their children.

Are we living on the side of Vesuvius? The people who did live on the side of Vesuvius, of course, did a lot of living before the volcano finally erupted. And many other people have lived on the sides of volcanos that have not erupted yet. It has been possible for them to move, of course, but it is not possible to move from all sources of danger.

It seems likely that the volcano will be quiescent for awhile. But after 10 decades, or 15, when the next imbalance of power relationship or transformation of outlook occurs, what then?

Nuclear war is the first idea that comes to mind. The name World War III will prove to have been premature, because the name would make no more sense to our great-grandchildren than Napoleonic War II or Thirty Years' War III would make to us. A nuclear war of multimegaton magnitude would be a unique experience, one not likely to attract Roman numerals.

The idea that a major nuclear war or even a series of nuclear wars can be fought and survived, if necessary, has been presented by a number of political scientists (e.g., Kahn 1978), particularly those associated with RAND. They make an interesting case in terms of modern recuperative capacity, but they presume a morale that does not seem likely in such a situation. Such a war would be more likely to occur when institutionalization had had its effect and totally new problems have brought about new ideologies, leading to major changes in values and attitudes.

In the long run—within a century or two—such changes are likely. If nuclear war were then to follow, it seems probable that there would be a reversion to feudalism followed by a long recuperative period like that which followed the fall of the Roman and Han empires. This reversion would take place, because as Rushton Coulborn (1956) argues, feudalism is the normal recovery political structure after catastrophe of civilizational dimensions. People look for local alliances and these gradually extend.

What would emerge then would probably not be a regenerated industrial society, but a largely agricultural civilization comparable to most of those that preceded the industrial revolution. This presumes that Harrison Brown (1978) is right when he suggests that after such a major catastrophe we would not be able to recover the combinations of materials necessary to rebuild industrial society. It also discounts species destructive possibilities, such as a nuclear winter (Powers 1984).

Crises have often resulted in the termination of a state system and the onset of an imperial phase. Persia or Rome or Ch'in conquers all, and an Achaemenid or Roman or Han empire dominates the entire civilization for hundreds of years of relative peace and sterility (Melko 1969; Wesson 1967). Such conquests, of course, involved a great deal of violence, and how would such violence take place without nuclear war?

One way has been suggested by R. S. Scanlan (1985), who notes that empires occur within civilizations. If, therefore, the United States dominates Western civilization and Russia dominates a different civilization (Orthodox? Byzantine?), could each become the dominant power within that civilization? If so, that might happen without a nuclear war, with great power tightening its control within its civilization, and no other state being in a position to challenge them each. Even Britain and France, which have scorpion stings against a Russian threat, may not bring themselves to use such threats against the United States. This analysis has its problems, but it does suggest that there could be other possibilities than nuclear war.

Another possibility has been suggested by David Wilkinson (1985). In the past, Wilkinson believes, empires have been created when a dominant power challenged an interstate system, picking off weak powers first, then strong powers, one at a time. But our own system has developed defenses against this occurrence, through preliminary counterinterventions and grand alliances. The counterintervention, a minor warlike act, may prevent the dominant power from reaching the stage of challenging major powers. Beyond that, there is the possibility of a grand alliance of major powers deterring the dominant power from attacking adversaries one at a time. Even though the formation of alliances failed to prevent the World Wars, it might have if the dominant power believed the alliance would hold. If, however, the dominant power tests the alliance, and a general war were to result, Wilkinson believes that it would be terribly destructive to world society, ten times worse than the World Wars, even if nuclear weapons were not used. Wilkinson's analysis, like Scanlan's, suggests there may be alternate possibilities to nuclear war in the next crisis period, but the alternatives are unpromising.

In any event, it is likely that a future total nuclear war, should it occur, would not be seen as World War III. It would be a separate war, comparable to others in a general way, but incomparable in its casualties and after effects. Certainly it would terminate what we have parochially called "modern Western history." It is most likely to occur in the latter half of the twenty-first century or early in the twenty-second. If it does occur, what follows will be something very different, possibly a reversion to feudalism followed by the resumption of agrarian but not industrial civilization. If it does not occur, it will be because problems that now have no apparent solution have somehow been solved.

3

THE REMISSION OF VIOLENCE

THE PRESENT PEACE

Several decades have passed since atomic-bombs were used in war. There have been many frightening statements made about what nuclear war could mean in terms of casualties. Two governments have spent fantastic amounts of money stockpiling nuclear weapons. The newspapers have been full of hostile statements by leaders of countries and of accounts of a series of wars, revolutions and invasions in Guatemala, the Dominican Republic, Nigeria, Ceylon, Bangladesh, Angola, Iran, Afghanistan, El Salvador, Nicaragua. There have been many other crises that have been very frightening, particularly the Berlin Airlift Crisis of 1948 and the Cuban Missile Crisis of 1962.

But by comparison to the decades before 1950, we have been living in a relatively peaceful period (cf. Lukacs 1978, 217–218). The term "Cold War" means that major powers have not been fighting a war against one another, they have been only making faces. There have been only two major conflicts in the developed world since 1945: the Greek Civil War and the Hungarian Revolution. There have been none for more than three decades. The per capita fatality rate from war and revolution has been below any comparable four-decade period in the Victorian Age or the Age of the Baroque, when civilization was elegant and war was the sport of kings.

The rest of the world has continued to be violent. Table 3.1 represents an attempt to gauge the amount of violence in the "developed world" compared to the Third World. The estimate is very rough, but allowing for considerable error the difference is overwhelming, with more than 14 million killed in the Third World compared to fewer than 100,000 in the developed world. The figures were drawn from the calculations of Gaston Bouthoul and Rene Carrere (1978, 1979; Kohler 1977) supplemented for the 1945–1988 period by the calculations of William Eckhardt (Sivard 1985, 9–11, private communication). Bouthoul and Carrere are used throughout for conflict fatality figures because they cover a longer period

TABLE 3.1
WAR DEATHS
1945–1988

		Estimated Deaths
Developed Countries		
Greek Civil War, Hungarian Revolution, U.S. Racial Uprisings, U.S.S.R. Intervention in Czechozlovakia, Political Violence in Northern Ireland	Under	100,000
Underdeveloped Countries		
Vietnam Civil War with French and U.S. Involvements 1946–1975	Nearly	3,600,000
Cambodian Rebellions and Massacres, 1970–88	Over	2,200,000
Bangladeshi Rebellion, 1971		1,500,000
Biafran Civil War, 1967–1970		1,100,000
Iraqi-Iranian War, 1980–1985		1,000,000
Ugandan Civil War, Coup, Massacres, Interventions 1971–1988		900,000
Indo-Pakistani Wars, 1947–1966	Over	800,000
Sudanese Civil War, 1955–1972		700,000
Rebellion, Famine, Intervention in Ethiopia, 1972–1988	Nearly	600,000
Indonesian Massacres, 1965		500,000
Rebellion in Afghanistan and U.S.S.R. Intervention, 1978–1988		500,000
Civil War and Famine in Mozambique, 1947–1988	Over	400,000
North African Rebellions, 1952–1962	Nearly	300,000
Chinese Civil War, 1946–1950		200,000
Massacres in Ruwandi and Burundi, 1956–1972	Nearly	200,000
Congo Wars, 1960–1966	Over	100,000
Iraqi-Kurdish Civil War, 1961–70	Over	100,000
Timor Massacres, 1975–1980		100,000
Other Asian Conflicts	Over	200,000
Other Latin American Conflicts	Over	200,000
Other African Conflicts	Over	100,000
Other Middle Eastern Conflicts	Over	100,000
TOTAL	Over	14,000,000

than Lewis Richardson (1960), Wilkinson (1980) or Singer and Small (1972). Because they use somewhat different criteria, the figures used here are probably high for Bouthoul and Carrere, low for Eckhardt. But even allowing a considerble margin for error, under and over reporting, and different criteria, it is clear that most of the violence since World War II has occurred in the Third World.

So it can be said that the period since 1950 has been one of relative peace for Western civilization and the developed world. Such periods have come before, the most recent being the period between the Napoleonic Wars and the World Wars, the period we refer to nostalgically as the Victorian Age and remember as one of the more peaceful in European history. The present period, so far, has been more peaceful than the early part of the Victorian Age. If we compare the first four decades of the present postwar period to the first four decades of the Victorian period, up to the onset of the Crimean War, there were fewer casualties in absolute numbers in the present period (Table 3.2).

TABLE 3.2

WAR DEATHS

Europe 1815–1855			Western World 1945–1985		
1820–23	Mediterranean Revolutions	9,000	1945–49	Greek Civil War	40,000
1825	Decembrist Uprisings	1,000	1956	Hungarian Revolution	32,000
1830–35	Revolutions of 1830	29,000	1963–71	Racial and Student Uprisings, U.S. and France	500
1848–49	Revolutions of 1948	62,000	1968	Czechoslovakian Revolution	500
			1968–74	Violence in Northern Ireland	1000
	c.	101,000		c.	74,000

These calculations have a considerable margin of error. Bouthoul and Carrere use somewhat different standards from Eckhardt. There is a considerable amount of data unavailable, which can lead to undercounting. On the other hand, A. K. M. Aminul Islam, studying Bangladesh, finds casualty reports overstated because of multiple reporting. But there is no doubt about the immense difference between violence in the developed and underdeveloped countries in the present period and, as we shall see, there is reason to believe by several different measures that the developed countries are experiencing the least violent period of modern history.

The figures do not include military casualties sustained by developed countries in the Third World. Eckhardt (1987) estimates that between 1817 and 1986 losses suffered by colonial powers in civil and colonial wars were about 555,500, between six and seven percent of the total fatalities suffered in those conflicts.

How does the present peace compare with preceding normal and crisis periods in terms of casualties? By taking Bouthoul and Carrere's raw figures, we have seen that it compares favorably with the Victorian-era *Pax Britannica*. But the normal periods last longer than the crisis periods, and therefore simply comparing total fatalities would make the crisis periods seem milder than they were. So we should consider fatalities per year (Table 3.3)

TABLE 3.3
FATALITIES IN NORMAL AND CRISIS PERIODS

Period	Fatalities Per Year	Median Population	Annual Fatalities Per 100,000
Age of the Baroque (1741–1788)	12,000	160,000,000	7.5
Napoleonic Wars (1789–1815)	91,000	193,000,000	47.2
Early Victorian Age (1816–1854)	14,000	261,000,000	5.4
Victorian Age (1816–1913)	27,000	362,000,000	7.5
World Wars (1914–1945)	1,532,000	697,000,000	219.8
Present Age (1946–19)	1,500	870,000,000	0.2

Data from Bouthoul and Carrere (1978–79), Braudel (1979) and Tomlinson (1965).

In using Bouthoul and Carrere's figures, some allowance had to be made for wars in which casualties occurred partly within Russia and the Western world and partly outside, e.g., the Seven Years' War and World War II. Fatalities for the Baroque and World Wars periods were therefore reduced by one-eighth. These modifications made, we can see that there was a marked increase, more than seven-fold, in casualties per year during the Napoleonic Wars as compared to the Age of the Baroque. Casualties dropped during the Victorian Age to less than a third of the Napoleonic Wars period but more than double the Age of the Baroque. With the World Wars there was a remendous jump in fatalities, from tens of thousands in all preceding periods, to well over a million a year. These casualties dropped off in the Present Age, not just back to the level of the Victorian or Baroque periods, but far lower. It should be remembered, however, that the first 40 years of the Victorian period were also peaceful, and the figures for that period were lower than for the age as a whole.

These raw fatality figures, however, occur against a changing population. As population increases, so does the possibility for fatalities in armed conflict. A better measure, perhaps, of the relative peacefulness of each period might be to use figures similar to those used for homicide fatalities per 100,000. Median population figures for Europe and North America were therefore calculated as indicated in column two, yielding the annual fatalities indicated in column three.

This column shows a fatality rate of 7.5 in the wars of the late Baroque Age, a figure somewhat under the annual homicide rate in the United States of the 1980s. The Napoleonic Wars show a six-time increase in fatality rate, meaning that Europe in that period was about as dangerous as the city of Miami is today. The rate for the Victorian Age, interestingly enough, drops back to 7.5, the same rate as for the latter Baroque. The World Wars, by this measure, prove to be nearly five times as destructive in terms of fatality rate as the Napoleonic Wars, a horrible but hardly surprising finding. The Present Age, in its early decades, proves to be the most peaceful period, with a fatality rate below the homicide rate in any country in the world, and below that of the safest state (North Dakota) in the United States. Even if we compare it to the first four decades of the Victorian Age (up to the Crimean War), the Present Age is more peaceful, with a rate of .02 per 100,000 as compared to 5.4 for the early Victorian.

The Present Age is not only peaceful; it is exceptionally peaceful compared to normal ages of the past in Western and Russian history.

WHEN WAS THERE A SETTLEMENT?

If the Present Age follows the pattern of the past three normal ages, we are in the fifth decade of a peace that can reasonably be expected to last 10 to 15 decades.

The present political settlement is one of those in which there was no single resolving conference. But it is a settlement, for all that. The great powers are in control of what they can control, and they have reached agreement about spheres of influence in peripheral areas.

Traditionally, we look at the great meetings of statesmen as landmarks in history, summing up the period of action that has been taking place, and introducing a new period, usually a different kind of period and usually one of relative stability and equilibrium. Actually, in our history, the Congress of Vienna seems to be the only example of a great conference that really marked the end of a crisis period. Other famous conferences, such as that leading to the Treaty of Prague in 1632, of Utrecht in 1713, or of Versailles in 1919, had no long-term influence in changing prevailing patterns.

The ending of the World Wars crisis seems to resemble more what has come to be called the Treaty of Westphalia. Though we give the date 1648 to that treaty, it is not a single document arising from a single conference like the Congress of Vienna. The Treaty of Westphalia, rather, is a retroactive title given to the cumulative results of a number of negotiations among various participants that took place over a five-year period, more of them in the territory of Westphalia than anywhere else.

Similarly, there was no single showy conference at the end of World War II, but a number of conferences beginning at Yalta and Potsdam in 1945, continuing through the German and Japanese surrenders in the same year, and culminating, after a series of secondary conferences, in a meeting between Khrushchev and Eisenhower at Geneva in 1955, by which time the revised world order had been acknowledged.

After the Napoleonic Wars, the great powers were able to make such secondary settlements as were necessary with relatively little conflict. The question of Italian unification was managed with few casualties; the question of the control of Germany was settled in two short, limited wars; the waning of Turkish power created more serious but regionally peripheral problems that were controlled though not resolved after the Crimean War. This was the most deadly European war of the Victorian Age, but its fearful casualty rate (772,000 killed) was attributable, for the most part, to disease rather than battle and it never threatened to become more than a regional conflict, fought at the periphery of Europe.

The basic power relationships in the Victorian Age were stable enough to permit secondary transitions in which franchise was extended after rebellions in various places, and in which various degrees of political autonomy were granted in the Balkans, the Low Countries, Poland and Finland. Outside the continent, Britain, France and the Netherlands resolved differences on the control of various parts of South Asia and Indonesia while in 1885 a congress of great powers amiably established areas of control in Africa.

Since 1950 a similar pattern has emerged for the Present Age. Once again a relatively stable situation exists. Two great powers have carved out spheres of influence, the United States retaining its hold on the Western Hemisphere including a predominant role in Western Europe, the Soviet Union dominating Eastern Europe.

Within these spheres there is considerable latitude for the resolution of secondary problems without danger of precipitating world conflict. Latin American countries, like Cuba, Peru and Nicaragua, seek domestic autonomy in relation to the United States. France, reduced from great to secondary power status, seeks freedom within the Western sphere. Yugoslavia does the same in the East. When great powers actively intervene in Afghanistan or Central America, there is considerable opposition among leaders, many of whom doubt that these secondary powers can pursue political policies that would be really dangerous to the great powers. Therefore, it is argued that they can be permitted considerable freedom.

The areas outside the spheres have included many trouble spots. Western political domination of other continents has brought to them the ideology of nationalism, which suggests that countries in these areas would profit by freeing themselves from that political domination. At the same time there is considerable sympathy for this view within the great powers, and considerable doubt that the maintenance of a political hold on these territories would be of much value. France and Britain have had to reduce their political hold, though with many countries they have kept economic and cultural ties. England made the decision to let go of its major colonial holding in India soon after World War II. France fought some holding wars in Southeast Asia and North Africa, but in the 1950s abandoned them for a policy similar to that of Britain.

The United States went through a brief period of attempting to play the successor to its Western Allies in Southeast Asia, but by the 1970s its leaders seemed ever more reluctant to make further commitments to intervention in conflicts within or between countries in this region. Thus the Present Age has become one of relative peace among the developed nations, diminishing intervention of great powers in the underdeveloped nations, and intermittent conflicts between and within the underdeveloped nations.

It would appear, then, that we are all aware of the international settlement. One of the problems in the United States, as the campaign to elect the successor to Ronald Reagan ground on, was that the candidates seemed unable to raise any issues. Or, as Michael Sandel observed, there were issues enough, but no overriding philosophy (1988). But the international settlement may have to do with that. There *is* no overriding problem. The United States, like other nations, has an array of domestic problems that are difficult to prioritize. There is no dominating international problem in sight to unify the nation. If the issues are inconsistent and trivial, if our personal lives lack focus, that is not necessarily a sign of moral decline. The people of the Soviet Union have even more to be distressed about. With twice the percentage of their gross national product going into defense, their economy remains dreary. It has been decades since the war and the terrifying days of Stalinism. The international settlement presents their leadership with a dismal array of problems, and confronting them may increase internal dissatisfaction.

When you are well fed, well clothed, and not threatened with imminent disaster, life is still tough. It always is. We then have more time to confront ourselves, our envy of others who have earned more fame, wealth or power; our disappointment in what we have achieved compared to what we might have done; our worries about the welfare of parents, siblings, spouses and children. It is the international settlement that allows us to be more aware of these problems, gives us more time to measure ourselves and to find, as always, that we are not what we hoped to be.

ACCOMMODATION OF AIR POWER

The 40 years of war and crisis between 1910 and 1950 was also the period in which air power came into its own. The basic effect of air power, as John Herz (1959) has pointed out, is the transformation of the concept of territoriality. Before air power existed it was roughly the case that the more territory a state had, the better its center was protected. Even if attacked the state would become stronger as its armies retreated to the interior, and the attacking forces would become correspondingly weaker.

This was illustrated by the defeat of the Germans by the Russians in World War II.

But World War II also saw the development of the capacity to deliver high explosives over tremendous distances. Fire bomb raids had tremendous effects before the atomic bomb was introduced. Since then the power of the explosives has increased tremendously and so has the capacity to deliver them. It seems unlikely now that controlling more territory would increase the capacity of a country to defend against an attack of this kind.

Nor is there any sign that an effective defense will be developed as variations of ABM have been countered by variations of MIRV; the prospects are that offensive superiority will continue for several decades. Even if defense were to reassert its normal superiority, it would be difficult to be certain that it would really work.

The result is that major land invasions of one great power by another are likely to be discouraged for some time to come. Historically governments invade other nations because they want to expand or consolidate territorial control. It is difficult to think of any major land invasion that would have taken place if the invader thought the cost would be the destruction of most of his cities and the killing of most of his population.

So it is not territory, but air power, that protects a great power from land invasion. Why, then, should a great power concern itself about the loyalty of a peripheral buffer power? Buffer states no longer serve that purpose. So when a great power intervenes in the affairs of a small power, as Russia intervened in Czechoslovakia, it is not because it needs to protect itself against land invasion. It must be for economic or ideological reasons. If it is not one of these, it must represent a reflex from experiences of the past, a kind of action that could become less common as leaders come to power who have no connection with that past.

Before air power, a nation could also protect itself if it were surrounded by water and if it developed a powerful navy. A great land power would then be stymied. This was demonstrated as recently as World War II when Germany failed to invade Britain but decided to take its chances with Russia instead. Just as a land power liked to have as much territory as possible, and buffer states beyond what it controlled directly, a sea power needed its land bases for refueling and for harboring its fleet so that as much of the sea as possible remained under its control.

But a navy will no longer protect a sea power. Like the land power, it is vulnerable to air attack. If an invasion is to be deterred, it will be because air power makes possible the devastating destruction of the attacker's cities. Therefore the control of the sea is of little value for home protection, nor is the control of distant bases. If missiles are to be launched from submarines, refueling stations will be needed, but these do not have to be located anywhere in particular, they simply need to be spaced. Why then should a great power concern itself about the government of a distant small power that might once have served as a base? When a great power intervenes in such a situation, as the United States intervened in Vietnam, it is not because it needs to protect itself against land invasion. It must be for economic or ideological reasons. If it is not one of these, it must represent a reflex from the past.

The effects of this transformation of need on outlook have already been noted. The British, once the most aggressive and successful of European powers in acquiring distant bases, were prepared to liquidate their over- seas holdings soon after the World Wars had ended. Certainly their de- fense of the Falklands in 1982 had nothing to do with the "Defense of the Realm." The French fought vigorously to hold their bases for a decade, but when such fighting proved costly and futile, they gave up and became major critics of the Americans for continuing such policies. The latter, who came late into this kind of involvement, were equally unsuccessful despite their superior strength.

As members of the postwar generation acquire control of government, therefore, it is less likely that great powers will actually intervene in the affairs of small powers with the intent of directly preserving their own political safety.

THE BALANCE OF POWER

The number of states in a configuration is not important. Even if there are a great many, there are likely to be a few principal actors. What is important is whether the states have accommodated their basic dif- ferences in accordance with their power and their interests.

The balance of power itself is simply a term that describes an existing equilibrium. The equilibrium of our time differs from that which had prevailed for 250 years prior to the World Wars. Britain, France and the German powers have been supplanted by the United States. Russia re- mains from previous equations.

The balance of power does not preserve peace nor insure stability. But when, as is the case in the present situation, the essential accommodations have been reached, the system begins to acquire a certain value of its own. Governments to some extent pull their punches because they recognize an inherent value in the existence of the system. Those who want to make radical changes in the system do not come to power or do not gain support.

Thus, emphasis is placed on international relations once a system returns to normal. Law and diplomacy once again have been developed to a level appropriate to the nature of the system, and few problems are so complicated that they cannot be settled by peaceful means. When war takes place the stakes are secondary. You might even say that war takes place *because* the stakes are secondary. Russia can intervene in a rebellion in Austria in 1849 or in Czechoslovakia in 1968 with reasonable assurance that the issue does not challenge the interests of Western powers to the extent that they will do any more than deplore the intervention.

It was customary in the decade after World War II to talk about bipolarity, a redundant term that indicated that all the power that mattered was shared between the United States and Russia. It was argued that this endangered the balance of power, which depends for its flexibility on having several participants who can switch sides in order to maintain the balance.

It is now obvious that no such polarization has taken place. Within the spheres of influence of each of the two great powers considerable loosening up is taking place as is to be expected in a "normal" period of international relations.

But even if this were not so, there is little evidence that a polar situation is less effective in maintaining peace or existence than a multi-power situation. Often, in the past, great powers have had other great powers on their borders, and peace has been maintained. An accommodation was reached between the Sassanian Empire and the East Roman, between the Sung and Liao, between New Kingdom Egypt and the Hittites, between Kassite Babylonia and early Assyria, between Russia and Austria, between the great sea powers of the United Kingdom and the United States. Often two such powers come to trust one another after a period because each knows the capacities of the other, and each is likely to regard the other as more reliable than other less powerful and less predictable states. Sassanians and the East Romans could allow each other to guard their inner frontiers while each devoted military power to fending off nomadic attacks from other directions.

Already, after only a quarter of a century, we have several examples of Russia and the United States begrudgingly supporting one another: in the Suez Crisis, in encouraging a settlement between India and Pakistan, and in negotiations involving the Egyptians, Syrians and Israelis in 1973 and 1974. Again in 1979, the two powers reenforced one another in the mildness of their response to a Chinese invasion of Vietnam.

In none of these encounters did the two powers meet directly. But their public and private messages were mutually reassuring: we won't get involved if you don't, and let us each do our best to use our influence to contain the situation.

Another interpretation of this polarization is not exactly flattering to the dominant powers. Arnold Toynbee (1934:III) has pointed out a recurrent tendency for peripheral areas to become dominant over core areas of a civilization that has existed before. The Greek city states were dominated by the Macedonians, the Chinese states of the Ch'un Ch'in period by the outlying Ch'in state, the Renaissance Italian states by the great European dynasties of Habsburg and Valois. The reason, he suggests, is that the small powers in the center generate a high level of culture, but check one another diplomatically. At the periphery of the culture area, however, states have room to grow and even if they are less sophisticated, they can learn to use the weapons and political techniques of the core area until they become so powerful that they can dominate the core area.

The appearance of these giant peripheral states, therefore, may signify the beginning of a new period of history, but it does not signify the end of a civilization or a millennial change. The balance of power may be changed, but the international system persists.

Nor does the shift in power mean that civilization has fallen under the aegis of semibarbarians. The shift in power from Italy to Europe was followed by a shift in aesthetics that produced an expanded Renaissance followed by the Baroque and Rococo periods. There is much evidence of aesthetic, philosophic and scientific vitality today.

INTERNATIONAL INTERACTION

Burns Weston recently (1986) spoke to a group of peace researchers on the decline of international law in the 1980s. He mentioned the Iranian taking of American hostages, Russia's intervention in Afghanistan, the American intervention in Grenada, the Iraqi invasion of Iran, the American refusal to sign or pay its share for the United Nations Law of the Sea Treaty, and the refusal of the United States to accept a World Court decision on Nicaragua. While Weston was collecting these incidents, the American president advised a graduating West Point class not to place too much faith in United States treaty commitments.

But despite Weston's concern it is probable that international law is more effective in normal than crisis times. The Iraqi and Iranian actions are those of Third World countries who are themselves in crisis. Great powers do circumvent law when they think they are acting on an important interest. For the same reasons, great powers are sometimes poor sports about international agreements or World Court decisions. International law has always been limited by the perception of vital interests by great powers.

Still, international law is generally effective in normal times. It does not prevent nations from fighting, but it provides rules for normal commerce between nations and even helps them define the areas in which they fight or stay out of fighting.

International law has suffered a period of disrepute because law that is developed in normal times cannot solve many of the problems of crisis periods, hence it was of little help during the World Wars. Among the provisions of international law in the West, for instance, were a number concerned with the protection of the noncombatant. In the eighteenth century, when quartermasters were regularly included in all armies, such laws did operate and violations of the rights of civilians were dealt with severely by military commanders. But with the development of citizen armies, with citizen participation in total war efforts, and with the development of weapons that owed their success to the destruction of morale (e.g., blockade, bombs), the separation of soldier and civilian became impossible and attempts to call upon such laws for support only led to the denigration of these laws.

The World Wars brought so much distress that one response was a determination that international law should in the future serve as a substitute for war, a determination that could be realized only if international law could be established on a basis similar to that of domestic law. A new international system was to be set up in which world courts were to operate like domestic courts, with a system of appeals to higher levels and a system of enforcement that was to be above any nation. The impossibility of carrying out such theories is obvious, and in fact, the international Court of Justice and *ad hoc* international arbitration commissions have played little part in international relations, at best settling questions between secondary nations that had no other recourse, or secondary questions in which both participants could afford to lose without political repercussion.

One example of the development of international law in secondary areas relates to the document the United States declined to sign, the emergence of a new body of law concerning the management of oceans, which began to develop with three "Law of the Sea" conferences held between 1958 and 1973, with more than 80 nations attending the first and more than 140 the third. These conferences and much work that went on between them, address the claims of various nations to territorial waters, economic zones beyond territorial waters, rights of regional associations and even the rights to compensation of landlocked states.

The work of the conferences has been to sort out and generalize the scores of regional agreements that have been made on these subjects. The deliberations of the conferences, in turn, provide guidelines for future regional agreements. Even though there are several dozen new nations, new concepts of rights, new problems such as conservation and pollution control, and interlocking memberships in various regional associations, nations have been calmly and quietly working out peaceful regional arrangements in the oceans (Alexander 1977). By 1986 the General Assembly was ready to call on all states to "consider ratifying or acceding" to the Law of the Sea. That call was approved 145–2, with the United States and Turkey opposing. The Law of the Sea Convention received 159 signatures and will enter force when it receives 60 national ratifications (it had received more than 30 by the end of 1986) (*U. N. Chronicle* 1986, 1987). John Gamble (1988), who has monitored the ratification process, anticipates ratification of the treaty by the middle 1990s. Even if the United

States does not sign the agreement, that does not mean that the American government will not accede to it. The choice the Americans had was to sign, realizing that if vital interests were perceived to be affected, the law would be violated, or not to sign, and generally obey the law. The former choice is better politically, but perhaps the latter is better morally. In any event, great powers generally obey such laws, but through history have violated them when national interests were perceived to be threatened. In normal times, however, national interests are rarely threatened, and international law is generally obeyed.

The completion of the Law of the Sea continues a 40-year period of what Benjamin Ferencz calls a "burst of codification" (1985, 6–9). There has been a wide range of agreements about law on secondary matters as well as attempts to define crimes against human rights, including genocide. This range of agreement may reflect hopes for the future, but it also reflects an expectation that for the present international standards of law are possible in areas that do not affect vital interests. This does not so much preserve peace as reflect an expectation of peace.

By contrast, nations of the world have had no comparable success in working toward an international law in regard to terrorism. This has been a volatile issue, subject to widespread media coverage, whereas fishing agreements are relegated to one program a decade on public television supplemented by an equal number of G-rated articles in *The American Journal of International Law*. Because of this, the issue was introduced by the Secretary General himself to the agenda of the General Assembly of the United Nations. Besides, while terrorism seems clearly a crime issue to governments and peoples of developed nations, it is a political issue to governments of underdeveloped nations, which sometimes include former terrorists who sympathize with the use of terrorism as a major political weapon of the weak. No legal resolution can occur here, at least in the near future, because the issue involves both developed and underdeveloped nations who are in different phases of development. So long as the issue involves vital interests of a number of underdeveloped nations, it cannot be resolved by the patient development of international law. But the resolution is all the more difficult because of the sensational and public nature of the problem.

The development of a "Law of the Sea," however, is more typical of the way in which international law emerges in the early decades of a normal period. Much of the international law of the Victorian period is being reaffirmed. Some, like those concerning the sea, will be new because of new conditions. No person or United Nations commission can draft it, but students of international law are beginning to tell us, from practice and cases, how much of the old law has survived, and how much is new. The Grotius of the future can do no more than that, nor could the Grotius of the past.

International organization, like international law, works best in normal times, providing mechanisms for solutions to secondary economic and political problems, permitting diplomats to meet quietly and frequently without attracting too much attention, and expediting the exchange of ideas.

International organization is not essential to peace. The "Concert of Europe," which accompanied *Pax Britannica,* had scarcely any permanent structural organization. On the other hand, the League of Nations, which was much more complex and highly structured, was unable to resolve the World Wars crisis.

But in normal times, international organization can help resolve secondary crises. Unarmed United Nations forces acted as a stabilizing factor for more than a decade after the Suez Crisis of 1956. The United Nations provided an important communications link during the Cuban Missile Crisis. In creating special drawing rights, the International Monetary Fund may have made a lasting contribution to living standards in poor countries.

International organization is not world government. Those who expect it to become world government will be disappointed, inclined to regard the experiment as a failure, and likely to blame the Establishment or the selfishness of mankind. A better model is the International Postal Union, which also works better in normal than in crisis periods, and which is not expected to do more than solve certain kinds of communications problems. When it works well, we hardly think about it. When it does not, we may grumble, but we do not expect the world to come to an end.

The World Wars crisis proclaimed the end of diplomacy. Woodrow Wilson's misplaced preposition went almost unnoticed when he promised open covenants openly arrived at. Then television introduced us to an era of epithets and bad manners that certainly seemed to seal the doom of rational discourse.

But all the while diplomacy continued. Diplomats carried on their work quietly, out of the media spotlight. Media diplomacy went on, but purely for home consumption. Americans and Russians exchanged discourtesies on the UN floor during the Berlin Airlift Crisis while Jacob Malik and Philip Jessup worked out some of the details of a settlement in a nearby hotel suite. The Cuban Missile Crisis had its quiet notes and private indications of position while Ambassador Adlai Stevenson was waiting until hell froze over on the TV screen.

Public diplomacy continued in traditional forms also. The 1955 Summit Conference at Geneva was meant to display a warming of diplomatic relations between great powers. In the nineteenth century the several conferences later known as the Concert of Europe were held for similar purposes.

Again, the Geneva Double Conference of 1954 was very much in the tradition of the 1878 Congress of Berlin. In both, several great powers met to attempt to resolve a diplomatic problem that directly involved only one of their number, on the ground that a settlement would affect the interests of all. In the Berlin Congress the aspirations of Russia to expand were reduced while in the Geneva Conference the desire of France to withdraw gracefully was encouraged. But the means of working out agreements by clothing power in the velvet of civilization were comparable.

In crisis periods, the normal channels of diplomacy are subverted and communications become more strident, or require special channels. In normal periods, the regular channels usually suffice, and public tones become more civil.

SPHERES AND ALLIANCES

In normal times, spheres of influence agreements are reached, often tacitly, by great powers without consulting lesser powers. They give the great power the right to interfere in the affairs of a small power without physical opposition by other great powers.

At the same time, alliances within the spheres tend to become looser as the spheres become clarified.

Thus the Hungarian crisis of 1956 showed Hungary to be within the Russian sphere of influence. Russia could intervene, and there was no likelihood that the United States would do anything but deplore Russia's action. The Cuban Missile Crisis, six years later, showed that Cuba was within the American sphere.

On the other hand, there clearly was no alliance between the United States and Cuba. France remained in formal alliance with the United States, but stressed independent courses of action. Hungary, under Janos Kadar, a loyal ally of Russia, nevertheless followed an independent course of domestic development. The sphere permits unopposed intervention, but at the same time lessens the need for it. The great power may bully, but at the same time seeks to avoid unwinnable situations like Vietnam or Afghanistan.

As Robert Wesson observes, there are subtle differences in the spheres of influence. The United States has intervened directly in Central America, Southeast Asia and the Middle East, but not in South America or Africa. The Soviet Union has intervened in Eastern Europe and South Asia, but not directly in the Middle East or Africa. But, as Wesson concludes (1986), "despite some evidence of loosening, the spheres on both sides seem decidedly stable. . . . They have lasted for a long time and will probably continue more or less in the present shape unless one or the other of the present superpowers should suffer a very marked decline."

This stability is sometimes overlooked because of perceptions about inherent expansionism in dominant powers. The Soviet Union is seen as implacably imperialistic, advancing wherever American weakness permits it, despite the absence of much evidence of that advance. The United States is also seen as an imperialistic power, with a history of expansionism going back to the conquest of the country itself, and continuing today as the inheritor of British imperialism's role in the world, an expansionist nation bent on world cultural domination (Williams 1980).

It would appear that in the immediate postwar period, behavior tends to be rigid and formal. After the Napoleonic Wars, great powers attempted to enforce the principle of "Legitimacy," to keep the world forever as it was. After the World Wars, the surviving nations vigorously set up formal alliances: NATO, SEATO, the Warsaw Pact. But as a normal period develops, and imminent danger recedes, such alliances tend to relax. Though formal alliances such as the North Atlantic Treaty Organization may continue to exist in a peaceful period, their effect is considerably reduced. Their headquarters may be retained and they may hold occasional formal meetings to assure one another that the alliance still exists, because otherwise it would be hard to tell. In the 1960s De Gaulle could still make news by "defying" NATO, but an independent policy in the 1970s by the German Chancellor Schmidt was lucky to get a half-page in *Newsweek*. And the Southeast Asian Treaty Organization: whatever became of SEATO?

As alliances become looser, the concept of neutralism loses its meaning. In time of war, nations in alliance support their allies while neutral nations must treat all belligerents alike. They may trade with them, but they must be willing to trade the same things to all at the same price. In periods of confrontation without war, the neutral nations behave in the same way, not only trading, but offering cultural interchanges, political visits, exchanges of tourists and pledges of eternal friendship to all comers. Nations in peaceful alliance reserve such honors for their own side but as time passes the sides become blurred as leaders of the alliances themselves cooperate with one another as often as they compete. When this happens, members of alliances are freer to pursue their own policies and they too are open to all in trade, culture, visits, touring and pledges. As an international system enters its normal phase, all nations gravitate toward neutrality.

Revolutionaries who were expelled from Hungary after the 1956 rebellion could, in the 1980s, revisit their former country without qualm, even though the very government and leader they had opposed were still in power. When the Russians run short of wheat, they buy it at bargain prices from Canada, or even from the United States. And the cardinals of the world, dominated by Italians of the Western bloc, elect a Polish Pope—an anti-Communist Pope, it is true, but antiliberal as well.

It follows that small powers have a great deal going for them in maintaining their independence from great powers. The great power really does not want to use force. It can be a nagging, sticky business if the small power resorts to guerrilla warfare. Even a quick and clean conquest involving occupation looks like bullying, and must be resolved with considerable compromise.

Where the sphere of influence is not clearly defined, great powers are more cautious about intervention. The United States could not intervene in the 1979 Iranian Revolution. Iran is not clearly in the Russian sphere of influence, but it is on the Russian border.

Often the small state will resist where the issue is important to it, but of secondary importance to the great power, as in the cold wars between Iceland and Great Britain (Klein 1981). Occasionally, but not often, the small power may miscalculate the importance of an issue to the great power, as in the case of the Falklands in 1982.

The existence and pertinacity of small powers is one of the encouraging aspects of the world of this *Pax Atomica*. It is clearly not a world in which people are indifferent to who rules them, and in this respect it is nothing like the worlds in which people everywhere were content to be ruled from a distant capital as part of a civilizational empire, as they were at the onset of the Han, Mughal, Achaemenian, Roman and many other empires.

On the other hand, it is apparent that the greater autonomy of small powers could be a factor encouraging the great powers to exaggerate each other's importance. Each needs the other to help hold together its sphere of influence (Kaldor 1978, 29–30). When the great powers are not doing too well, their economies sluggish, their leadership unimpressive, they must be challenged to persuasively portray each other as threatening. They even may need to choose actors or communicators as leaders.

WORLD CRISES

There have been five international crises since 1945 that seemed to have the potential to ignite World War III: the Berlin Airlift Crisis of 1948; the Korean War in its earlier phases (1950–51); the Suez Crisis of 1956; the Berlin Wall Confrontation of 1961; and the Cuban Missile Crisis of 1962. The use of the term "crisis" here presents some contextual problems. The term has been used at the system level to distinguish periods in which the system itself is threatened from normal periods when it is not. Here I am referring to specific and local political situations perceived to be crises when they are occurring and which, in retrospect, seem to have had the capacity to lead to a return to crisis situation for the system.

All but the Cuban crisis occurred in areas that were not in an established sphere of influence of the United States or Russia. In retrospect only the Berlin Airlift and Korean War seem to have been really serious, and they occurred before the present peace had become fully established.

The Airlift and Korean crises were the rule makers. Since the rules were made implicitly and improvised as situations changed, and since

World War II, a conflict without limits, had ended just a few years before, it seems possible that an error in judgment or a loss of patience could have precipitated a resumption of the World Wars crisis. But in the Airlift encounter, when the Russians and/or the East Germans blocked the route from West Germany to West Berlin, the Western powers did not attempt to force the blockade, but sent planes instead. The Eastern powers, in turn, did not attempt to prevent the planes from landing, much less shoot them down. When neither side chose to raise the stakes, the crisis wound down and the real European political settlement was made.

In the Korean case, the American president, Harry Truman, resisted pressure from his own field commander to allow nuclear weapons to be used. The Chinese, on the other hand, did not employ a force massive enough to drive the Americans into the sea. A stabilized line was formed, winding down occurred again, and the real Pacific settlement was made.

The Suez affair, which appeared so grave at the time because of the many powers involved and the traditional sensitiveness of the area, now seems to have been an emotional outburst in the trying business of empire liquidation. The disapproving attitudes of the United States and Russia helped settle the situation rapidly, but even if the super powers had remained aloof, Britain and France were involved in defending interests they no longer had. France's subsequent withdrawal from Africa indicates the way in which the resolution would have occurred.

The Berlin Wall and Cuban Missile crises were affirmations of the status quo. The Eastern powers showed that they could do what they wanted in areas not controlled by the West. The West had already indicated what its response would be by making a unilateral settlement with Japan in 1951 and by refraining from intervening in the Hungarian crisis of 1956. The building of the wall, therefore, became an internal matter with regard to the Russian sphere.

The Cuban episode showed that the United States would continue to insist on domination within its sphere of influence. The Russians tested this, but withdrew when they encountered resistance. A high level of diplomacy was exercised by both powers, but the rules had been set up and, in comparison with the Airlift crisis earlier, the outcome was more predictable.

The importance of the Cuban case was exaggerated for Americans by its Western Hemisphere location, by the drama that accompanied it, and by the first symptoms of the influence of the younger generation. Americans were not accustomed to having world crises so near home (regional crises in Central America were something else), so Cuba drew disproportionate attention. It happened that the developments in this crisis were clear, dramatic, and paced so that there was enough time for breathholding and applause. By contrast, the Suez affair was partly obscured by concurrent Russian intervention in Hungary, an impending American presidential election and by the multiplicity of participants, which diffused its effect. The Korean War had long periods in which nothing happened, or rather in which the same thing happened every day.

Also, Cuban Missile Crisis particularly lent itself to television. It was only a little longer than a political convention or a world series. The Berlin Airlift was reported only by radios and newspapers and made less impact. Besides, to a generation accustomed to World War II it seemed like pretty tame stuff.

The other factor in the Cuban crisis that added tension was the counter-influence of the younger generation. This was found in the views of some of the participants who came to be labeled "doves." They had enough awareness of the transformations brought about by airpower to ask whether it mattered which great power influenced which minor country, regardless of its geographical location. They were also not much interested in the alleged ideological differences that were supposed to affect the Cuban leadership. As a result, the routine defense of a sphere of influence acquired considerable internal tension.

The Cuban crisis was followed by a general relaxation, in striking contrast to the Berlin Wall confrontation, which, only a year before, had caused many otherwise rational Americans to install bomb shelters ("we use unmarked trucks"). On the surface the reason for the relaxation would seem to be a general feeling that if a conflict that seemed as bad as the Cuban Missile Crisis could be resolved, *anything* could be resolved. But more important, possibly, was the increasing influence of the younger generation, which caused the Russians to keep clear of Vietnam and the Americans to refrain from getting involved in Czechoslovakia.

Since the Cuban Missile Crisis, there have been no disruptions that could have threatened world peace. Episodes involving major violence, like the Biafran War or the resumption of war in Southeast Asia were serious events to the countries involved, but they never threatened serious war between major powers in the developed world. The Yom Kippur War produced a day of tension, concern about great power intervention, and a defense alert, but it did not produce the degree of danger, nor public perception of impending disaster, that was characteristic of the earlier crises (Allen 1982; Insight Team 1974).

It seems probable that the Cuban Missile Crisis will prove to have been the last world crisis of the twentieth century and several decades beyond.

GREAT POWER INTERVENTIONS

Many of the elements of the Relational Age came together in the tragedy of Vietnam. The "Munich effect" still operated here, but it was compounded by nationalism, guerrilla warfare, the difference in phase between developed and underdeveloped countries, the tendency for systems to create needs, and the gradual transition from older generation to younger generation outlook.

The Munich effect was responsible for the Americans taking over the untenable French position in the 1950s. After a reasonably successful resolution of the Korean conflict, a stop-them-at-the-line outlook was still possible. But after the Americans had become well entangled, younger people carrying the relational outlook were reaching positions of influence. Concern about ideological differences had generally cooled. The split between Russia and China undermined the view that a great power was being resisted. Skepticism grew stronger in the educational and journalistic estates, these were picked up almost as quickly among the political and even the military. The younger generation was aroused from its concern with domestic problems and general protest grew and spread. When, in October 1969, a protest moratorium was organized, it became apparent that opposition to the war was widespread. The opposition in America, incidentally, had long been shared by almost everyone in the developed countries of Europe, the countries in which colonialism originated.

In the face of this transformation of opinion, an outside observer might suppose that the great power would bring its troops home with the resolve that it would never again become involved in nationalistic struggles of the underdeveloped world. But, for several reasons, this took a few years. This delay has to do with the differences in phase between developed and underdeveloped areas as well as with a tendency for systems to function in a certain pattern even after the need the function was meeting has disappeared. More concisely, systems have their own rationale.

Now here is a normal problem for seasoned diplomats. Negotiations take place, and the problems are worked out. But here, also, is where the government of the developed nation runs into a problem similar to one it encounters in its dealings with the younger generation. For many of the leaders in underdeveloped countries are fanatics, that is, people who feel so strongly about their own rightness that they are not willing to accommodate other people's rightness. The British encountered the problem when they wanted to negotiate a reasonable settlement with the Americans after a few years of the American Revolution. The Americans were unwilling to negotiate like reasonable Europeans, they were not sufficiently mature to appreciate the delicate nuances of the situation. They wanted the British out and as for what they would do afterwards, that was their business and not that of the British.

The underdeveloped countries are still in a strongly nationalistic phase, and they will be for some time to come. But they were not more irrational than the Americans. They believed that their "fanaticism" would carry the day, that they did not have to compromise, that the developed country would eventually find a way to extricate itself. (Similarly, younger people know they do not have to compromise. Time is on their side.)

As for the system, it does tend to keep operating regardless of need. One rationalization after another will be provided for keeping it going. And when reasons give out, there is still loyalty. Our system, right or wrong. Inertia pattern is a factor here. Institutionalization is also a factor in that, having been formed, the system not only does what it is designed to do regardless of the need, but those involved with the system try in every way they can to expand the performance. We were told that failure of the system to solve the problem had nothing to do with its performance: soldiers fought bravely and their performance was really impressive—they consistently outkilled Vietnamese by impressive ratios. The involvement in the first place, as Dean Rusk often explained, was not a policy decision, but a series of implementation decisions: advisory cadres replacing the French; soldiers to protect the cadres; more soldiers to avenge the unsuccessful protectors; bombers to protect the developing commitment. Thus the system operates. These things happen. No one is to blame.

The Russian intervention in Czechoslovakia was about as obsolescent and useless as the American intervention in Vietnam. It probably had a similar reception in the middle echelons. The Russians had been similarly hesitant about invading Hungary in 1956, but then there was probably more concern about the possibility of an American reaction. This time the debate in the Kremlin probably centered around utility.

In some respects the two interventions are quite different. In its relative mildness and in its success, the Russian intervention was more like the Hungarian venture and the American interventions in Guatemala and the Dominican Republic. These interventions all took place within spheres of influence that already had been established. If their intent was to discourage further episodes of the sort, all of these interventions seem to have been successful. But it is no longer obvious that there is much to be gained by discouraging such domestic transformations. They no longer threaten great powers.

The Russians who advocated the 1968 intervention may have been concerned about the effects of successful political change on territories incorporated within the Soviet Union long ago. If such a transformation could be brought about within Czechoslovakia, why not in the Ukrainian S.S.R.? Similar nationalist stirrings have been evident in Ireland and Canada. In developed countries, however, such stirrings do not have wide support among the minority groups themselves. They get most of their support from the radical right, which tends to be parochial and nationalistic. Such groups did come to power in the World Wars period, and it is understandable that the older generation should be uncomfortable about a resurgence of this kind of thing. Certainly it would be no easier to reassure the Russians about Ukranian Nationalists than it would to reassure Canadians about French-Canadian nationalism or Americans about the limited support for states'-rights candidates like George Wallace.

It is probably a relational outlook toward nationalism that prevented the Czechs and Slovaks from organizing guerrilla resistance to the Russian invasion. National independence was not worth dying for. The example of Hungary showed that acquiescence, in the long run, was likely to bring about most of the reforms that would make life more pleasant. Civilized men accept compromise—in a normal period.

Since the Cuban Missile Crisis, and even before, great power interventions generally have been limited, cautious, and unlikely to antagonize the other power or to compel a counterintervention.

Even the last three crises were not interventions. No one intervened in either Cuba or Berlin, and the great powers intervened only diplomatically to stop the military activities of other powers in the Suez Crisis.

The Russian interventions in Hungary, Czechoslovakia and Afghanistan were all borderline interventions that could not precipitate American military response. The Americans could range more widely, but neither Latin America, the Mediterranean nor Vietnam were areas in which Russian troops were likely to appear. Whether these interventions were successful or not, whether they were for political, economic or emotional reasons, they never threatened anything more than the peace of the area in which the intervention occurred.

These interventions never had the people cheering wildly in the streets. They did not bring glamour or prestige to the governments initiating them. More often the governments were angrily defensive, felt unappreciated, or in the case of the Russians, were sullenly silent. It is hard to imagine a book that would present Afghanistan as a great moment in Russian history or a film called "Grenada!"

More significant, perhaps, are the situations in which intervention did not take place. Cubans, but not Americans nor Russians, became involved in Africa in the 1970s. Russians never appeared in Korea. Neither the Russians nor the Americans appeared in Iran, not during the days of the Shah, though Iran was, after all, on the Russian border, nor in the days of the Ayatollah, despite the American hostages. OPEC posed a real threat to the West, and the OPEC nations were out of range of the Russian sphere, but there never was a threat of Western intervention. The Americans did send marines to Lebanon, but never to Israel or Egypt, and they went on defense alert at the suggestion that the Russians might intervene (Insight 1974; Allen 1982).

Even indirect confrontations had become rare in the 1980s. A notable and tragic exception was Angola, where after 25 years of civil war, Cuban soldiers still supported the Marxists MPLA government, while South

Africa supported and the United States provided arms to the UNITA opposition. Russia, either confused or hedging, rhetorically supported the MPLA government and provided military aid to the PRA, another opposition group (Wolfers and Bergerol 1983; Marcum 1986). But generally, if one great power is intervening, the other is not. And they never confront each other with direct military power, anywhere.

During the Baroque and Victorian Ages, great powers would occasionally invade each other's territory. In 1740 Prussia attacked Austria and precipitated the War of Austrian Succession for no better reason than that Austria was perceived to be in a weak period because a woman had come to the throne while Prussia was strong and the new monarch, Frederick II, wished to add glamour to his reign. Britain and France fought each other all over the world in the eighteenth century. France and Austria fought over the unification of Italy in the 1850s, an issue of secondary importance to both. Prussia attacked both Austria and France in the period between 1866 and 1871. But in the Present Age, Russian and American troops have never encountered each other.

Especially they do not encounter one another in Europe. In the 1950s and 1960s, it was argued that the United States protected Europe. The Russians would not intervene because the Americans would retaliate with a nuclear attack on the Soviet Union. In the 1970s, when long-range Russian missiles obviously could reach the United States, European leaders came to doubt that the United States would risk Washington to save Munich (Barnet 1983, 367–377). But it made no difference. There was no panic, no alarming alteration in European patterns of life. It had simply become evident that the peace of Europe was a product of political rather than military factors.

In 1987 the INF agreement was reached because the intermediate-range missiles were no longer perceived as influencing the European peace. In 1988, European scholars were justifying the military blocs as having stabilizing functions within their respective jurisdictions, but little significance in East-West relations (Jahn, Karkoszka 1988).

Often, but not with grace, Russia and the United States have supported each other: in the Suez Crisis of 1956; in encouraging a settlement between India and Pakistan; and in negotiations involving the Egyptians, Syrians and Israelis in 1967 and especially 1973 and 1974. Again in 1979 the two powers reinforced one another in the mildness of their response to the Chinese invasion of Vietnam, each avoiding threat while urging withdrawal, and each polite to the other, with the United States expressing certainty that the Russians would not intervene and the Russians remarking that the United States had learned to be cautious in supporting the Chinese adventurers. In none of these encounters did the two powers meet directly. But their public and private messages were mutually reassuring:

one wouldn't get involved if the other didn't, and let each do its best to use its influence to contain the situation.

In the 1980s, besides the several friendly summit conferences between the engaging American president and the genial General Secretary of the "Evil Empire," cooperation has sputtered along between the great powers on security communications, trade (somewhat), environmental protection (sometimes as a good way of getting together about other subjects), medical research, space exploration and the exploration of Antarctica (Jamgotch and Finley 1988).

THE REMISSION OF VIOLENCE IN RUSSIA

Among civilizationists, Russia is a subject of dispute. Some see it as part of Western civilization. Since the seventeenth century it has been one of the five great powers in the Concert of Europe. Others see it as coming from a different civilization, either as a civilization in its own right occupying the center of our largest continent, or as the legitimate successor to the Byzantine Empire.

If Russia does belong to a different civilization, would it have a different history, a history that is separate from that of the West? And if that were so, might it be that the West might continue at peace while there were internal disruptions in Russia or particularly in the non-Russian parts of the Soviet Empire?

The history of Russia in the Baroque and Victorian Ages has certainly been related to the West. During the Age of the Baroque and the Victorian Age, Russia was involved in the conflicts with other great powers, such as the Wars of Succession, the Seven Years' War and the revolutions of the 1840s (Table 3.4). These kinds of wars have not been renewed in the Present Age, and Russia, therefore, has not been involved in such wars.

During the Victorian Age, when the other European powers were dividing up Africa, Russia was engaged in a series of conquests along her southern borders, in the Caucasus, Turkestan, Circassia. She also intervened with varying degrees of success and failure, often incurring European opposition in Turkey, Persia, Afghanistan, China and Japan. The Crimean War and the Russo-Japanese War were notable failures. The Afghan War of the 1980s seems to be the only recurrence of this type of intervention.

There were also recurrent and prolonged uprisings within conquered territories in Poland and the Caucasus, and an invited intervention in Austria-Hungary during the revolutions of 1848–1849. The interventions in Hungary and Czechoslovakia in the Present Age seem to fit in this category. Like the Austro-Hungarian intervention, they were quick and effective; but also in the nature of putting down uprisings in that these countries were in the Russian sphere of influence.

TABLE 3.4
RUSSIAN CONFLICTS
1740–1978

Conflict	Dates	Number of Combatants	Number Killed
War of Austrian Succession	1740–1748	250,000	90,000
Russo-Swedish War	1741–1743	60,000	8,000
Seven-Years' War	1756–1763	350,000	550,000
Russo-Turkish War	1768–1774	140,000	N/A
Pugachev's Rebellion	1773–1774	30,000	18,000
Russo-Turkish War	1787–1792	90,000	N/A
Russo-Swedish War	1788–1790	60,000	N/A
Second Polish Partition	1792–1793	80,000	15,000
Third Polish Partition	1794–1795	50,000	30,000
War of French Revolution	1797–1802	600,000	200,000
Conquest of Caucasus	1801–1829	60,000	N/A
Napoleonic Wars	1803–1815	1,800,000	1,380,000
Russo-Turkish War	1806–1812	150,000	N/A
Russo-Turkish War	1821–1829	200,000	120,000
Decembrist Uprising	1825	12,000	800
Russo-Afghan War	1883–1886	60,000	N/A
Russo-Japanese War	1904–1905	400,000	130,000
Revolution of 1905	1904–1906	400,000	3,000
World War I	1914–1918	11,000,000	8,500,000
Russian Revolution and Civil War	1917–1922	600,000	1,300,000
Russo-Polish War	1919–1920	200,000	11,000
World War II	1939–1945	16,000,000	38,000,000
Russo-Finnish War	1939–1940	1,200,000	90,000
Soviet-Iranian Conflict	1945–1947	50,000	N/A
Berlin Blockade	1948	600,000	0
Hungarian Intervention	1956	120,000	32,000
Cuban Missile Crisis	1962	200,000	1
Czechoslovakian Intervention	1968	2,000,000	500
Afghan Intervention	1980	150,000	N/A

Russia also experienced two well-known but not very violent internal uprisings in 1825 and 1905. Nothing of this sort seems to have occurred so far in the Present Age.

On the whole, the Present Age has been considerably more peaceful for Russia than the first four decades of the Victorian Age had been. In the Victorian period Russia was involved in 11 different conflicts of various kinds: border wars, suppressing rebellions, an occupation and a major war with other European powers. In the Present Age there have been only three conflicts, two spheres of influence interventions and one border war.

Of these, only the Hungarian crisis was threatening, since it could have spread to other states or, more remotely, involved external intervention. The Berlin Airlift and Cuban Missile Crisis were much more threatening for world peace, but involved no direct Russian participation, except possibly of technicians and advisory cadre.

Prospects for borderline and internal peace look problematical for Russia. While Caucasus-type border rebellions can be difficult to put down, none has occurred in more than a century. The Afghan war does not seem to be a model for future interventions anymore than was Vietnam.

In some respects there were similarities. In Afghanistan there was a decentralized resistance, almost village by village, with control of the country reverting nightly to the Islamic resistance. There were similar patterns of frustration among the occupiers, resulting in atrocities against civilian populations and the use of chemical warfare (Yellow Rain instead of Agent Orange).

However sordid this campaign may have been, whatever it says about the continuation of great power politics, it was never likely to lead to a confrontation among great powers. It is a symbol of the gratuitous evil of power, of the continued perception of rights of intervention within a sphere of influence.

Mikhail Gorbachev, born in 1930 or 1931, seems to be the first great power leader born in the interim generational period (chapter one, "Decline of Generational Conflict"). Obviously he differs from his predecessors in his ways of thinking. He must have found support among the younger leaders for abandoning the war in Afghanistan. It was probably an easier war to liquidate than was America's Vietnam War, in terms of both the degree of involvement and the management of public opinion.

Internal rebellions in the Soviet Union are possible, and it appears that some may have occurred in the 1960s of the magnitude of those in France and the United States, but these were never serious during normal periods. The Russian Revolution and Civil War were, of course, very serious indeed, but they were part of the 30-years' crisis period.

So it would appear that Russia, like Europe, will probably not be involved in imperial conflicts, may be able to resolve border conflicts and rebellions, and is not likely to experience much internal opposition. If the Western world is in a period of peace, or at least a remission of violence, this should be shared by the Soviet Union.

DOMESTIC VIOLENCE IN TIME OF PEACE

Is it possible in a time of relative international peace, that people compensate for this by an increase in domestic violence? What good is peace if streets are unsafe, if people are too fearful to walk dogs at night? Americans are particularly susceptible to such questions since they experience the highest homicide rate in the developed world. Where most countries experience a rate of 1 or 2 yearly homicides per 100,000 population, Americans kill one another at a rate that sometimes has exceeded 10 per 100,000. In our cities the rate is much higher, exceeding 40 in cities like Detroit and New Orleans.

How do these rates compare with countries at war? Unfortunately, war fatalities are not calculated in terms of fatalities per 100,000 per year. But they can be translated into such terms, although such translations are not always satisfactory since a war between two countries may take place within the territory of one, and therefore the casualties would be skewed. Granted that difficulty, one can still compare homicides to war fatalities on the basis of fatalities per 100,000 per year. Bouthoul and Carrere (1978, 1979) present data that can be translated to rates, and compared with data available from conventional sources for homicide data (*Statistical Abstracts* 1983, 1984; *Crime in the United States* 1982; *Vital Statistics* 1978; Viccica 1980).

Table 3.5, drawn from longer tables (Melko and Murray 1984), represents a selection of familiar wars. Some wars, in which large populations are involved, or in which fighting is sporadic over long periods, do have casualty figures comparable to domestic homicide. These include the Chinese Civil Wars of the 1920s and 30s (1.3) and the late 1940s (6.7) as well as the American Revolution (2.7). Civil Wars tend to run higher because they involve only the population of one country and much greater civilian participation.

In general, domestic violence, measured in terms of fatalities, tends to run far below war casualties, with median war casualties from a table of best-known wars running 30–50 times greater than median homicide casualties from a table of available homicide figures. A period without war casualties is bound to be more peaceful than a period of war, even if homicide figures are running well above average.

TABLE 3.5

	Homicides (1978 or 1979)	Wars	
Norway	0.9	Vietnam War (1960–1975)	32
Japan	1.0	Korean War (1950–53)	51
England	1.2	Indo-Pakistani War (1947–49)	68
Sweden	1.4	Russian Revolution and Civil War (1917–1922)	135
Australia	1.8	World War I (1914–18)	178
Canada	2.5	World War II (1939–1945)	319
Northern Ireland	5.7	U.S. Civil War (1861–65)	456
United States	9.4	Spanish Civil War (1936–39)	1200

Is there more domestic violence in the present period than there has been in the past? It does not seem likely. American history has been famously violent. It is an ethnocentric prejudice that violence is as American as the handgun. In the post-American Revolution period, South Carolina remained a guerrilla battlefield. Vigilantes were dominant in the latter part of the nineteenth century and into the twentieth, "an era of Ku Kluxers, lynch mobs, White Caps, Bald Knobbers, night riders, feudalists, and outlaws." The family feud emerged in the South after the Civil War while assassination was a routine political tactic in New Mexico. Political assassination in the rest of the country came to the fore as dueling lapsed as a means of settling disputes. Organized crime had its origins in the eighteenth century. The social bandit and the free-lance multiple murderer have been recurrent figures along the way. In the 20 years between 1882 and 1903 about 100 blacks a year were lynched by Southern mobs (Brown 1979).

Europe, however, did not lag behind America. In times of peace Europeans experienced feuds, violent conflicts between rival religious groups or guilds, pogroms against Jews and other minorities as well as conscription and food riots (Tilley 179). It is probable that family violence in the eighteenth century was far more extensive than it is in the twentieth (Shorter 1975). The fact that we recognize the concept of family violence in the past three decades suggests that our perceptions have changed and that levels that were acceptable in the past are no longer acceptable today.

As is the case with war, observing that the quantity of violence in the present period is comparable or possibly reduced from periods of past history is not to endorse that level of violence as acceptable. But whether the level of violence is comparatively low or comparatively high is an important consideration, as is the impact of domestic violence as compared to the impact of war.

A great deal has been written about institutional violence. Eckhardt thinks that in the twentieth century it is responsible for many times the deaths attributable to war. This is an immensely complicated matter, involving a host of factors, including questions of time frame and intent. It is a very important subject, to be sure, but it does not fall within the compass of this study.

THE CONTINUATION OF WAR

We ordinarily live at peace. The stuff of history may be war, but peace is our normal condition. War is what historians write about—from their peaceful libraries. Most people spend most of their lives in peaceful situations. Their encounters with war are relatively rare. Most people who do encounter war are not killed fighting. War is exceptional.

Yet the history of war is as old as that of civilization. It seems as endemic as government or social stratification. It is a method of resolving problems that is not likely to be replaced. Plans for eliminating war are not likely to succeed because there will be situations in which particular men will want to make war, and it is difficult to prevent it from taking place if they want to fight.

Wars between great powers have been few and limited in the Present Age: the border scuffles between Russia and China at the end of the 1960s have been the only conflicts in this category since the Americans met the Chinese in Korea in the early 1950s, if indeed China could be classified as a great power. Wars between great and secondary powers have been more frequent, but where underdeveloped countries have not been involved, they have been short and relatively low in casualties. Wars involving both developed and underdeveloped countries have been most common and most disastrous in the 1950s and 1960s. But France had withdrawn from these by the end of the 1950s and the United States and Portugal withdrew in the 1970s. Russia pulled out of Afghanistan in 1989. This kind of war seemed to be occurring with declining frequency.

Wars involving only underdeveloped countries have been few, but they may increase, War is often a sign of vitality. It is not necessary to a vital nation, but it seems to be the case that periods we now regard as most interesting in ancient Greece, the Italian city states, Spain, France, England and the Netherlands were also periods of continuous, but not overwhelming, strife. Wars often provide a focus for national unity, they enable people to solve problems that had seemed insoluble, they bring out selflessness, courage, and other miscellaneous qualities that we seem to consider admirable in most civilized societies. It seems likely that they could be perceived as useful, therefore, to underdeveloped countries in which national identity is in doubt and in which insoluble problems abound.

For developed countries, then, war may continue, but it is likely to be brief, secondary, unimportant in comparison with problems of poverty, ecology and spirit. Yet the existence of an occasional war will continue to draw attention, and except in some arcane journals, the overwhelming prevalence of peace is likely to remain unnoticed.

PEACE AS A CAUSE OF WAR

If most of the developed world is peaceful most of the time, what then? John Lukacs (1961) wondered whether a generation knowing only peace would be greatly motivated to avoid nuclear war as, for instance, Eisenhower and Khrushchev obviously were.

There is considerable evidence that World War I was popular in many European countries at its outset. Most people living in 1914 had never experienced war in their homeland, so they were not unwilling to support their military leaders. In this sense, then, it could be said that the Victorian peace contributed to war.

On the other hand, peace can also reenforce itself. A pattern of peaceful resolution has become traditional in Switzerland and Sweden. The United States and Canada are not more anxious to fight for not having fought for so long. Through history, empires all over the world—the T'ang and Sung in China, the Gupta in India, the Sassanian in Persia, the Roman in the Mediterranean—have ruled great areas in peace for long periods. So generations that have experienced peace will not necessarily be prone to war.

Normal periods come into existence around reenforcing sets of international and psychological accommodation. Once these patterns become established, they tend to be self-perpetuating for a number of decades. But when, as at the turn of the century, a transition is in the making, the existence of a long period of peace may then be a contributing factor to war.

But Switzerland and Sweden have strongly reenforced peaceful patterns that transcend crises. Other areas have maintained internal peace almost continually for more than 100 years. This has been true of Australia and New Zealand, Hawaii, Thailand, southern India, Iceland and the West Indies. Whether it would be possible for wider areas of the world to maintain peace through transitional periods is difficult to guess. We need a greater understanding of the patterns that preserve peace through the phases that cause war.

THE WANING OF IDEOLOGIES

Secularization is a long-term process that develops over several centuries. Ideologies, on the other hand, gain more following in periods of transition, when unity and belief are necessary. If such a transition occurs in a period of secularization, the ideologies that are developed are likely to be secular. And so they were in the most recent crisis period, with democracy, communism and fascism attracting the most attention.

During the World Wars, a great deal of attention was paid to ideologies. The Russian Revolution heralded the beginning of a socialist transformation of the world. The German and Italian fascists, on the other hand, proposed a state in which the government's will and the will of the people were identical. To the more pluralistic nations of Western Europe and America, these ideologies seemed similar in threatening to subordinate the individual (and the corporation) to the state.

In the first decade after World War II, the defeat of the fascists seemed to leave a bipolar world divided by an "iron curtain" running through central Europe. On one side were the Western "Allies," on the other Russia and her satellites, including China. By the 1950s, with the death of

Stalin, the Polish and Hungarian rebellions, and clear differences between Russia and China, and also with a determination by France and Britain to make their own policy, as in the Suez Canal Crisis, this conception began to melt.

By the 1980s, the ideological dispute had largely dissolved. The ideologies of Russia and China had been much watered down and culture modified. The Chinese were actively opening contacts with the West to enhance their modernization. The Russian leadership became ever older, more bureaucratic and less messianic. Its hold on Eastern Europe was one of power tempered by compromise and apparent weariness. The United States had similar problems: with a stagnant economy, it was more concerned with economic competition than with Communist subversion, and could no longer provide inspiring leadership. Almost all governments were bureaucratic structures involving some system of interaction between executive and legislative wings. If a monarch still remained, he or she played a ceremonial role. Students, in the West, hearing about the problems of the Third World, had no idea that the "Second World" was supposed to consist of nations espousing a Communist ideology. And equity rather than ideological considerations is becoming dominant in foreign aid decisions (Horowitz 1982, 10–11).

Since World War II there has been a waning of ideologies in which a particular kind of political doctrine is invested with a moral superiority that is not subject to rational questioning. Ideologies lose their effect because there is no longer a need for unity and belief. There was a multiplicity of problems that could be dealt with by diversity and reason. The amelioration of any one problem, moreover, was likely to intensify another, so there could hardly be ideological unity about priorities.

It seems absurd to most younger adults that a man should be sent to prison for burning a piece of cloth that happens to be a national symbol. But even older generations, who might approve of that, are likely to forget the words of the corresponding symbolic song. And pressure for greater displays of patriotism are likely to be regarded as excessive and in poor taste.

Nations continue to exist in the Relational Age. There are international agencies, but there is no universal state on the horizon. As threats to the existence of the state subsides feelings of a strong need to expound its virtues subside as well. For people living in a developed nation, the state is only one of many reference groups, and not the closest nor the most immediate. Not only do feelings of nationalism have to compete with more demanding involvements associated with the nuclear family, the school or the company, but they are also crosscut by cosmopolitanism, the common element of identification among world-traveling urbanites.

Nationalism had two phases in Modern European history, the first following the development of the nation-state in the sixteenth and seventeenth centuries, the second coming in the late eighteenth and nineteenth centuries. This second phase of nationalism accompanied the industrial revolution in Western Europe and served to identify the middle class with the nation, thus relating the most important economic activity to the purposes of the state. Eventually this burst of nationalism led to the definition of a state in relation to language, culture and history, leading to the unifications of Germany and Italy, the retention of the United States as a single entity, the breakup of the Habsburg Empire into national states and the re-creation of Poland.

These transformations were accompanied by internal and external war. But by the end of World War II this phase had run its course. The excesses of totalitarianism, the violence of the two World Wars, the achievement of an acceptable redefinition of state boundaries had cooled the ardor of most people in the developed countries for further conflict. They were willing that some people speaking the same language should live under different states.

Underdeveloped countries, however, are running through a later phase. The concept of nationalism, the possibilities of the industrial revolution, and other secrets of the West were picked up by the intelligentsia of the colonial countries. When the World Wars hastened their assimilation of Western ideas and gave them their opportunity for independence, they were able to utilize the concept of nationalism as a means of identification for peoples who would otherwise have a tendency to splinter into regions or tribes. The concept of nationalism, therefore, remains strong in these countries and is likely to lead to further conflict before accommodation of the European type can be reached.

Totalitarianism arises in time of crisis. In the twentieth century it was reinforced both by nationalism and the relational outlook. Though the relational outlook continues to develop, totalitarianism is fading with the resolution of the crisis and the decline of nationalism.

Nationalism conveys the feeling that every member of the nation is part of the state. Each has a duty to the state, which is an entity above and beyond himself. The state serves all the people, not the interests of particular individuals. The government, therefore, is the agent of the people. As the totality of relationships is perceived, it is evident that all the actions of the individual relate to the welfare of the state and therefore to all the people. Whether a man marries, whether he has children, whether he expresses support for the state's activities, whether he produces art that expresses concepts supporting objectives of the state—all these details become important. The totalitarian state involves the bringing of all people into harmony, all the entities into fullest participation in the system.

But the nation was obviously part of a larger system, and it was not surprising that the totalitarian idea should be expanded into what Hans Morgenthau (1975) calls nationalistic universalism, the idea that whatever ideology your nation has ought to be the ideology of all nations. The application of totalitarianism is obvious, but it was also implicit in Woodrow Wilson's idea of making the world safe for democracy, revived after World War II by the United World Federalists and others who saw the future world as a constitutional, parliamentary federation and the practical men who came to power and wanted to protect and expand what they conceived to be a "free world," which was a world run by their kind of people.

The intensity and expansion of totalitarianism may have been logically consistent, but it was also exhausting. The totalitarian state is a roaring fire that requires a tremendous amount of fuel. Leaders and young people may give their all for a time, but it appears impossible for the whole of a people to remain totally involved. Some can all of the time and all can some of the time, but all can't all of the time. As the threat of the crisis loses credibility, most people drop out of the ranks of the zealots and seek a return to the deferred pleasures of normal life.

So the totalitarian state heads toward catastrophe and restoration, as in the case of Germany and Italy, or toward a gradual burning out and return to conservative despotism, as in the case of Russia or Spain. Meanwhile, nationalistic universalism has encouraged national resistance movements around the world, and these become successful as the totalitarian impulse subsides in the developed countries.

Herbert Marcuse (1964) has suggested that the ideal of totalitarian state persists and has, ironically, conquered the conquerors of the totalitarian state. He points to the general agreement on the validity of material goals, the acceptance of a consumption ideology and the limitation of choices within the narrow confines of this ideology. Not only is this acceptance as pervasive in the developed countries as fascism was supposed to be in the totalitarian states, but it is even accepted by the progressive elements of underdeveloped countries, future seedbeds of totalitarianism.

But the acceptance of a consumption ideology hardly requires a totalitarian atmosphere. It is simply an aspect of social conformity that pervades most societies. Moreover, there is no shortage of dissent. There is much more than there was in the 1950s, and Marcuse himself, as one of the dissenters, became a popular hero.

Totalitarianism, then, is a product of transition, and it has had its day, at least among developed countries. The relationship of whole and parts obviously has not required that the whole control the parts. Dissent, decentralization and diversity of the parts both determine and are accommodated by the whole.

For many reasons the Relational Age must be a period of tolerance. If the power of particular ideologies diminishes, there is less reason to assert them. The ideologies served important needs during transitional periods, but with relative security established, it is no longer necessary to insist on a single outlook.

As ideologies become secondary, there is a corresponding decline in messianic approaches to international relations. The world need not be made safe for democracy any more than it need become a system of socialist republics. The distinction between despotism and democracy becomes blurred, and the ideologies lose their force as rallying cries. If the ideology loses its importance at home, how can you insist on preserving it for people in distant lands?

As security increases, pressures increase for great decentralization. It is difficult to fight for your own autonomy while you argue that the autonomy of others should be restricted by the imposition of a particular ideology.

It could be said that there are two kinds of tolerance. One is closed tolerance, which is characterized by a confident acceptance of an ideology without feeling either threatened by or curious about possible alternative ideologies. The other is open tolerance, which involves the acceptance of alternative ideologies as providing other possible frames of reference. In normal periods both kinds of tolerance seem to exist. Closed tolerance is common among people who live in relative security, regardless of whether their commitment to their own ideology is strong or tepid, though in the developed world it is more likely to be the latter. Open tolerance is found among people trying to cope with difficult secondary problems.

Intolerance is most common where ideology is strong and security is weak. This is a condition more likely to prevail among underdeveloped countries. People living in developed countries are apt to be rather condescending toward intolerance in these countries, forgetting how they themselves felt in the 1930s and not realizing that intolerant commitment to a particular ideology can often unite a nation in a period in which great unity and energy are essential if economic progress is to be achieved.

Normal times, then, are likely to be less intense, less ideologically focused, less nationalistic, more tolerant. A combination of improved communications, open tolerance and the relational outlook makes the present period particularly inclined toward cosmopolitanism. We are eager to visit other countries and to import their artifacts and ideas.

While all of this does not solve political problems, it does create an atmosphere in which problems can be solved, or if not solved, deferred or endured. Even the failure to solve a particular conflict can be weighed against the costs of taking more extreme measures to bring about a resolution.

Perceptions can differ about, for instance, whether Western commitment to nationalism is being underestimated here. One way of testing is to make a survey that makes no reference to nationalism but would nevertheless be influenced by the presence or absence of perceptions of nationalism. Despite an absence of budget and time, some studies were done that, while possibly perceived as whimsical, and lacking an adequate sample, at least can be easily replicated.

The sample, as is too often true, comes from students. But in this case, fortunately, the students were in two large daytime classes with a combined enrollment of over 100. They were all younger generation, and since this was an urban university, they came from a mixture of working and middle-class homes, with a substantial sprinkling of minority representatives. This urban area, Dayton, Ohio, is regarded by George Gallup as among the ten most representative areas in the United States.

The first study involved the term "Third World." Students were asked if they were familiar with it. More than 90% said they were. This familiarity was reenforced by a definition. Then they were asked: where does the term come from? What does it mean? No one in either class could answer. No one, from suburban nor city high school, was aware that the first two worlds were the Free World and the Communist World. And when so informed, they required quite a bit of explanation about the delineation of these worlds.

The second survey involved the 1988 Winter Olympics, which had just taken place. It could be given to only one of the classes. The students were asked an open-ended question: What did you think of the Winter Olympics? What did you most enjoy? As each answer was given, others were asked if they agreed or disagreed. The results are reported in Table 3.6. The number present was not counted, but the class was well attended. It was final examination review day. The class roster shows 35 women, 17 men in the class.

The first statement was made by a male athlete who led the class into a discussion of the very subject this thesis predicted would not be high on the priority list—America's failures in the competition. And 82% of the class agreed with him.

But when the rest of the results were tallied, they looked to be what

TABLE 3.6

STUDENT RESPONSES TO THE 1988 WINTER OLYMPICS

	Agree	Disagree	Percent Agreeing
1. The Olympics were terrible from an American perspective	28	6	82
2. The games were great	24	8	75
3. American professionals should be allowed to compete	18	15	55
4. ABC coverage was poor	7	4	64
5. What I enjoyed most was the figure skating	18	9	67

one would expect in normal times. Yes, 82% thought the games were depressing from an American perspective, but then students turned around on the next statement and 75% of those voting agreed that the games were great.

The statement about professionals competing was dealing with the solution to the problem of America's Olympic record. Other countries use professionals, why shouldn't America? This time only 55% agreed. The discussion made clear that a substantial minority thought the use of professionals would not be sporting, whatever other countries may or may not do. How you play the game becomes a matter of concern in normal times.

The last item was interesting. Since the class was two-thirds women, it is not surprising that two-thirds might agree that figure skating was the most enjoyable event. (However, there was no gender count on the vote.)

But it was women's figure skating that got the most attention, and there the American heroine was dramatically defeated by an East German. And the Soviets dominated the Americans in paired skating (charming the Canadian town in which they practiced along the way). The Americans won only the men's figure skating. Despite the outcome, figure skating was most enjoyed, reenforcing the conclusion that the Olympics were great *despite* the lack of American success.

The vote on ABC's coverage is worth a footnote. Only one-third the number of students voted on this question compared to the other questions. The issue of media coverage, apparently, is always more interesting to the media than to the public.

Anyway, though this Olympic study may not qualify for the most carefully controlled study of 1988, it was more fun than a number of others done for this book, and the data is consistent with that gotten elsewhere or findings from anecdotal evidence.

Nationalism is not dead, but it is kind of wilted and wrinkled.

THE IMPROBABILITY OF POLITICAL TRANSFORMATION

War has ended for other civilizations when an empire was established and one government controlled the whole civilization. Such a political solution brought peace to the classical world, to Mesopotamia under Persia, to India under the Gupta and Mughal empires, to China under five empires, to Andean America under two.

Is there a chance that the present world is on the verge of an empire? There has been a long period of conflict culminating in the two World Wars. Such times of troubles, as Toynbee calls them, have led to the creation of empires in the past. Characteristically, too, their establishment has been preceded by a polarization among two great powers: the Romans and Carthaginians, the Ch'in and Ch'u, the Persians and the Medes. Also characteristically, there is considerable evidence of a general longing for peace preceding the establishment of these empires.

If such a transformation were to take place, it is not likely that it would occur in our time. By the end of the Present Age, there is no certainty that the United States and Russia will continue to be the dominant powers. They have both looked a bit sluggish in recent years while Japan, for instance, has experienced a great period of growth. The dominant powers in 1815 had been France, Britain and Russia. It would have been hard to predict then, or even 40 years later, that the next challenge to the system would come from Germany.

An alternate possibility has ben suggested by R. S. Scanlan (1985), who sees Soviet Russia as part of Byzantine civilization, a different civilization from the West. Looking at the characteristics of empires, she agrees with Quigley that the Soviet Union already represents the imperial phase of Byzantine civilization. The United States, on the other hand, may be seen as imposing an imperium on the West. The fact that many Europeans want American dominance is characteristic of early response to an incipient empire. From her perspective, World War II was the war in which the United States defeated Germany for the right to dominate the West, while Russia beat off another attack by its troublesome neighboring civilization in the process of consolidating its own empire. Following the logic of Scanlan's argument, East Asia would also be entering a period of unification under China, with Japan retaining its autonomy, as it has done in each of the other periods of a unified and expanding China.

While Scanlan's thesis provides a very different explanation from the one presented here, it would also lead to a period of peace, characteristic of early imperial phases. The conflicts that would terminate such a period would likely be internal, and less violent than that which would occur in another international crisis. It is a hopeful possibility that deserves further investigation.

Over much of the history of the past 2000 years, it has been normal for Europe, like Southeast Asia, to be politically diverse. Therefore in a normal period, the continuation of such diversity is to be expected. Russia, on the other hand, has been unified for several centuries. It would be reasonable to expect that unity to continue, with rebellions most likely in recently acquired peripheral areas, the subordinate socialist republics. China also has been unified normally since the advent of the Han Empire more than two millennia ago. The unification of Japan has now lasted for more than three centuries, and it seems to be a country of exceptional ethnic unity. It would therefore not be surprising if both China and Japan remained unified but separate during the Present Age.

All in all there are some good reasons for anticipating a continuity in political structure for the remainder of our time.

4

PEACE AND VIOLENCE IN THE WORLD AS A WHOLE

THE PERCEPTION OF NORTH AND SOUTH

A century of peace seems likely, then, for North America and Europe, for reasons given in the first three chapters. Russia, though of a different civilization, seems likely to share in this peace, nor is there a great likelihood of inner Asian disturbance, though such a development might be somewhat more likely on the southern frontier. East Asia has other reasons for anticipating a peaceful period, perhaps a longer period of peace than the West, with Japan having both Eastern and Western characteristics.

But peace seems less likely for Latin America, including Central America and Mexico, for Africa, the Middle East and South and Southeast Asia. Except for Australia and New Zealand, then, the longer period of peace seems likely to extend around the northern part of the Northern Hemisphere. If the rather local eighteenth century war between Russia and Sweden came to be known as the Great Northern War, then surely this longer period of peace over a much greater area could merit the title of "The Great Northern Peace" or, if these peaces must be translated into Latin to gain full authenticity, how about *Magna Pax Septentrionis?*

So presented, this view of a northern peace may seem parochial if not downright selfish. Our Western world has entered a period of peace in which we are joined by other northern neighbors. But Asia, Africa, and to a lesser extent, Latin America, continue to be embroiled in conflict that is beyond the scope of our research. This would be particularly insensitive if, as many scholars believe, the West is a major contributor to violence in the rest of the world.

In this chapter, then, I shall consider the regional record of peace and violence in the rest of the world, patterns of violence for the world as a whole during the past quarter millennium, and the relationship between the current "Northern Peace" and the recurrent conflict in the vast area that Westerners have variously described as developing, underdeveloping, Third World and South.

The patterns of violence can be fairly well documented. At least we can present a series of tables and figures that look hard-edged and quantitative, though the basis on which they are drawn may be less secure. The reasons for the difference in levels of violence since World War II are much more difficult to ascertain.

The regional review will cover Latin America, Africa, the Middle East, South Asia and East Asia.

LATIN AMERICA: VIOLENCE WITHIN THE SPHERE

Latin America has had its share of violence since the various nations broke free of Iberian domination. Yet the image of brutal dictatorships, and torture, of uprisings and U.S. interventions, does not necessarily mean that Latin American history has been a bloodbath.

Since 1810 there have been two wars among Latin American countries in which more than 100,000 people have been killed. One was the Chaco War between Paraguay and Bolivia in the 1920s and 1930s, in which 150,000 were killed and the other was the nineteenth-century War of the Triple Alliance, in which Argentina, Brazil and Uruguay went a long way toward exterminating the population of Paraguay, certainly one of the worst wars in history in terms of casualties in relation to population. In 180 years since 1810 there have been only two other wars with casualties over 10,000, including the wars of independence themselves.

There were 4 internal conflicts that produced more than 100,000 killed: the Cuban Uprising of 1868–78 against Spain, the Colombian Civil War of 1899–1902, the Mexican Revolution of 1910–20, and the Guatemalan massacre of Indians of the past two decades. Nine other internal conflicts produced more than 10,000 fatalities.

External interventions contributed to more than 100,000 fatalities in the case of the Cuban part of the Spanish American War and thrice over 10,000 in the U.S. war against Mexico in the 1840s, the French intervention in Mexico in the 1860s and the inter-American intervention in the Dominican Republic in 1965.

The Table of Armed Conflicts in Latin America (Table 4.1) includes only major conflicts. There have been a number of lesser ones, particularly in Central America, that have been long lasting and wearying for the populations involved. Data for all tables in this chapter come from Bouthoul and Carrere, 1978, 1979, supplemented by Eckhardt correspondence (Sivard 1985 and private correspondence).

The overall picture is one of recurrent but not overwhelming conflict, with neither interstate wars, internal uprisings nor external interventions dominant. The pattern has been intermittently continuous, with hardly a decade passing in which a conflict involving more than 10,000 fatalities did not occur somewhere. This pattern does not seem to be much affected by

TABLE 4.1
LATIN AMERICAN ARMED CONFLICTS
1740–1978

Conflict	Dates	Population Involved	Number of Combatants	Number Killed
Santo Domingo Rebellion	1741–94	25 M	40,000	20,000
Santo Domingo War of Independence	1802–04	27 M	50,000	12,000
Latin American Wars of Independence	1810–28	200 M	160,000	37,000
Chilian-Bolivian War	1836–39	8 M	40,000	2,000
War of La Plata	1836–52	9 M	27,000	11,000
U.S.-Mexican War	1846–48	30 M	30,000	17,000
Mexican Civil War	1858–61	9 M	40,000	2,000
French Intervention in Mexico	1862–67	45 M	200,000	20,000
Ecuadoran-Columbian War	1863	4 M	6,000	1,200
Spanish Intervention in Peru, Chile	1864–66	21 M	138,000	1,200
War of the Triple Alliance of La Plata	1864–70	14 M	35,000	1,100,000
Jamaican Rebellion	1865	30 M	20,000	600
Cuban Uprising	1868–78	16 M	50,000	150,000
Saltpetre War	1879–1884	7 M	30,000	14,000
Salvadoran-Guatemalan War	1885	2 M	12,000	NA
Chilian Revolution	1891	2 M	30,000	11,000
Spanish-American War in Cuba	1895–98	94 M	300,000	130,000
Columbian Civil War	1899–1902	2 M	30,000	150,000
Panamanian Rebellion	1903	2 M	30,000	NA
U.S. Intervention in Nicaragua	1909–1916	80 M	30,000	800
Chaco War	1928–1935	3 M	600,000	150,000
Salvadoran Uprising	1931–1932	3 M	50,000	24,000
Costa Rican Civil Conflict	1948	NA	NA	NA
Bay of Pigs	1961	9 M	15,000	NA
Cuban Missile Crisis	1962	450 M	200,000	1
Dominican Republic Intervention	1965–66	204 M	60,000	30,000
Guatemalan Government Massacre of Indians	1966–1987			138,000
El Salvador Raid on Honduras	1969	6 M	60,000	NA
Coup d'etat in Chile	1973	9 M	30,000	5,000
Nicaraguan Civil War	1978–1988			65,000
El Salvadoran Civil War	1979–1988			65,000
Jamaican Election Violence	1980			1,000
Falkland War	1982			1,000
Peruvian Maoist Rebellion	1983–1988			15,000

Western crises, though of course the Napoleonic Wars provided the opportunity for the Wars of Independence. The period before those wars was much more peaceful for Latin America than any subsequent period has been.

The effect of the Monroe Doctrine is difficult to ascertain. There have been interventions by other countries besides the United States since that time, and there have been wars among Latin American nations that the United States could not or did not prevent. It is difficult to say whether there would have been more wars or fewer wars if Latin America, like Europe, did not have the somewhat porous protection of the United States from external intervention.

It would appear that though Latin America is within the U.S. sphere of influence, it is not operating within the rhythms of the West. Many, but not all, of its nations are underdeveloped. It seems probable that there will be recurrent but not overwhelming conflict in Latin America, regardless of whether the United States does or does not intervene. Whether such conflict would be likely to increase or decrease would require an investigation of the special circumstances involved in Latin America.

But the history of conflict in Latin America since the Napoleonic Wars does not appear to be closely related to conflict in the Western world.

REBELLIONS AND MASSACRES IN AFRICA

The pattern of military conflict in Africa (Table 4.2) is very different from that of Latin America. But it is not one that would lead to an expectation of peace.

Most of the conflicts during the Victorian Age were the result of European invasion and expansion, with no fighting among the European powers themselves. The most striking casualties in this period were the result of massacres of Hottentots and Maji-Maji by the Germans in the first decade of this century.

The distraction of the World Wars seemed to bring such conflict to an end, save for the Italian reprise in Ethiopia. There were rebellions during this period, but no conflict among European powers in Africa, however much they might be fighting in the rest of the world.

The postwar period brought about conflicts of two kinds: rebellions by Africans against European occupiers and conflicts between majorities and minorities in African successor states. Wars between African states have been minor.

The conflicts relating to rebellion against European domination appear to be about over, unless South Africa is seen as European dominated. In any event, there is clearly a continued potential for racial conflict in South Africa. The widespread failure of the European-created African states

TABLE 4.2
MAJOR ARMED CONFLICTS IN AFRICA
1807–1988

Conflict	Dates	Population Involved	Number of Combatants	Number Killed
Koukou-Nor Rebellion	1807	160 M	20,000	5,000
English Conquest of Ghana	1821–1826	30 M	15,000	3,000
Caffres War	1834–1843	35 M	40,000	4,000
Conquest of Senegal	1854–1885	40 M	30,000	2,000
Bantu Rebellion	1854	5 M	15,000	3,000
Tanganyikan Civil War	1859–1869	5 M	12,000	N/A
Conquest of Nigeria	1861–1900	40 M	60,000	N/A
Anglo-Ethiopian War	1867–68	35 M	80,000	4,000
Ashanti Rebellion	1873–74	33 M	40,000	1,500
Egyptian-Ethiopian War	1874–76	15 M	60,000	7,000
Conquest of Zululand	1879	36 M	60,000	14,000
French Conquest of Niger	1879–1898	38 M	30,000	9,000
Basutoland Revolt	1879–1881	36 M	12,000	1,200
English Conquest of Nyasaland	1885–1896	35 M	20,000	1,500
French Conquest of Dahomey	1890–1893	40 M	30,000	1,500
Anti-Slavery Struggle Belgian Congo	1892–1894	7 M	40,000	20,000
Italian-Ethiopian War	1894–1896	35 M	120,000	16,000
English Conquest of Uganda	1894–1901	41 M	30,000	1,500
French Conquest of Madagascar	1894–1900	40 M	70,000	8,000
Anglo-Ashanti War	1896–1900	40 M	30,000	1,500
English Conquest of Benin	1897	40 M	30,000	1,500
French Conquest of Chad	1897–1900	41 M	40,000	1,500
Boer War	1899–1902	41 M	400,000	25,000
Rebellion in British Somalia	1899–1904	41 M	30,000	2,000
French Conflict in Chad	1902–1914	41 M	30,000	1,500
English Occupation of North Nigeria	1903–	45 M	30,000	500
Hottentot Rebellion	1903–1908	52 M	40,000	80,000
Maji-Maji Rebellion	1905–1907	54 M	60,000	150,000
Zululand Revolt	1906	40 M	40,000	5,000
Ethiopian War	1935–1937	48 M	400,000	20,000
Mau-Mau Revolt	1952–1963	60 M	60,000	45,000
Civil War in Sudan	1955–1972	13 M	40,000	700,000
Tutsis Massacre in Rwanda	1956–1965	11 M	20,000	105,000
Cameroon Rebellion	1957–1958	52 M	40,000	N/A
Congo Rebellion	1958–1976	30 M	120,000	110,000
Angolan Rebellion	1961–1976	16 M	80,000	55,000
Guinean Rebellion	1962–1974	11 M	40,000	15,000
Mozambique Rebellion	1965–1975	18 M	60,000	30,000

Conflict	Dates	Population Involved	Number of Combatants	Number Killed
War of Biafran Succession	1967–1970	55 M	200,000	1,100,000
Eritrian Conflict	1969–	25 M	40,000	N/A
Tibetsi Rebellion in Chad	1970–	4 M	30,000	1,500
Ugandan Civil War	1971–1988			900,000
Hutu Massacres in Burundi	1972	4 M	30,000	90,000
Eritrean and Ogaden Rebellions in Ethiopia	1974–1988			556,000
Angolan Civil War	1975–1988			377,000
Mozambiquan Civil War	1981–1988			415,000

(Wheatcroft 1984) could also lead to attacks upon the numerous Europeans who still live in Africa.

Wars between African states have been secondary, as was true of Latin America during the first three decades after the nineteenth century wars of independence. Whether this absence of conflict is a residue of the absence of conflict among European powers is hard to say. Or it could be that the struggle to unify the various artificial political entities does not allow much energy for conflicts among states. If there were consolidation and economic improvement, the possibility of such wars could increase.

But the greatest danger for Africa seems to be continued secession struggles with possible concomitant massacres. The massacres of the Tutsis and Hutus, and especially of the Ibo in Biafra, all of which had very high casualty rates, indicate the danger and lethality of such conflicts. The economic collapse of the European polities certainly could lead to further bitter secession struggles of this kind.

If Africa were to achieve peace for the next several decades, it would certainly not be connected with the factors involved in the peace of the developed world.

The use of Eckhardt's figures for the 1980s somewhat skews the data, since he includes famine in the civilian deaths, particularly in Mozambique and Ethiopia, while Bouthoul and Carrere apparently do not include famine or other forms of structural violence. Thus the figures for the late 1970s and 1980s may be considerably inflated, compared to the earlier periods, or the earlier periods may be deflated, depending on one's preference of criteria.

Be that as it may, violence in Africa has been widespread and recurrent in the past two centuries. If Africa were to achieve peace in the next several decades, it would certainly owe little to the peace of the developed world.

THE MIDDLE EAST: MORE VIOLENT THAN DANGEROUS?

The Middle East has not been protected by a well-defined sphere of influence, as has Latin America. The United States, as a successor to Britain and France, has played more of a negotiator's role. It is an area of ideological conflicts and frustrations, of modernization, and historical and economic pulls that attract the developed countries. In 1970 the American president, repeating frequently expressed contemporary opinions, suggested that it is the most dangerous area in the world. He compared the situation there to the situation before World War I, in which conflicts among small powers dragged unwilling great powers into a general conflict.

Yet it seems that there are a number of factors operating against a major conflict in this area. One is the normal period itself. If major war did not break out during either the partition of Israel or the Suez Crisis, it was less likely during the Six-Day or Yom Kippur Wars (Insight Team 1974), when a younger generation, less concerned about territorial control, was gaining more influence in the governments of developed nations.

Of course, historically, Russia had long been interested in the Middle East. But historically the Middle East has not been a focal point for major conflict since the expansion of the Caliphate in the first millennium. None of the modern crisis conflicts centered around the Middle East. Napoleon dabbled in it and Montgomery and Rommel were colorful, but it was not a central theater in either general war. The Crimean War was a major conflict in the Victorian Age, and there is no question that it arose from disagreement about the Middle East, but despite its nastiness it was geographically contained, as its name suggests. The tinderbox conflicts preceding World War I occurred in the Balkans, not the Middle East.

Economically Russian interest is understandable. Control of oil sources and the Suez Canal may have some economic value, but compared to the political risk, it seems negligible. The political risk involves not only the Western defense of Israel, should the Arab nations really seem threatening, but also the subsequent nuisance of Arab hostility against Russian intervention, should the Russians send any great number of cadre or advisors.

The selling of arms by great powers to the small powers represents a familiar pattern. The arms may alter the sophistication of the conflict, and tragically and unnecessarily increase the number of casualties, but the conflict would continue at some level of technology whether the great powers were involved or not.

Internal changes, whether perceived as positive or negative, warming or cooling, Nobel Prize winning or losing, really do not change the situation nearly as much as one would think from the magnitude of the headlines or the breadth of in-depth analyses. The accession of a Khomeini regime in Iran resulted in some frightening rhetoric, horrifying internal scenes, and a lethal war, but did not change the regional balance of power nor the involvement of great powers. Similarly, the 1979 Egyptian-Israeli treaty produced some hopeful rhetoric and pleasing internal scenes, but did not change the internal balance of power nor the involvement of the great powers.

The Suez Crisis of 1956 confirmed the limits of conflict in the Middle East. This will continue to be an area of nagging international conflict like Southeast Asia. Such conflicts are in prospect in all areas where modernization is being attempted and where ideologies are strongly stated, but in the Middle East and Southeast Asia, such patterns of conflict already have a long history. Great power intervention reduced them, when Britain and France were the occupiers. Now that they are gone, normal patterns have resumed. This is regrettable, but it is not likely to be the source of a major war for many decades to come.

SOUTH ASIA

Take South Asia in the broad sense: the Indian subcontinent, Southeast Asia and Indonesia. Much of this territory has been Hindu or Muslim, with Buddhism having been strong in earlier periods. Vietnam is an exception here, having cultural ties that are closer to East Asia, but political involvement more closely related to South Asia.

The long-term history of this area points to recurrent warfare between divided states. This has long been true in Southeast Asia, where Burma, Thailand and Vietnam have been the regional powers, and in south India. Northern India has been unified in earlier periods of history, before the Mughal and British Raj, notably under the Maurya and Gupta Empires. But when these entities broke up, conflict followed.

History following the breakup of the British Raj doesn't indicate things will be different. The Indo-Pakistani War following the partition of India produced 800,000 fatalities. The war involving the separation of Bangladesh from Pakistan possibly killed another million and a half. Further east there have been the French-Indochina War, the Vietnam War, and the Cambodian and Indonesian massacres, both with fatalities in the hundreds of thousands.

There is no indication that these conflicts are over. The strains of industrialization in India could produce conflicts among the multilingual states, especially if the danger of conflict between India and Pakistan should subside. Southeast Asia has had several decades of intervention by outside powers. With the subsidence of this intervention, there are still power relationships to be sorted out among Burma, Thailand and Vietnam, with a weak Cambodia and Laos providing an area for possible conflict. Indonesia, Malaya and the Philippines remain areas of possible internal conflict.

South Asia has been an area of recurrent violence. In some areas the conflict appears to have been increased by the intervention of outside powers, as in Vietnam, or by their attempts to remain, as in French Indochina, or by their precipitate withdrawal, as in British India. Their absence has not prevented catastrophic violence in Cambodia, Indonesia, the Philippines or Bangladesh.

There seems to be little reason to believe that this period of conflict is coming to an end. The peace of our time has not included, and is not likely to include, South or Southeast Asia.

EAST ASIA: THE DAWN OF PEACE?

The prospects for peace are very much more favorable for East Asia than for South Asia.

To begin with, China has a long history of recurrent periods of peace, empires that have maintained internal peace for two or three centuries: the Han, T'ang, Sung, Ming and Ch'ing (Melko 1973; Table 4.3). Each of these peace periods in China have usually been accompanied by peace in Korea as well.

Once again there seems to be a strong, centralized, bureaucratic government in China. If China were free of external intervention, past history would indicate prospects for a couple of centuries of internal peace, a longer peace than would be expected in the Western world. As the younger generation comes to power, disturbances over governmental style, such as the student suppression of 1989, will probably subside.

Nor is conflict likely between China and her great neighbors, India and Russia. Their borderline clashes have been limited and minimal in the past, as they seem to have been in the postwar period. When China has

TABLE 4.3
CENTURIES OF PEACE IN THE EAST

Peace	Period	Location
Han	202 B.C.–A.D. 184	China, Annam
T'ang	628–868	China, Annam, Manchuria, Korea, Tibet
Fujiwara	600–900	Honshu, Kyushu, Shikoku
Sung	1004–1235	China
Kamakura	1185–1331	Honshu, Kyushu, Shsikoku
Ming	1403–1629	China, Korea
Manchu	1682–1852	China, Manchuria, Korea, Taiwan
Tokugawa	1638–1942	Japan

(Melko 1973, 32–33)

intervened, in Korea and Vietnam, she has shown herself to be discreet and careful not to get involved in sticky peripheral conflicts.

Though Japan has been very much influenced by Chinese history, her rhythms of war and peace have been different. Japan has had shorter periods of internal peace, longer periods of civil conflict. But the Tokugawa Shogunate of the seventeenth through the nineteenth centuries provided two centuries of solid peace (Table 4.3).

Then came the Meiji reform, and Japan became involved in Western history, including the World Wars crisis. Japan emerged as a major industrial state in the Western style, with a peaceful internal orientation not unlike that of Germany.

The relations between Japan and China have been generally peaceful. The invasions of China in the crisis period were atypical, and not likely to be repeated even if Japan were not so much involved in the Western orbit.

If Japan were involved only in East Asia, it would seem likely that she would share China's prospects of two centuries or more of peace. Insofar as she is involved in the politics and society of the West, she is likely to share in the century or more of peace that Western society anticipates.

In any event, the prospects for peace in East Asia would seem to be, if anything, better than that of the West, and probably the blackest cloud—an unconscious but relevant metaphor—is on the Western horizon. The greatest threat to peace in East Asia is probably the future termination of peace in the West.

PATTERNS OF WORLD CONFLICT: 1741–1985

Bouthoul and Carrere go as far back as 1740, which takes us back to the middle of the Baroque Age. Figures 4.1 and 4.2, representing world conflict, therefore cover the end of one normal period, the whole of another and the beginning of a third, with the Napoleonic and World Wars crises in between. Two shadings are used to differentiate mild and severe conflict. Severe conflict (black) is defined as 10,000 or more fatalities in 5 years. Mild conflict (shaded) is from 100 to 10,000 fatalities. If an entire region, such as Western Europe, had fewer than 100 fatalities, the area is left white. Where figures on fatalities were not available, the area was shaded gray. Areas are blackened or shaded only if fatalities from armed conflict occur in them, but not if troops from that area fight elsewhere. If the British attack Nigeria, West Africa is shaded, but Western Europe is not. Readers have wondered about the identity of conflicts that are represented by the black areas. These are listed in Table 4.9.

Sixteen geographical regions are designated. The time periods are five years each. The chart is presented in two versions. Figure 4.1 has a north-south arrangement, to show the areas presently expected to experience

FIGURE 4.1
World Conflict: 1741-1985
(North-South Arrangement)

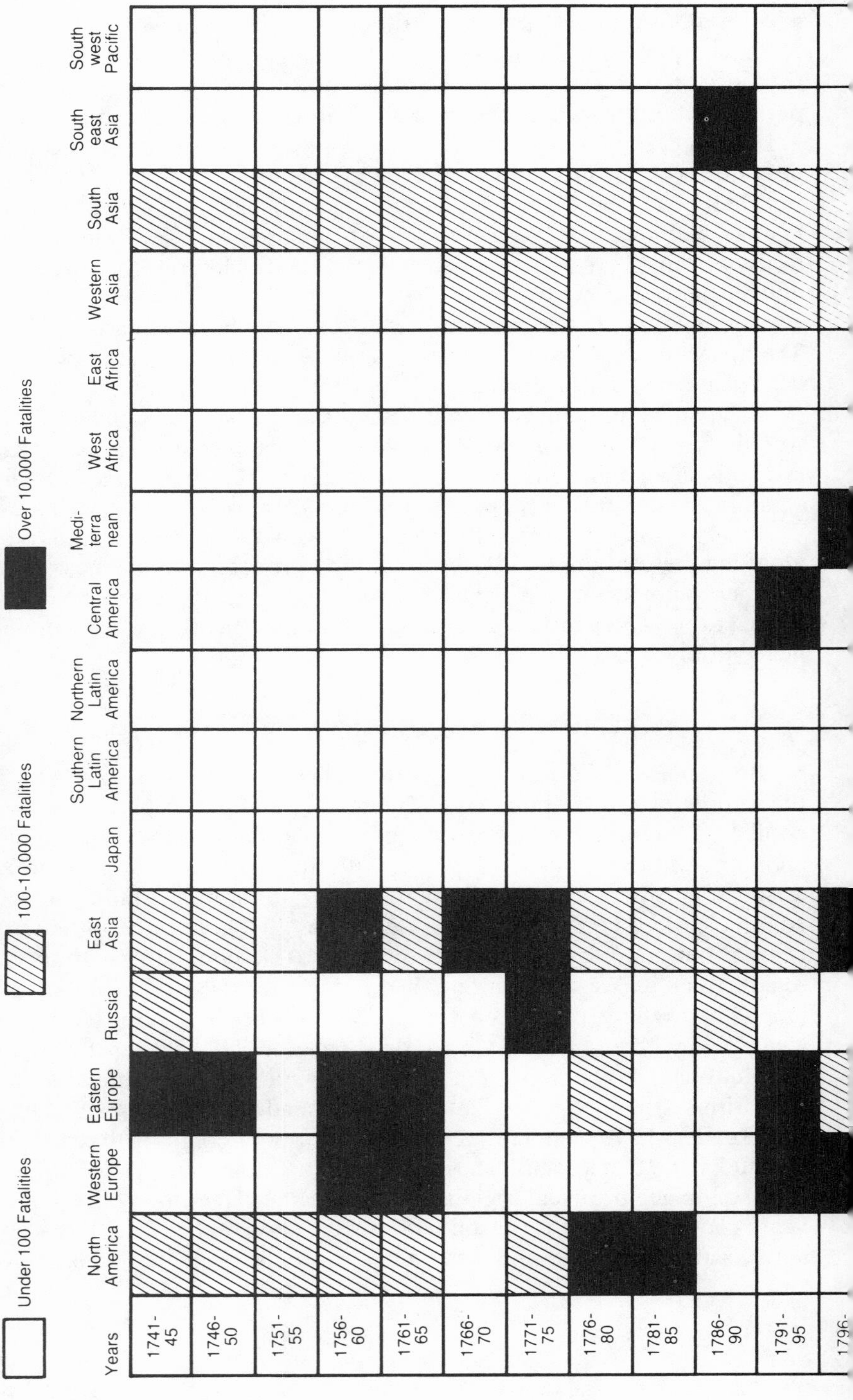

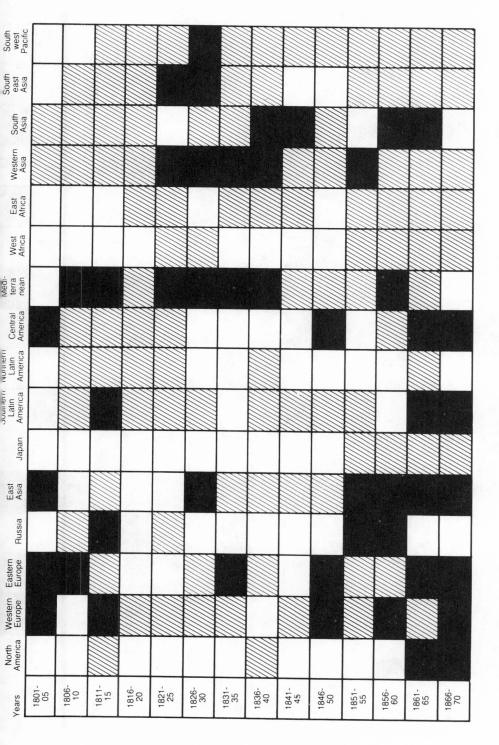

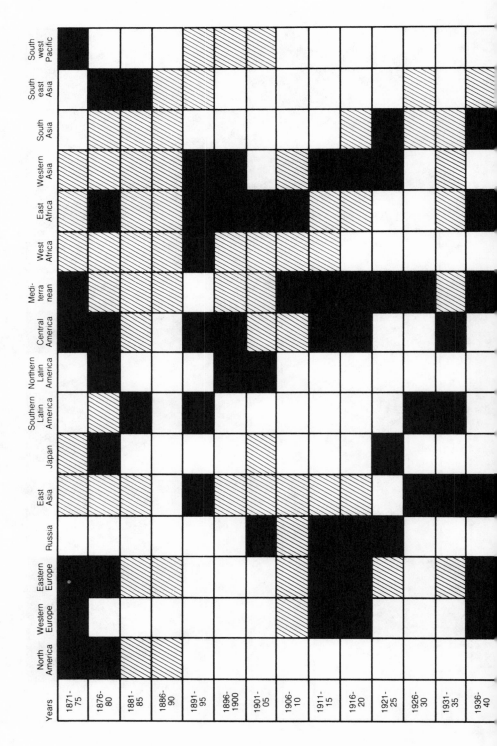

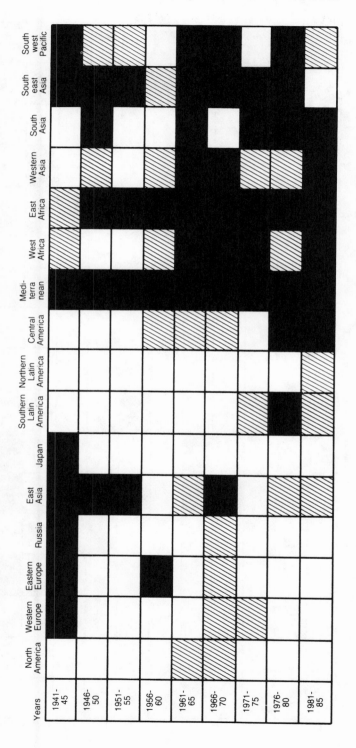

FIGURE 4.2
World Conflict: 1741-1985 (West-East Arrangement)

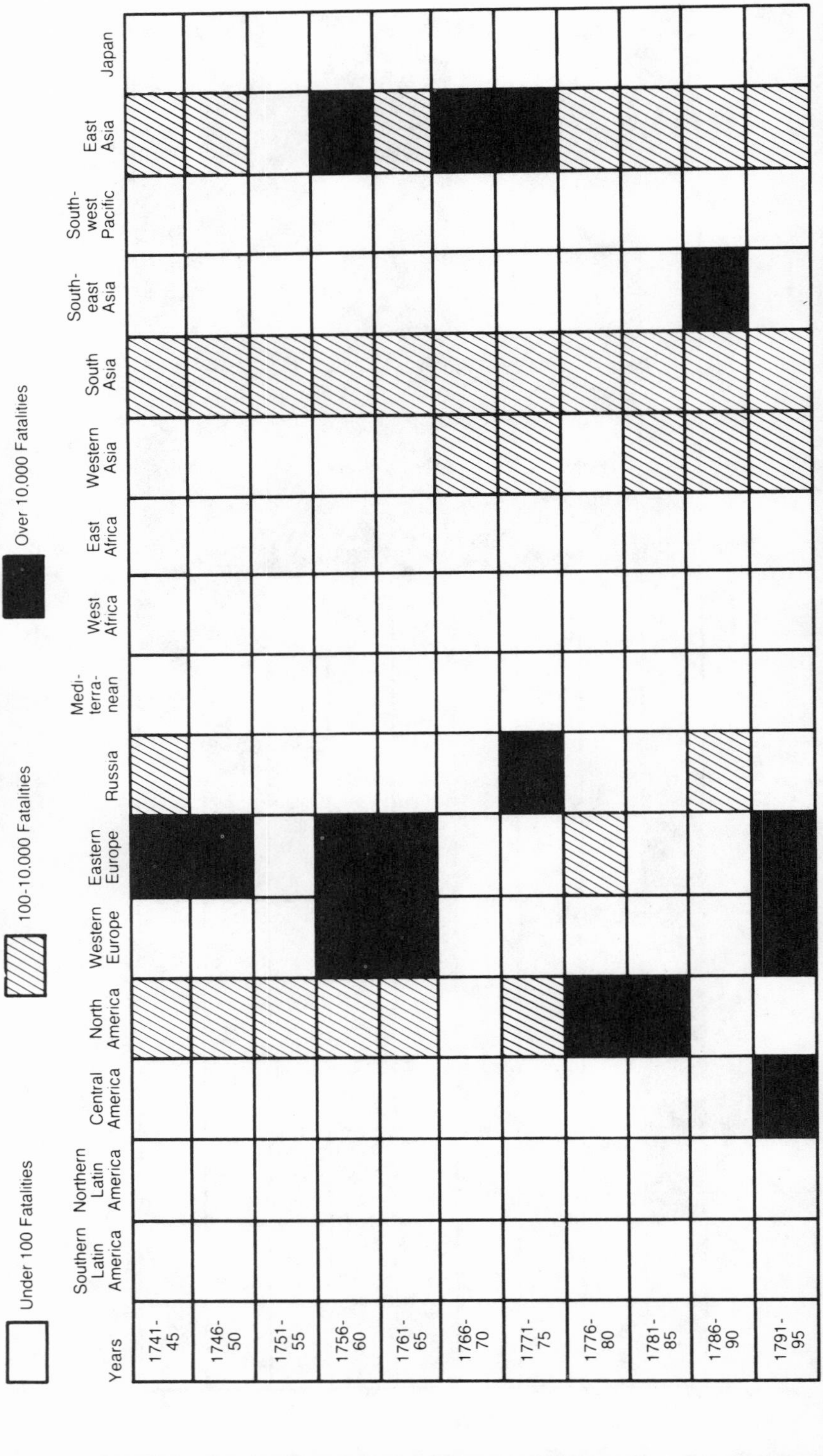

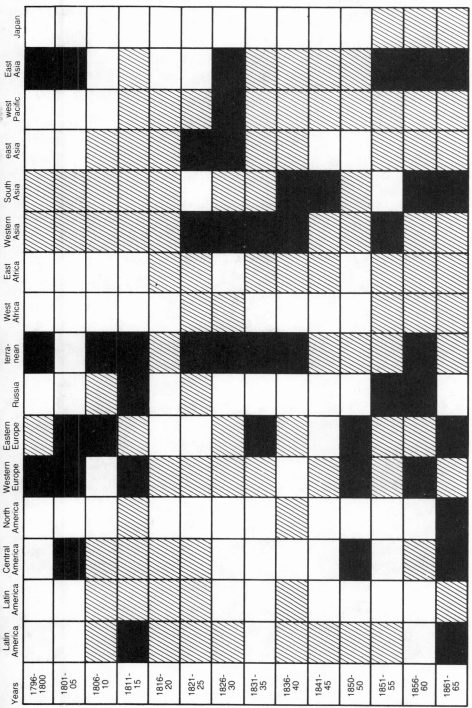

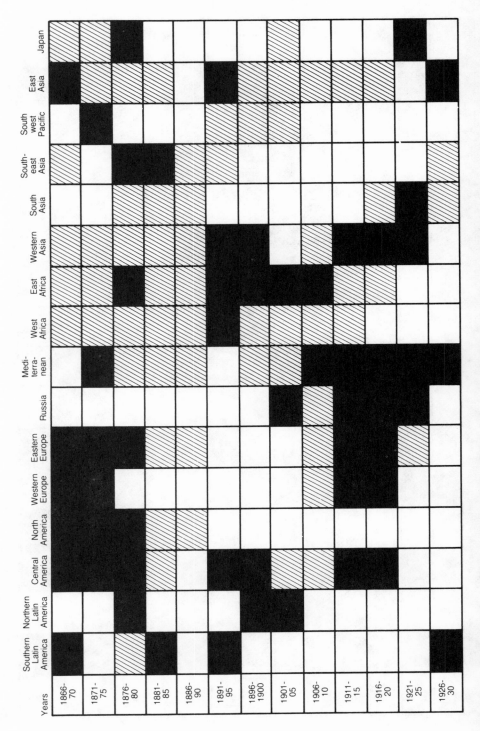

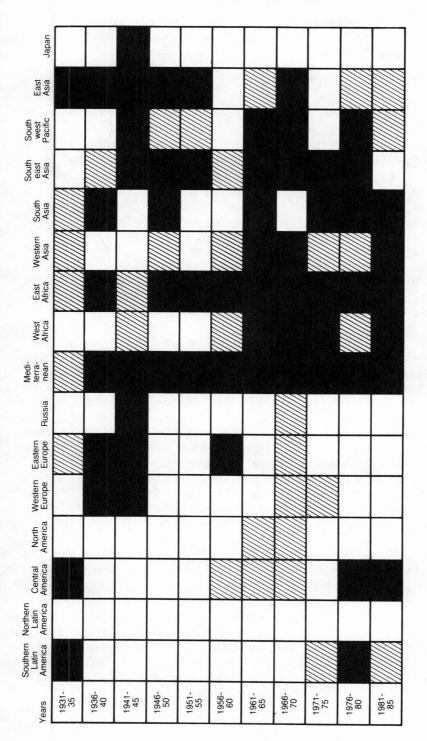

peace on the left, the more doubtful areas on the right. Figure 4.2 shows the world schematically arranged from west to east, beginning with the Western Hemisphere.

These are very rough charts, unsatisfactory in many ways. But the more subtle they become, e.g., more shadings for more variations in fatalities, the less clear would be the patterns. This means, however, that the 11 million fatalities in the Taiping Rebellion of 1851–1864 are represented by three vertical black squares, while the 62,000 fatalities of the revolutions of 1848 are represented by two horizontal black squares. Armed conflict may be underrepresented where information was not available. On the other hand, it could also be overrepresented where multiple reporting has occurred.

The 16 geographical areas are somewhat arbitrary. No attempt is made to consider population, so some areas may have a greater population than others, or populations may change. This could distort the situation in East Asia, for instance, where heavy population may cause relatively mild conflicts to exceed 10,000 fatalities.

Northern Latin America includes Brazil and Bolivia, but not Panama when it can be separated from Colombia. Central America includes Mexico and the West Indies. The Mediterranean includes Spain but not Portugal, Southern but not Northern Italy, Greece but not the Balkans, the Levant but not Turkey and Egypt as well as the Maghreb. West Africa includes countries not bordering the Mediterranean from Mauritania east through Chad, and south through Zaire and Angola. East Africa includes countries from the Sudan to South Africa and Madagascar. Western Asia includes Turkey, Iraq, Iran, the Arabian Peninsula and the Caucasus nations now in the U.S.S.R. South Asia includes Afghanistan, Pakistan, India and Bangladesh. Southeast Asia begins at Burma and includes Malaya. The Southwest Pacific includes the East Indies, Philippines, Australia and New Zealand. East Asia includes Korea and Tibet.

The chart covers 16 areas over 49 five-year periods, creating a total of 784 squares. Of these, 381 were white, 224 shaded and 179 black. Rounding off, that means that in these large areas, peace was experienced 49% of the time, mild conflicts 29% and major conflicts 23% of the time (see Table 4.7 below).

Visually, the area of the Northern Peace—North America, Europe and Russia—looks relatively peaceful since 1946 as shown in Figure 4.3. There are 32 squares, of which 25 are white, 6 cross-hatched and only 1 black (78%–19%–3%) (Figure 4.4). Japan also fits, with peace since 1945, but East Asia does not, with heavy conflict through 1970, and further conflict since.

Earlier "normal" periods do not fare as well. As we see in Figure 4.4, the Victorian Age looks relatively peaceful for Western civilization and Russia from 1816 through 1845. In this period there are 24 boxes, with 13

FIGURE 4.3
Peace So Far
1946-1985

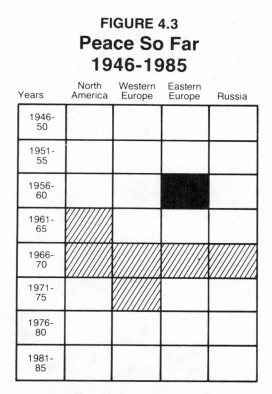

Years	North America	Western Europe	Eastern Europe	Russia
1946-50				
1951-55				
1956-60			■	
1961-65	▨			
1966-70	▨	▨	▨	▨
1971-75		▨		
1976-80				
1981-85				

of them (54%) peaceful and 8 experiencing mild conflict (33%), with 3 experiencing heavy conflict (13%). For the next 35 years, however, conflict is heavy, with only 9 of 28 five-year periods peaceful, four experiencing mild conflict and 15 heavy conflict (32%–14%–54%). By the kind of measure used here, that period from the revolutions of 1848 through the Balkan revolution of 1875–1878 was certainly above average in violent conflict. The Congress of Berlin, which brought forth the phrase "peace for our time," was followed by 30 years of relative peace: 24 blocks, of which 16 were peaceful, 7 experienced mild violence and one heavy violence (67%–29%–4%). The Victorian Age at 38, 19 and 19 (50%–25%–25%) is scarcely more peaceful than the Russo-Western average since 1740 (54%–20%–26%) (Figure 4.4, Table 4.4).

The Age of the Baroque does not appear to be especially peaceful between 1741 and 1785. Of 36 five-year periods, 9 experienced heavy warfare, 8 milder conflict and 19 peace. This rate (53%–22%–25%) was not quite as peaceful as the Victorian period.

If we take the crisis periods for these four Western areas, we find that in the Napoleonic crisis there were ten periods of peace, five periods of mild war and nine periods of major conflict (42%–21%–38%) while in the

FIGURE 4.4
Three Phases of the Victorian Age

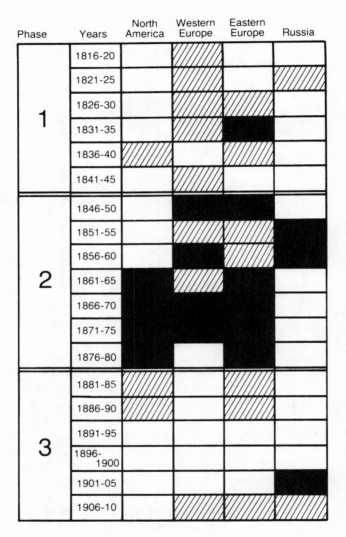

World Wars period it was 14–2–12 (50%–7%–43%). The major difference in the crisis times is that the periods of severe conflict about double those in normal times. The peaceful five-year periods are about the same in crisis

TABLE 4.4
PEACE AND WAR IN RUSSIA AND THE WEST

Dates	Number of Five-Year Periods				Percentages			
	Peace	Mild Conflict	Severe Conflict	Total Conflict	Peace	Mild Conflict	Severe Conflict	Total Conflict
1741–1785	19	8	9	17	53	22	25	47
1786–1815	10	5	9	14	42	21	38	59
1816–1845	13	8	3	11	54	33	13	46
1846–1880	9	4	15	19	32	14	54	68
1881–1910	16	7	1	8	67	29	4	33
1816–1910	38	19	19	38	50	25	25	50
1911–1945	14	2	12	14	50	7	43	50
1946–1985	25	6	1	7	78	19	3	22
1741–1985	105	40	51	91	54	20	26	46

and normal times, though this is somewhat skewed by the fact that North America sent millions of troops to fight elsewhere, many of them in Europe.

In chapter one I had compared the early Victorian period with the early part of the Present Age. Table 4.4 and Figure 4.5 confirm that comparison. The early part of the Victorian Age (1816–1845) shows up as relatively peaceful, with 54% of the five-year periods lacking war and only 13% experiencing major conflict. The early part of our age (1946–1975) is even more peaceful, with 71% of the periods experiencing peace and only 4% involved in major conflict.

Ah, but what about that period from 1846 to 1880? This is a period in the middle of the *Pax Britannica* and the Victorian equivalent of the period we are currently experiencing. It was already mentioned but glossed over how warlike it was by the five-year measurement used here. As Table 4.4 and Figure 4.4 show, it was less peaceful than either the Napoleonic or World Wars period (32% cf. 42% & 50%) and had a higher percentage of severe conflict 68% (cf. 38% & 43%). This certainly is counter evidence to the thesis that the Victorian Age was a period of relative peace and to the very idea that the West has been experiencing a series of crisis and normal times. All that can be said is that the measure of total fatalities and casualties per hundred thousand given in chapter two (Table 3.3) is more convincing in favor of the idea that the crisis periods were much more devastating.

Be that as it may, does that mean one should expect an increase in violence in the next few decades to correspond with the middle decades of the Victorian Age? Not necessarily. There is data only for two beginnings (Victorian and Relational), one middle (Victorian) and two endings (Baroque and Victorian). The two endings are not similar. The Victorian

FIGURE 4.5

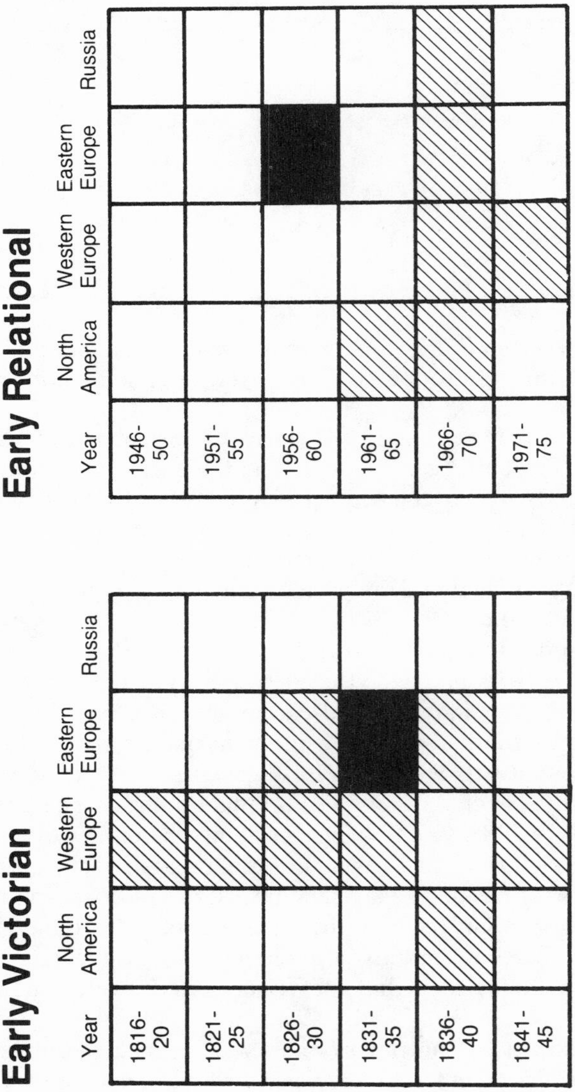
Early Victorian
Year
North America
Western Europe
Eastern Europe
Russia
1816-20
1821-25
1826-30
1831-35
1836-40
1841-45
Early Relational
Year
North America
Western Europe
Eastern Europe
Russia
1946-50
1951-55
1956-60
1961-65
1966-70
1971-75

period ended with 30 years of relative peace (1881–1910), which led people to believe that Norman Angell (1913) was saying there would be no more war. There is no corresponding peace to be found in the closing years of the Baroque (1741–1785).

From a look at the way peace is distributed throughout the world (Table 4.5), there is nothing to suggest that East Asia would share the present peace. With 8 periods of peace, 23 of mild conflict and 18 of severe conflict (16%–47%–37%), it has about the worst record of any of the 16 areas (Tables 4.5 and 4.8). The reason for thinking it may continue to be peaceful is that East Asia has had long periods of peace when China was under strong domestic dynasties: the Han, T'ang, Sung and Ming. It has been conflict-ridden between these dynasties or under alien centralized dynasties: the Yuan (Mongols) and Ch'ing (Manchu). The two and a half centuries charted here catch the period of the declining Manchu dynasty in the eighteenth and nineteenth centuries and its demise, climaxed by the extremely violent Taiping Rebellion of the mid-nineteenth century. The creation of the People's Republic of China involved the establishment of a new domestic centralized regime and could, therefore, mark the onset of another peaceful period.

TABLE 4.5

WORLD DISTRIBUTION OF PEACE AND WAR

Area	Number of Five-Year Periods				Percentages			
	Peace	Mild Conflict	Severe Conflict	Total Conflict	Peace	Mild Conflict	Severe Conflict	Total Conflict
Japan	40	6	3	9	82	12	6	18
Northern Latin America	39	7	3	10	80	14	6	20
Russia	34	7	9	15	69	14	18	31
North America	31	12	6	18	63	24	12	37
Southern Latin America	30	11	8	19	61	22	16	39
West Africa	27	17	5	22	55	35	10	45
Southwestern Pacific	27	16	6	22	55	33	12	55
Central America	24	11	14	25	49	22	29	51
Southeast Asia	23	14	12	26	47	29	24	53
Western Europe	23	11	15	26	47	22	31	53
East Africa	20	15	14	29	41	31	29	59
Eastern Europe	17	13	19	32	35	27	39	65
Mediterranean	14	11	24	35	29	22	49	71
South Asia	13	25	11	36	27	51	22	73
Western Asia	11	25	13	38	22	51	27	78
East Asia	8	23	18	41	16	47	37	84

Japan, on the other hand, has been the area least afflicted with war (82%–12%–6%) (Tables 4.5 and 4.8) though the Japanese, like the North Americans, have given rather more than they have received. Japan, in 1945, presumably resumed the long peace of the Tokugawa period, which had been broken in the 1850s. Thus it may be that the present Japanese peace was begun with the atomic bombing of 1945 and, if the analysis here has validity, it could be that it would end with nuclear bombings in the twenty-first century.

The present peace appears on the world chart (Figure 4.1) at the bottom eight rows of the four left-hand columns. It could extend to six left-hand columns in coming decades. Even schematically represented, it is a small part of recent world history.

Before the Eckhardt figures were available, when the chart ran only through 1975, it appeared as though the Latin American columns also might fit in the peace. Rearranged from West to East (Figures 4.2 and 4.6) there appeared to be a possible "occidental" peace, even with Central America included. The Eckhardt figures for 1976–85, however, undercut that possibility.

FIGURE 4.6
An Occidental Peace ?

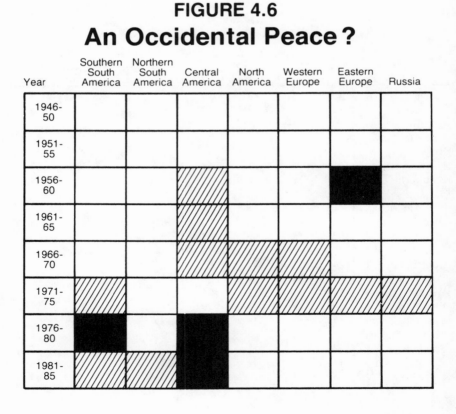

South America, however, has an excellent record for peace. As Table 4.5 shows, Northern Latin America is second to Japan as the most peaceful region on the globe by the five-year area count, and South America as a whole has been, by far, the most peaceful continent (Table 4.6). Still, Latin America has run by different rhythms from Western civilization, and there is no reason to believe, from this analysis, that troubled times, such as were manifested through much of the nineteenth century, would not return in the twentieth or twenty-first.

Africa's record has been somewhat worse than the world as a whole, but particularly since Europeans became involved early in the nineteenth century. It is probable, moreover, that Bouthoul and Carrere have incomplete records for the period before 1816. The record for recent decades gives little reason for optimism.

Nor is there much in the record of South Asia through the East Indies that would make a peaceful future seem likely, nor in the record of the Mediterranean and Western Asia taken together, which collectively covers a territory something like what we call the Middle East.

Looking at Table 4.2 rearranged from west to east, it does seem that from the beginning of Victorian times, the African and Asian worlds have been in particular turmoil. The peace-mild conflict-severe conflict ratio for these areas in this period has been 101–120–73: a percentage ratio of 34%–41%–25%; a peace-war ratio of 34–66%. These times of European intervention and expulsion, and of change in adoption of approaches and technologies, have been bloody periods indeed. Particularly violent were the Victorian period between 1821 and 1900 with a 19%–81% peace-war ratio (Figure 4.7, Table 4.8, cf. Denton, 1966) and the 1936–1985 period during and after World War II when there was a 20%–80% overall ratio, with 60% devoted to violent conflict (Figure 4.8, Table 4.8).

TABLE 4.6

CONTINENTAL DISTRIBUTIONS OF PEACE AND WAR

Area	Number of Five-Year Periods				Percentages			
	Peace	Mild Conflict	Severe Conflict	Total Conflict	Peace	Mild Conflict	Severe Conflict	Total Conflict
Europe	41	24	33	57	42	24	34	58
Western Civilization	72	36	39	75	49	24	27	51
Latin America	93	29	25	54	63	20	17	37
Africa	47	32	19	51	49	33	19	51
Asian Mainland (except Russia)	54	88	54	142	28	45	2	72
Eurasia	207	151	130	281	42	31	27	58
Afroasia	101	120	73	193	34	41	25	66
World	381	224	179	403	49	29	23	51

FIGURE 4.7
Violence In Africa and Asia: 1820-1900

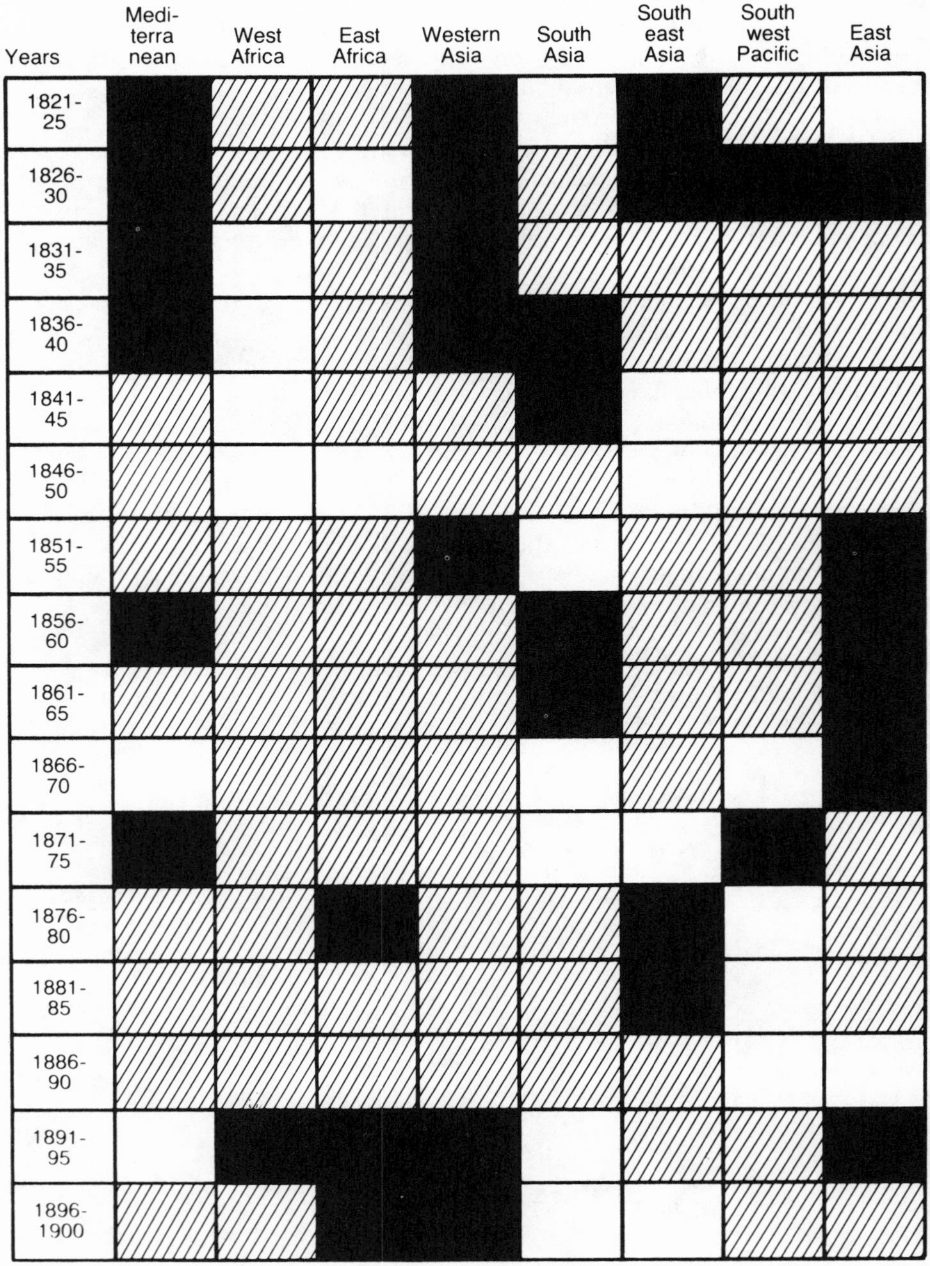

Years	Medi-terra nean	West Africa	East Africa	Western Asia	South Asia	South east Asia	South west Pacific	East Asia
1821-25								
1826-30								
1831-35								
1836-40								
1841-45								
1846-50								
1851-55								
1856-60								
1861-65								
1866-70								
1871-75								
1876-80								
1881-85								
1886-90								
1891-95								
1896-1900								

FIGURE 4.8
Violence In Africa and Asia: 1936-1985

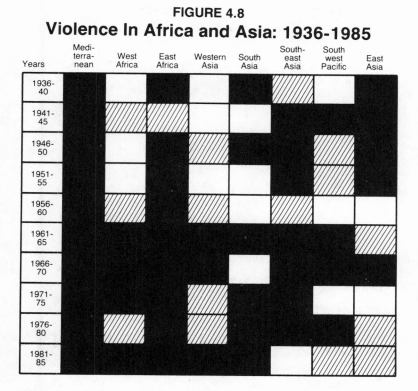

Though this approach has its limitations, it does indicate that the distribution of conflict in the past two centuries has tended to be greater in the Afro-Asian world than elsewhere, and that the past few decades do constitute a period of relative peace for Western civilization, Russia and Japan. China has been experiencing recurrent violence, and nothing in this record would suggest peace is at hand. Latin America has been comparatively peaceful as well, but its patterns have been different from those of the West.

From time to time, scholars have asked whether war as a whole has been increasing or decreasing. Pitirim Sorokin (1957) and Quincy Wright (1942) among others have attempted to answer that question, and more recently Francis Beer (1981) has attempted to sum up those answers while David Singer and Melvin Small have considered the question from their accumulated data (Small and Singer 1979). Sorokin thought war was increasing in terms of casualties, but Wright thought it might be decreasing in terms of duration. Singer and Small tend to support Sorokin, believing it has increased steadily in the past century and a half. The charts here provide another answer in terms of patterns over time (Table 4.7).

Taking half centuries beginning with the latter half of the eighteenth

TABLE 4.7

PEACE AND WAR FOR THE WORLD AS A WHOLE

Area	Number of Five-Year Periods				Percentages			
	Peace	Mild Conflict	Severe Conflict	Total Conflict	Peace	Mild Conflict	Severe Conflict	Total Conflict
World	381	224	179	403	49	29	23	51
World 1751–1800	115	28	17	45	72	18	11	28
World 1801–1850	62	68	30	97	39	43	19	61
World 1851–1900	50	65	45	110	31	41	28	69
World 1901–1950	81	32	47	79	51	20	29	49
World 1951–1975	38	16	26	42	48	20	33	52
World 1801–1900	112	133	75	207	35	42	23	65
World 1901–1975	119	48	73	121	50	20	30	50

and concluding with the third quarter of the twentieth, the latter half of the eighteenth shows the highest percentage of peace at 72%, the latter half of the nineteenth, in the heyday of the Victorian Age, having the least peace at only 31%. On the other hand, the latter half of the twentieth century, taken only as far as 1975, had experienced the greatest percentage of heavy conflict at 30% with the latter half of the eighteenth again being the most peaceful at 11%. It would be well to remember that there is reason to doubt the African data for that period, so the latter half of the eighteenth may not be as peaceful as it would appear.

We don't have centuries as a whole to compare, since data for a full century are available only for the nineteenth. But comparing the nineteenth to the first three quarters of the twentieth, it can be seen that the twentieth has been peaceful about half the time compared to 35% for the nineteenth. On the other hand, the twentieth has had a higher percentage of heavy conflict, 30% to 23%. Population could be a factor here, since world population reached only one billion by 1850, whereas it passed the five billion mark in the 1980s. But this way of calculating seems to support both Sorokin and Wright. There has been more heavy conflict in the twentieth century (Sorokin was calculating only for Europe and only as far as the first quarter of the twentieth century) but the total amount of time given to war and other major conflict seems to have been less in the twentieth than in the nineteenth, as Wright suggests. Sorokin's perception that the nineteenth century was more peaceful than the eighteenth does not seem to be supported for the world as a whole by the data presented here.

It would appear, then, that war was more frequent and violent in the nineteenth century than in the eighteenth, and has been less frequent but still more violent in the twentieth century than in the nineteenth.

In this discussion, many periods of relative peace and violence have been introduced. Those that have been particularly peaceful (including the peace of our time) and particularly violent are brought together in Table 4.8.

The increase in quantity, distribution and death rate during the World Wars period would suggest that possibly there has been a gigantic leap in civilian deaths during the twentieth century. Data assembled by the indefatigable William Eckhardt suggest that there certainly has, but not as a percentage of deaths. Through the period studied here, the ratio of civilian to military deaths has remained fairly close to 50–50 (Eckhardt 1987).

One disappointment in this attempt to measure world distribution of war and peace is that, as Table 4.9 shows, violent conflict exceeded peace (51%–49%), if you accept peace as fatalities of under 100 for a 5-year period. The thesis that peace is normal and violence exceptional is not

TABLE 4.8
PERIODS OF PEACE AND VIOLENCE

PERIODS OF RELATIVE PEACE

Area	Period	% Peace	% War	% (Mild-Violent)
Japan	1741–1985	82	18	(12–6)
Northern Latin America	1741–1985	80	20	(14–6)
Russia and West	1946–1985	78	22	(19–3)
Western Hemisphere Europe & Russia	1946–1985	73	27	(25–2)
World	1751–1800	72	28	(18–11)
Russia	1741–1985	69	31	(12–18)
Russia and West	1881–1910	67	33	(29–4)
North America	1741–1985	63	37	(24–12)

PERIODS OF RELATIVE VIOLENCE

East Asia	1741–1985	16	84	(47–37)
Africa-Asia	1821–1900	19	81	(55–24)
Africa-Asia	1936–1985	20	80	(20–60)
Western Asia	1741–1985	22	78	(51–27)
South Asia	1741–1985	27	73	(51–22)
Mediterranean	1741–1985	29	69	(22–49)
World	1851–1900	31	69	(41–28)
World	1801–1900	35	65	(42–23)

TABLE 4.9
THE "BLACK SQUARES" SINCE 1741

Years	Area	Conflict	Fatalities
1740–1748	Eastern Europe	War of Austrian Succession	90,000
1755–1757	East Asia	War Against the Dzoungars	600,000
1756–1763	Europe	Seven Years' War	550,000
1765–1770	East Asia	Burmese Invasion of Yunnan	40,000
1771–1776	East Asia	Rebellion in Szechwan	120,000
1773–1774	Russia	Pugachev's Rebellion	18,000
1775–1783	North America	American Revolution	20,000
1788–1789	Southeast Asia	Chinese Expedition in Annam	30,000
1789–1799	Western Europe	French Revolution	20,000
1791–1794	Central America	Rebellion in Santo Domingo	20,000
1792–1802	Mediterranean Europe	War of the French Revolution	950,000
1795–1803	East Asia	White Lotus Uprising	20,000
1802–1804	Central America	Haitian War of Independence	12,000
1803–1815	Europe, Russia, Mediterranean	Napoleonic Wars	1,380,000
1810–1828	Latin America	Wars of Independence	37,000
1821–1829	Mediterranean Western Asia	Greek War of Independence Russo-Turkish War Massacre of Ottoman Janissaries	140,000
1824–1826	Southeast Asia	British Invasion of Burma	15,000
1825–1830	Southwest Pacific	Uprising in Java	15,000
1826–1828	East Asia	Muslim Uprising in Turkestan	20,000
1830–1831	Eastern Europe	Polish Uprising	15,000
1831–1841	Mediterranean Western Asia	Turkish-Egyptian Wars First Carlist War	35,000
1838–1842	South Asia	English-Afghan War	20,000
1846–1848	Central America	Mexican War	17,000
1848–1849	Europe	Revolutions of 1848	62,000
1851–1864	East Asia	Taiping Rebellion	11,000,000
1853–1856	Russia Western Asia	Crimean War	772,000
1855–1873	East Asia	Yunnan Rebellion	60,000
1857–1958	South Asia	Sepoy Rebellion	15,000
1859	Western Europe	Piedmontian War	40,000
1859–1861	Mediterranean	Spanish-Moroccan War Massacres in Lebanon	12,000
1861–1880	North America	Civil War Indian Wars	770,000
1862–1867	Central America	French-Mexican War	20,000
1863–1864	Eastern Europe	Polish Uprising Austrian War of the Duchies	10,000

Years	Area	Conflict	Fatalities
1863–1865	South Asia	Ambela Campaign	11,000
		Conquest of Bhutan	
1864–1870	Southern Latin America	War of the Triple Alliance	1,100,000
1866	Eastern Europe	Austro-Prussian War	40,000
1868–1878	Central America	Cuban Uprising	150,000
1870–1871	Western Europe	Franco-Prussian War	270,000
1871–1875	Mediterranean	Kabylina Uprising	12,500
		The Carlist War	
1873	Southwest Pacific	Dutch Occupation of Sumatra	200,000
1873–1875	Southeast Asia	French Conquest of Tonkin	30,000
1875–1878	Eastern Europe	Balkan War	300,000
1877	Japan	Satsuma Uprising	12,000
1879	Northern Latin America	Colombian Revolution	80,000
1879	East Africa	Conquest of Zululand	14,000
1879–1884	Southern Latin America	Saltpetre War	14,000
1881–1898	East Africa	Sudan Uprisings	54,000
		Italo-Ethiopian War	
		French Conquest of Madagascar	
1891	Southern Latin America	Chilian Revolution	11,000
1892–1894	West Africa	Belgian Congo Slavery War	20,000
1893–1897	West Asia	Armenian Massacres	40,000
1894–1895	East Asia	Sino-Japanese Wars	15,000
1895–1898	Central America	Cuban Uprising and Spanish American War	130,000
1899–1902	Northern Latin America	Colombian Civil War	150,000
1899–1908	Africa	Boer War	257,000
		Hottentot Rebellion	
		Maji-Maji Rebellion	
1904–1905	Russia	Russo-Japanese War of 1905	131,000
		Revolution of 1905	
1907–1912	Mediterranean	French Invasion of Morocco	10,500
		Spanish-Moroccan War	
1910–1920	Central America	Mexican Revolution	250,000
1911–1912	Western Asia	Italian-Turkish War	20,000
1912–1920	Europe	Balkan Wars	9,864,000
	Russia	World War I	
	Mediterranean	Armenian Massacres	
	Western Asia	East European Wars & Rebellions	
1917–1922	Russia	Russian Revolution and Civil War	1,300,000

Years	Area	Conflict	Fatalities
1920–1932	Mediterranean	Libyan and Moroccan Uprisings	80,000
1920–1922	Western Asia	Greco-Turkish War and Massacres	70,000
1921–1925	South Asia	Momplah Muslim and Afghanistan Rebellions	12,000
1923	Japan	Korean Massacres	11,000
1926–1935	East Asia	Chinese Civil Wars Japanese Intervention	1,375,000
1928–1935	Southern Latin America	Chaco War	150,000
1931–1932	Central America	Salvador Uprising	24,000
1936–1939	Mediterranean	Spanish Civil War	1,200,000
1937–1945	East Asia Europe Russia Mediterranean East Asia Japan Southeast Asia Southwest Pacific	Japanese Invasion of China World War II	40,000,000
1944–1949	Mediterranean	Greek Civil War Arab-Israeli Partition War	48,000
1946–1950	East Asia	Chinese Civil War	48,000
1946–1954	Southeast Asia	French-Indochinese War	1,200,000
1947–1948	East Africa	Rebellion in Madagascar	15,000
1947–1949	South Asia	Indo-Pakistani War	800,000
1950–1953	East Asia	Korean War	2,000,000
1952–1962	Mediterranean	French War in Maghreb	255,000
1952–1972	East Africa	Mau-Mau Rebellion Sudan Civil War Tutsis Massacre	850,000
1956	Eastern Europe	Hungarian Revolution	32,000
1960–1975	South Asia	Vietnamese War	1,800,000
1960–1976	West Africa	Congo and Angola Rebellions	165,000
1961–1970	Western Asia	Iraqi Civil War Yemeni Civil War	120,000
1965–1966	South Asia	Second Indo-Pakistani War	20,000
1965–1966	Southwest Pacific	Indonesian Massacres	500,000
1965–1969	East Asia	Chinese Cultural Revolution	15,000
1965–1976	East Africa	Rebellion in Mozambique	30,000
1966–1985	Central America	Guatemalan Indian Massacres	45,000
1967–1970	West Africa	Biafran War	1,100,000
1967–1978	Mediterranean	Six-Day War Yom Kippur War	85,000
1970–1985	Southeast Asia	Cambodian Civil War and Massacres	2,150,000

Years	Area	Conflict	Fatalities
1971–	South Asia	Bangladesh War	1,500,000
1971–1985	East Africa	Ugandan Rebellion and Massacres	1,086,000
		Hutu Massacres	
		Ethiopian Civil Wars	
1972–1985	Southwest Pacific	Philippine Rebellions	134,000
		E. Timor Massacres	
1975–1985	West Africa	Civil Wars and Rebellions in Angola, Nigeria, Ghana and Chad	20,000
1976–1979	Southern Latin America	Argentinian Military Suppression	14,000
1978–1985	Central America	Sandinista Civil War	92,000
		Salvadorian Civil War	
1978–1979	Southeast Asia	Vietnamese Invasion of Cambodia and Chinese Intervention in Vietnam	54,000
1978–1985	South Asia	Afghan Civil War and Soviet Intervention	300,000

supported. If the world were divided into more areas, however (what power the researcher has!), peace would win handily. A chart for the period 1875–1975, was drawn with one-year periods. But there were 2500-3000 squares to fill in and the point, if proved, would have been peripheral to the argument of this book.

How would a major nuclear war appear on a world chart? Probably as a single horizontal row of black squares followed by an impressive array of white squares both horizontal and vertical. There might not be 10,000 people to kill in any of the areas for many decades to come.

Of course, there might not be anyone interested in making the chart either.

THE INTERACTIONS OF NORTH AND SOUTH

The hypothesis that a remission of violence is occurring applies to the developed world: to Europe, its rimland settlements, Russia and Japan. It does not apply to the rest of the world. Even Russia and Japan are influenced by factors outside Western history.

In attempts to gain internal coherence, Westerners have applied such terms as developing, underdeveloped, and Third World to these areas of Asia, Africa and Latin America. The validity of such terms depends on the problem addressed. These are important and difficult problems, but they can be addressed here only insofar as they pertain to the developed world.

It is probable that the developed nations have ended a period of major political involvement in the rest of the world. They avoid situations in which there would be military confrontation either with underdeveloped nations or other developed nations, even if the economic costs of such avoidance are severe.

In the vacuum that has been left, various kinds of violence have been occurring and are likely to continue to occur where nationalism and tribalism come into conflict, as in the Biafran, Bengali and Sri Lankan civil wars; where modernizers collide with established elites, as in Cuba and Indonesia; where Caesars arise in unstructured situations, as in Cambodia, Uganda and Libya. One kind of transformation that looked to be a source of serious trouble has been managed with relatively little violence so far: the situations in which the great revolutionary leader dies or loses his capacities and successors must be found. Ghana, Kenya and Tanzania, among others, have managed such transitions without serious disruption, though China has experienced considerable transitional violence.

Violence between nations is also likely to continue as regional power balances are established. India-Pakistan, Chad-Sudan, Vietnam-Cambodia, China-Vietnam, Uganda-Tanzania, Iraq-Iran illustrate this kind of war. These struggles occur partly because of the withdrawal of the developed nations. But their outcomes, whatever they may be and however tragic they may be for Cambodians or Ugandans, have little effect on the developed world.

Far more serious than the political situations, for much of the rest of the world, is the economic situation. As insecticides reduce malaria and antiseptics reduce infant mortality, population increases contribute to undernourishment and starvation. Excessive cash-crop production exacerbates local displacement and hunger. The developed world continues to sponsor conferences and provide some material assistance, but disaster and catastrophe are likely to be recurrent through the twentieth and twenty-first centuries. The developed world also contributes to this catastrophe through its demand for raw materials and cash crops.

This basic catastrophe is unlikely to be ameliorated by much that underdeveloped countries can do for themselves. Capitalization is difficult with only marginal surpluses available, and the integration of capital development with education has proved to be extremely difficult. There has been little progress and even retrogression in many countries, and this must lead either to further internal violence, or despondency and hopelessness.

In some places economic problems have been and will be catastrophic. In many more they are simply going to be chronically bad. In some—

several East Asian countries, perhaps China, perhaps some South American countries—they may work out and standards of living may get better for a broad stratum of people. The developed nations have helped some, but as often they have been part of the problem. But whether economies in the rest of the world turn out to be better or worse than expected, their fate is not likely to have much effect on conflict in the developed world. Given the relational outlook, we may expect an increase in empathy and concern and given normal times, an understanding that development will follow many patterns (Horowitz 1982, 77–78). But this concern and understanding has been and will continue to be subordinate to others that more directly affect the developed world.

Western civilization has expanded around the world as no civilization has before. Its ideas concerning social relationships and production and distribution have been instrumental in precipitating social change and revolutions in other civilizations. China and the Russian heirs of Byzantine civilization are creating modern industrial states.

Everywhere leaders use Western methods in an attempt to create a more highly industrialized economy that accepts Western objectives of steady growth, full employment, and a higher level of consumption. Computers, washing machines and Coca Cola are everywhere. If Western civilization cannot effect a world political unification it may achieve something even more far-reaching: world cultural unification.

Few ideas can be less appealing. Here it is possible to take advantage of air transportation to travel quickly to any part of the world, only to find that the very process of traveling appears to be molding the world into a single unit in which thinking is already similar and architectural reflections of this thinking can be only a matter of time.

Beyond that there is a more obscure worry. In the past, when one civilization has lost its vitality, others have arisen to take its place. But what would happen if Western civilization provided a world culture? When this lost its vitality, there would be no sources of new development: another reason, perhaps, for fearing that the *Pax Atomica* represents the twilight of Western civilization, and perhaps of civilization in general.

We do not know, of course, the consequence of the Western impact on other civilizations. We do know a good deal, however, about the interaction of cultures. What is important, in assessing the probable impact of one culture on another, is the condition and pattern of the receiving culture. If that culture is in a transitional phase, it will be particularly receptive to outside ideas that may help it reconstitute its patterns toward another period of development and crystalization. It happens that Western patterns have been presented forcefully, but it also happens that a number of other civilizations—the Far Eastern, the Indian, the Islamic, the Russian and arguably the Latin American—were in a receptive phase in which reconstitution was taking place anyway and in which the Western approach provided some answers.

But along with phase we must also consider the powerful influence of pattern. In every culture certain ways of thinking and doing come to be adopted and once they are, alternative ways tend to be excluded. It has been widely observed by Westerners, usually in an attitude of amusement or despair, that despite the adoption of Western devices and techniques, the Chinese remain Chinese and the Indians remain Indian. It is supposed that this is a temporary, transitional state and that a new generation of Indians will really behave like Westerners. In fact, this would seem to be consistent with my argument that the generation coming to power in the West is viewing society quite differently from the generation now retiring from power. However, the younger generation will still be Western, will still have Faustian tendencies that may strike the Indian as too clever and too superficial. Culture patterns go deeper than phases, just as childhood patterns of a man will always stamp his personality regardless of vastly different experiences he may meet later in life.

So it seems likely that despite external similarities in technology and political development, which are consonant with an industrial, organization-oriented world, we can expect that the present diversity of civilizations will be maintained. Just as decentralization occurs within industrial states and among political entities, so we should expect to find it among civilizations.

The process by which the underdeveloped civilizations resist and accommodate the impact of the West, however, is not likely to be peaceful. Resisting and accommodating both involve the conflict of many interests. The alternative possibilities are immense; the threats to basic culture are fearful; people are fighting for their ways of life, which can be more important than life itself.

Probably there is no ideal model. If any civilization has made its way through the crisis of transition, it must be the East Asian. If so, the resolutions have been very different for China, Japan, Korea and Taiwan. The Chinese experience, as we have seen, has been particularly bloody in a country that has been known in the past for long periods of internal peace. Japan, while more peaceful, suffered the dreadful experience of the World War II bombings and is the only country so far to have experienced nuclear attack. Korea experienced an externally imposed division that nevertheless was consistent with divisions of past history. A bloody war followed, with external intervention on both sides, and the threat of nuclear war entirely too palpable. Taiwan, although perceived as a repressive dictatorship, has transformed itself by an "economic miracle" into a prosperous nation. Each country took a different route, and none of them were easy. If these are models, it is to be hoped other civilizations can find other routes to resolution.

We often think of the barbarian as advancing upon civilization in hordes, an image that has come down from the last centuries of the declining Roman Empire. The Goths and Vandals who attacked Rome were barbarians, however, not because of their ferocity, but because they were men who coveted the artifacts and ideas of another culture.

Usually the barbarian is a primitive, but he need not be. Any person who thinks any other civilization is superior to his own culture is a barbarian. Nor is he usually a conqueror. On the contrary, he is usually seduced into giving up his own culture for a fragmentary and subsidiary position in an advancing civilization or he is forced into fighting a series of losing battles in order to preserve some of what he has. The American Indian is a familiar example here.

The elite of the barbarians are the intelligentsia, usually men who are trained in the "superior" civilization and return to their own culture. Such men often have no culture to identify with because they are treated condescendingly by the members of the civilization from which they have gained their education while they are not understood by the people in the culture from which they came. This was often the fate of nineteenth century leaders in colonial countries, and even in Russia.

Used in this sense, the term "barbarian" can be applied to most of what we call the underdeveloped world. Insofar as the analogy holds, it will taken considerable time for the political and technical methods of the West to be incorporated into various other cultures. This period of incorporation must be one of considerable turbulence as social, economic, ideological and international adjustments will have to be made. Along the way, if patterns of the past are followed, feelings of cultural alienation will be high, and the incidence of failure will be great.

It is quite natural that the barbarian should feel considerable hostility. This was expressed by the hordes when the civilization was weak, and by violent raids against advanced parties when the civilization was strong. In the modern world the opportunity to express this hostility is limited. There is no likelihood of hordes, though the image is preserved in recent illegal immigration from Mexico to the United States. But it is possible to chip at the civilizations in their weak spots by killing their advisory cadre, by kidnapping their diplomats, by hijacking planes and holding passengers for political ransom.

Civilized people have always called such acts "barbaric," but they have not always considered the contexts in which "barbarism" takes place.

If violent conflict is likely to continue, at least sporadically, in Latin America, Africa, the Middle East and South and Southeast Asia, how will this affect the West? It certainly does not seem morally appropriate for the West to enjoy its peace while the rest of the world suffers. The case can also be made that the West could do more. The cost of one Trident submarine would buy food for immense numbers of Latin American children for many years. The budget of the United States Air Force is larger than the total educational budget for the children of the Third World. The governments of developed countries spend 18 times as much for military purposes as they do for Third World development assistance (Sivard 1985).

Undoubtedly, the Western nations could contribute more to the Third World, whether they build submarines or not. They can reduce human suffering considerably, though this would not reduce warfare. Such a reduction could contribute to rising expectations, and rising expectations can lead to increased domestic conflict. For all that, morally, the West should help the Third World more than it does. Probably the benefits would outweigh the complications. But these are decisions for Western nations to make that are independent of peace. And the building of Tridents and the providing of aid are independent decisions. The United States may do both or neither.

The great powers also have been providing military aid, either to governments they like or to all governments. The latter is more likely to happen as Cold War images fade and the developed nations realize that they gain or lose little from conflicts among Third World nations. As costs of armaments rise, they are more likely to sell to all comers, thus spreading armaments in the Third World, perhaps increasing the levels of conflict among those nations, and also compelling them to make military purchases they cannot afford, either to defend against possible enemies, or because sophisticated military equipment is considered part of the developmental process. Third World military spending increased five-fold between 1960 and 1985 (Sivard 1985).

Much of this is regrettable but the forces encouraging this spread of armaments are powerful. They benefit Western arms makers and they are desired by Third World governments. It is difficult to see how the structure is likely to change. It does not follow, however, that the selling of armaments to Third World countries will lead to the termination of peace in the West. The Third World countries are not likely to invade nor bomb the Western nations. They may, indeed, be better able to discourage Western intervention.

A greater danger for the rest of the world is famine. If this occurs because of population imbalance or crop failure resulting from improper or short-sighted use of Western farming methods, the West will provide aid, ineffectively and belatedly. However great the catastrophe it is not likely to cause the termination of peace in the West. How does one write such a thing without appearing callous? However compassionate one may be, there is no good in writing that if we fail to avert world economic catastrophe we shall have world war. We may have both, but one does not necessarily cause the other.

In reviewing the situation in the Third World, have I been whitewashing the developed nations, particularly the United States? Does the very delineation of North and South switch the responsibility for the problems of the Third World from the United States? It is probable that the approach taken here, which is certainly functionalist to a considerable extent, does downplay individual responsibility and stresses social forces. I assume that while people have various sets of ethics and values according to the cultures from which they come, these ethics and values are imperfectly carried out. There are immoral people both North and South, and within the North, Americans are not likely to be more or less moral than other people. There are also likely to be various levels of competence, with mediocrity (by definition) the norm. There is no question that the North, and particularly the United States, has contributed substantially to the problems of the Third World (Kick and Kiefer 1985). But much of this contribution has to do with a lack of perception in the 1950s and 1960s that we have since acquired partly from experience and partly, perhaps, from the advance of the relational outlook. There is also no question that the Third World leaders have contributed to their own problems by excessive emphasis on cash crop farming when there were not sufficient subsistence crops to feed the local population, and by the premature building of industrial and military structures. Again, as with leaders in developed countries, some of these mistakes represented the best judgments that could be made with the perceptions and knowledge available, although some undoubtedly are attributable to shortsightedness and egoism.

Then there is the question of the extent to which the developed world owes its situation to the Third World. Is our peace and prosperity based on war and poverty in the Third World? This is a complicated question. The sale of armaments to Third World countries may increase the violence of encounters between them and perhaps to the intensity of indigenous rebellions or state terrorism. The importing of cash crop products at low prices contribute to the profit of multinational corporations at the same time that it causes hunger and sometimes starvation in Third World countries. On the other hand, developed nations have made loans to Third World nations, have contributed capital and expertise to various developmental projects, and have acted as intermediaries in bringing about peace settlements. Where the balance lies would be hard to say. That would require a different study. That the Northern nations, including the United States, could do better than they have done is something most of us acknowledge. But it does not follow that the peace and prosperity of the developed nations rests mostly or even substantially on war and poverty in the Third World.

In any event, perceptions have changed (Eckhardt 1977). Understanding has advanced beyond the "five stages of development" of the 1960s (Rostow 1971). If also the perception develops that a state of crisis no longer exists, if a reexamination of relations with Third World nations from political, economic and moral standpoints can occur, perhaps more fruitful interactions between North and South can be established than in the past (e.g., Lake 1987). In chapter six the probability of some of those responses will be considered.

But before attempting that, there is one more factor that should be considered in relation to the peace of our time. If the possibility of the existence of something like the relational outlook is accepted, would that be a factor that reenforces or undermines the peace?

5

THE CHARACTERISTICS OF OUR TIME

THE EMERGENCE OF THE RELATIONAL OUTLOOK

Suppose, once more, that someone were writing about the Victorian Age in 1860. He might observe that it was a relatively peaceful time, compared to the Napoleonic period, despite the Crimean War, the imminent American Civil War, and various European expeditions in Africa and South Asia. He might also make some observations about the nature of the society as compared to the past. Because of its advances in technology it seemed to be on the edge of new advances in architecture. Poverty was about to be wiped out. On the other hand, the French Revolution failed to produce substantial governmental change. And literature was mixed, with some great poets diluted by a sea of long boring novels about the middle and working classes.

A later observer might disagree. He might believe that Victorian architecture was ugly, and poverty rampant; that substantial changes were made in the reduction of despotism and the widening of franchise; that there was an overproduction of lyrical, sentimentalized poetry, but that a considerable number of novels read well and give us an excellent picture of the time. This disagreement might be quite separate from an assessment of the validity of the presence or absence of peace.

In the same sense, it would be possible to disagree with this chapter while accepting the main hypothesis of the book. While it may be reasonable for a twentieth-century writer to appraise the Victorian Age in terms of characteristics, with relative peace being one of those characteristics, it may not have been reasonable for our Victorian to attempt such a combination. In the same sense, it may be too early to attempt this for the Present Age.

With that demurral, a sketch of some of the characteristics of our time will be attempted, with an eye toward explaining why these characteristics reenforce the peace. The evidence is selected, therefore, to support these conceptions. To note these peace reinforcers is not to deny that some counterforces may exist and grow in the future. We have already noted this possibility with reference to peace itself.

The first assertion about the Present Age has to do with what Quigley (1961) calls outlook, what Redfield (1953) calls worldview, the way in which people collectively view their world. We perceive such outlooks in other civilizations, perceive a Chinese worldview or an Indian worldview. And we perceive it in relation to past ages, when we use the adjectives baroque or Victorian, the former sometimes meaning a tendency to over-elaborate; the latter often meaning any way of seeing that has been supplanted. The present outlook, already described in chapter one as "relational," is one that could be particularly helpful in facilitating social relationships.

The second assertion has been referred to already in the discussion of the waning of generational conflict. As the new outlook gradually replaces the old, conflict wanes. There is greater agreement about reality. When there is conflict, it is less likely to arise from misunderstanding. The opponents understand each other; they just disagree, or have irreconcilable objectives.

The emergence of the relational outlook, then, refers to the gradual adoption of the outlook of our time, the outlook that will someday be meant when people refer to the past, when they say "How relational" in the way we would say "How baroque." Relational, of course, will not be the term they will use, but it is the term I am applying for the time being, until a consensus emerges. In this sense, we could be said to live in the Relational Age.

This Relational Age is a good age—better than many—in that it is both cool and warm; it does not worship heroes; it emphasizes relationships, including human relationships, rather than absolutes; it diminishes authority figures; it encourages participation; it is often objective and sometimes generous.

The advantages of crisis periods are obvious. They are exciting, they provide greater scope for the individual to bring about changes, and more opportunities for spectacular achievement. A normal period, any such period, is more proscribed, less surprising, more secure, less inspiring.

The transitional period of the World Wars was given to obscene materialism, unedifying attempts of the newly rich to become richer for no purpose other than display. The Depression accentuated the desirability of goods, and the older generation responded with an orgy of purchasing in the late 1940s and through the 1950s. But by the 1960s, this kind of materialism was seen in perspective as vulgar, even by members of the older generation, as they continued to buy. In the 1980s the younger generation acquired goods as a backdrop for living. It is easy to make fun of old clothes worn with $300 boots, but such combinations do reflect a different perspective.

The transitional period was also given to a feverish spiritualism existing alongside total commitment to secularized beliefs, resulting in nationalistic universalism, totalitarianism and even genocide. While members of the younger generation still seek mystical experience, this is usually transitory and peripheral. Most are not given to total commitment. If this leaves them in danger of failing to form a set of principles by which to live, it also frees them from ruthlessness on behalf of the cause, a trait all too common among members of the older generation who often retained the ruthlessness after the cause was lost. By contrast the less committed members of the younger generation, whatever their faults, are likely to do less harm than good.

Ruthlessness in the transitional period was common because men became callous. After a certain amount of catastrophe, they were willing to let anything happen so long as it did not touch them. There was a great weariness of conflict, a desire that it should end forever, and out of this arose a hope that a world federation or state would come into existence, guaranteeing perpetual peace at whatever the price might be. Comparative historians have discerned these feelings before, and often they have led to the creation of great empires.

But in the Relational Age, people have recovered. If they are not to have a world empire, they are willing to work with the world that is. If they cannot rebuild the world, they can find many manageable, specific tasks worth undertaking.

In the sections that ·follow, some of the ways in which the relational outlook is manifested will be considered. In most cases it fits comfortably, almost as if the organizational style or the scientific approach were caused by the outlook. But it would probably be more appropriate, certainly more relational, to say that the resemblances between the way an organization functions and the way scientists work is the characteristic we describe as relational.

RELATIONAL THINKING

The widespread perception in the twentieth century that fragmentation of knowledge is counterproductive is itself a product of relational thinking, not of a knowledge explosion.

Robert Sinai, in his gloomy book on the decadence of our time (1978), unconsciously juxtaposes a paradox in relational thinking. On one hand we have the holists, trying to combine all relationships into a single system, so that, for instance, a "Third World" is theoretically generated in order that we can find its universal qualities and solve them. On the other hand we have the specialists, Kuhn's normal scientists, plugging away enthusiastically on individual aspects of problems without any insight or interest in how these problems relate to larger contexts.

A marvelous example of this contrast is the current intense competition among physicists to discover hypothetical microscopic entities such as free quarks, magnetic monopoles or monojets that would confirm, modify or upset the "standard model" of the physical composition of the universe. Tens and hundreds of millions of dollars are being invested in giant accelerators designed to discover not even the entities, but the conditions that would indicate the theoretical possibility of their presence (Taubes 1987). What a combination of materialism and abstraction!

This paradox is not unique to our age. All periods have theorists trying to make sense of the whole, and specialists working out the details of problems that have been set. They are likely to be two different kinds of people and each is not likely to be deeply interested in the work of the other. On the other hand it may be that there is a greater amount of both kinds of thinking going on in the present period than there would be most of the time. There is a greater amount of normal science because we are well into a normal period, when normal science would be expected in many areas. And we are in a relational age, when there is probably a greater drive than there would be in other ages to achieve universal theories.

If this explains the paradox, then it is no longer a paradox. If it does not, well, the relational mind is particularly appreciative of paradoxes, since they enrich the whole.

There is always too much knowledge and, at least in civilized society, always has been. All of us function by focusing on some areas of knowledge, and letting others go. By specializing, an individual can know almost all there is to know about a field, so long as it is narrowly defined. Collectively there is greater knowledge if we can devise systems so that specialists can interrelate. The organizational system is one such system, with some individuals focusing on the development of special areas of knowledge or the means to get at those areas, and others focusing on systems that enable such knowledge to be combined in various ways.

Renaissance men still exist today, but they are likely to be perceived as superficial, as were the Renaissance men themselves. Toynbee is an example of such a modern man, so is Isaac Asimov. Neither could win a Nobel Prize, since their kind of breadth does not contribute a measurable addition to existing knowledge. Deep down, people feel, they are superficial. As far as that goes, Leonardo was and still is perceived in the same way: kind of an all-around putterer who couldn't seem to follow through. This book is a kind of Renaissance exercise, sacrificing depth in favor of a broad, demonstrable but unprovable view.

But if we are condescending about the superficial generalist, we are likely to be a little regretful about the fate of the specialist as a human being. If he gets too much into his specialty, can he know enough about the world to function as a person, a spouse, a parent? The doctor, in learning too much about the neural system, may forget that such systems are part of a particular man or woman. Of course, if you happen to be that particular man or woman, you would probably prefer that he use his spare time to read the latest neural journals instead of Hegel, Shakespeare or Julian Jaynes.

Such specialization was considerably advanced in the nineteenth century and was praised by the generalist, Adam Smith, in the eighteenth. But there wasn't much of a problem in the nineteenth century, because specialization did not conflict with the prevailing outlook. In Germany, for instance, specialization in the second half of the nineteenth century was an exciting phenomenon. It flourished in the universities, where there was at the same time a close tie between colleagues and a plethora of rival schools of thought (Wagar 1977). Ideas were carried from one place to another because students and teachers transferred frequently, without apparent concern for loyalties or associations of place. But this was all perceived as diversification or development, not fragmentation.

Specialization still goes on in the twentieth century among devotees of hang gliding, frontier studies, jogging, pornography and entomology. In each of these areas there is meaning, excitement and enthusiasm. Yet our collective perception is often negative; we perceive that there ought to be more cross-fertilization, more interdisciplinary activity.

The perception of specialization as regrettable, then, comes from the increase in relational thinking. Specialization deliberately cuts off relational thinking, focuses on the lesser rather than the greater system. Still, the relational outlook carries almost a moral imperative to look at each problem in the context of the greater system. Benjamin Nelson, first American president of the International Society for the Comparative Study of Civilizations, came close to making it a moral imperative that each of us, in considering a social problem, such as the rise of homicide in the United States in the 1960s and 1970s, consider that problem in its total civilizational context. What has been the function of homicide in Western civilization, what have been its fluctuations, how do these relate to changing moral worldviews? In fact, criminologists looking at the problem are likely to consider only the 1960s and 1970s in America, the change in demographic structure during the period in terms of age categories or rural and urban environments. Meaningful answers may be obtained without any reference to larger historical or civilizational questions. But the urge to consider the larger system is relational.

The perception of unmanageable knowledge itself is relational. If anything, twentieth century man may know more than nineteenth century man. I don't mean more in the sense that he would know more about statistical techniques that had not been known in the nineteenth century, but in the sense of total knowledge, the twentieth-century person, because of relational techniques, might have more. It is difficult to prove one way or the other, but the perception of specialization as regrettable is necessarily relational, and therefore creates the illusion of a decline in knowledge.

The perception of perception has brought a ghostly ambiguity to relational thinking. There is much more stress on the impact of the perceiver on what is perceived. Reality as a single entity is more difficult to get ahold of, slides easily away.

In 1949, when George Orwell wrote *1984*, he was writing from an older generation viewpoint at the end of a crisis period. By the time 1984 actually came along, the normal period had arrived. While Orwell was wrong in supposing that the totalitarian aspects of a crisis period could have persisted into a normal period (concepts he couldn't have had anyway), many of the outlooks of the characters representing the establishment had come to appear more acceptable, while the outlook of his antiestablishment hero, Winston Smith, did indeed appear somewhat dated. Winston's problem in *1984* appeared to be that he was certain about reality. It had only to be discovered. The main protagonist for the establishment, O'Brien, knew that reality could be different under different situations. Winston thought there were laws of the universe that had to be obeyed. O'Brien thought that the laws were man made, and changed from time to time. Winston thought the Copernican theory was real. O'Brien thought it was a theory. Many of the aspects of *1984* are in fact commonplace in our society: changing history, the perception that thought is more important than act, a wider and less deep set of social relationships, a managerial aristocracy, the absence of private place, and the complimentary holding of two contradictory opinions (which Orwell dubbed "doublethink"). Winston Smith, though still decent and heroic, seems to live in a different period with a different worldview, as did his creator.

The acceptance of the coequal reality of perceptions leads to considerable tolerance for ambiguity. One way you can recognize the outlook of the older generation is when you encounter an insistence on clarity. The older generation outlook takes things apart to show how they fit together. It outlines. It organizes.

The members of the younger generation have no such obsession. They are more concerned with how things go together than with what the parts are. They don't outline, they simply bring in the parts that seem relevant, and they don't worry if they don't get them all. They thrive on contradiction, they like new complexities added before old ones are resolved, they love aimless discussions. They want richness. They prefer ambivalence.

Relational thinkers appeal because of their vitality. Life needs freedom, it must not be inhibited by structure, which makes you delete what you feel like putting in and forces you to include what you don't care about.

These feelings, of course, derive from the relational outlook. Systems can be linked in an infinite number of ways, and there is no need to comprehend them in any order. It is also commonplace that the system will appear different as it is perceived from different places, and that one perception is not necessarily superior or more correct or more basic than another.

For the younger generation, then, ambiguity presents no problem. For many members of the older generation, it is intolerable.

The relational outlook, first perceived by a few creative scientists and philosophers, was then introduced into the educational system. Those who were educated under the mixture of influences themselves carried the relational outlook further, so that the postwar generation is embued with that way of seeking. The conflict in the educational system itself has declined, as the outlook of teachers and students again more closely coincides.

The relational outlook is seen in the educational system in the decline of hierarchy, the perception that learning is as important as teaching, a generally more relaxed approach, more discussion, more projects, more student participation. The educational system is more geared to prepare students for an organizational society.

This greater conformity of education with the dominant system is peace reenforcing, as are the negotiating and personal interaction skills that tend more to be stressed. For some decades it is likely that education will reenforce the organizational system. When change takes place, it is likely that the organizational system itself will begin to change, not that education will change it.

TRANSPORTATION AND COMMUNICATION

Transportation and communication both involve delivering something from one place to another. In communication you still have it after you deliver it; in transportation, you don't.

There is no doubt that there has been a vast revolution in transportation and communication in the past century. Morgenthau (1973) points out that it took Caesar 13 days to travel from Rome to Britain, and in the nineteenth century it took Robert Peel the same length of time. Today we can fly that distance in hours or anywhere in a day, only six decades after the first person flew over an ocean. And there is equally no doubt that there have been marvelous developments in electronic communication, making verbal and visual transmission instantaneous around the world.

But these developments have taken place. Telephones, radios and airplanes existed during the World Wars crisis, but they did not prevent the crisis. The telegraph transmitted instant messages before World War I, but the war came. The "hotline" between Washington and Moscow is not much of an improvement. It wouldn't have mattered whether Chamberlain flew to Munich or took a train. Television made the Cuban Missile Crisis very exciting, but did not contribute to its solution. The solution was arrived at despite television, or perhaps had been arrived at when the United Nations' advance in the Korean War stopped, or was stopped, at the Yalu River (Blair 1988).

The speed with which nuclear weapons can be transported is something new, though the comparative slowness of the cruise missile indicates that speed is not everything. What matters is whether the missiles can be stopped, and that has always mattered, regardless of whether what was being transported was guns on tanks or Huns on horses. Nuclear weapons have greater destructive capacity, of course, but then we are considering destructive capacity, not speed of transportation.

Does the speed of delivery make the present situation more dangerous? Yes, probably it does. If either the Russians or the Americans were to launch a large attack either accidentally or on the basis of false information, that would precipitate a large counterattack and probably a massive catastrophe, with casualties exceeding the 38 million of World War II and terminating the peace, as peace is defined here. Speed of transportation certainly compounds the problem.

This is a special dilemma peculiar to our age. We are going to have to live with it as a person may live with heart problems or diabetes. It could kill us but, with luck, it may not. It can't be forgotten and it isn't going to get better.

But if we are talking about a single mistake, a computer malfunction or a mad colonel, the probability is that the single launching, even if not successfully stopped, would not precipitate a full-scale nuclear war. The situation would be similar to that of an attack by a smaller nation.

After more than three decades of use, we are still investigating the effects of television. Whether it makes us more violent or not is still in debate: probably not, since it has been so difficult to demonstrate. Probably the demographic distribution matters more: the percentage of our population that is young and male. In any event, it is difficult to argue that television has caused wars; possible to argue that it has curtailed at least one: the American war in Vietnam. That too seems difficult to prove.

Modern communications, such as computer technology and the WATS line, acting within the relational outlook, may have contributed to an increased amount of networking. People contact other people in distant places or in the local area to facilitate particular kinds of interests. "Referral" techniques are used by job hunters to find the kinds of jobs that will meet their own preferences and abilities. They interview with a person who suggests other people they should talk to. Often in such interviews, they learn of routes to a desired position they never would have thought of. Other people, within larger organizations, form special networks. The Conference on Peace Research, Education and Development includes all sorts of networks for people especially interested in Third World development, peace education, antinuclear marches, religious retreats, and occasionally peace research itself. Hundreds of thousands, probably millions, of such networks exist, to provide names of baby-sitters, information on health-related lawsuits, services for runaway youths and their families, or advice on housing rehabilitation (Naisbitt 1982). Whether all this interaction makes up for the probable decline in family and community interaction that occurred when people remained in their area of birth is hard to say. It may be that the relational outlook creates a greater desire for communication. It may be that the communication, with all its technological facilitation, arises from a collective need to compensate for loss of family and community.

The marvels of transportation have done little to alleviate traffic jams. But commuting was invented in the seventeenth century, and its problems have not been solved since. People continue to prefer to commute rather than live adjacent to their work, or at least they choose kinds of work that require commuting. It may be that energy shortages will force greater use of public transportation and car pools, which should make commuting a happier experience for those with a relational outlook, and who are therefore more likely to seek social interaction.

The new transportation and communication of the Relational Age have not changed the situation. Travel in outer space is an amazing achievement, but Neil Armstrong's flight did not change our lives in the way that Lindbergh's did.

When we are not calling this the Space Age, we are calling it the Age of the Computer. But it is difficult to see how the computer would affect the peace as a communication device. It does not increase the rapidity of delivery nor improve the quality of the message. It may provide the message sender with a greater range of data, but then we are talking about a filing cabinet revolution, which is not likely to change the nature of the age. It may lose the message, but so may a filing cabinet. It may malfunction and cause the unintentional large-scale attack, but so may people.

Changes in transportation and communication, then, largely preceded the Relational Age. They are being used in some different ways, but have not necessarily improved the quality of communication.

Speed of transportation increases the dangers of the contemporary situation as compared to previous ages. Speed of communication could, on occasion, prevent the ultimate catastrophe from occurring. But quality of communication, rather than speed, would be of greater importance, and this would depend on the combination of relational outlook and the perception of normality, not on the quality of the technology. That is to say, the danger of accident, caused by improvement in speed of transportation, can be reduced by taking time to think about the problem, and a willingness to share possible ways of reducing the danger, rather than by the development of technologically sophisticated recall systems, or last-minute communication systems that reach into the shower or the bedroom.

THE LOOK OF THE OUTLOOK

If one is looking for the decline of the West, "the end of the world as we know it," there is a great deal to see and hear that supports this view. Much of the civilized world looks like it is coming to an end. Strip zoning converts miles of highways into vulgar and gawdy nightmares, without redeeming social value. There are miles of suburban American housing, each gulping immense yards, collectively treeless and giving the impression of some kind of spreading social virus. There are the cities downtown, dirty, monotonous, gray, discouraged, boarded-over.

Art reenforces this impression. Much that is painted or sculpted is not intended to be beautiful, but is disturbing, conscious-rousing, fearful. Music, instead of being harmonious and soothing, is often strident, enervating, irritating, discordant. Literature is unhappy, pessimistic, ambiguous. This looks like a civilization that is down on itself, and has lost its sense of form. It is visibly dissipating.

Contrast this with the reverence we maintain for the past. In Europe, villages and cathedrals are lovingly preserved, just as they were. Americans go even further, and restore or recreate the past, even moving buildings hundreds of miles to locate them in a single area, where we can get the feel of how such periods were. And these villages, these cathedrals, these restorations have a sense of form, a mystery of inner relationships that is so lacking on the highways we take in the effort to reach them.

Or contrast our urban sprawl, our smoky cities, our dilapidated rural housing with nature itself. We like to get away from the cities to walk in the woods, visit national parks, swim in the ocean, often to find that civilization has arrived there too, and that the parks are overrun by civilization-carrying tourists, the beaches threatened by crowding and amusement parks. "You should have seen the ocean in the Thirties," says Bert Lancaster in *Atlantic City*. Civilization pursues us everywhere, and it looks malignant.

If you look for the decline of everything, it is not hard to find.

But ugliness is not unique to our time. The surviving Victorian factories are not pleasant; aesthetically they are less satisfying than most modern factories, which often are architecturally distinguished, and could be schools or churches (and sometimes are). The sprawl of the past was not so extensive, because the population was not so great, but the pollution of a coal-based technology created a world of iron and smoke in which, Lewis Mumford (1961) tells us, the predominant color was black, including the clothes and hats and vehicles of the people who lived in it.

What was preserved from the past is what was most interesting and aesthetically coherent. We may look much better to future generations if only our best buildings are preserved, and our strip zoning is ploughed under. When we compare the best of one period of the past with the best of another, our preferences take over, and we may be divided about various aspects. We may prefer eighteenth century colonial architecture to the Victorian, but read Trollope rather than Richardson.

Certainly our own time is producing much that has a chance to be memorable. The West is experiencing a booming period of novel writing and is producing some outstanding films and plays. Some contemporary architecture and bridges are striking, and we have had a number of composers who have produced intensely interesting music that can make the classical seem insipid by comparison. If urban sprawl represents a loss of sense of form compared to that of the nineteenth century, we have also produced art and music that supremely represent relationship between form, and architecture that is characterized by sharply defined line. If these survive, we may be seen as a people supremely concerned with form.

We are also condemned by our ecologists as brutal destroyers of our environments. But it is the twentieth-century viewpoint that is aware of this destruction, and the twentieth-century architect who is more concerned with harmonizing with the environment rather than standing out against it. It is our age that has produced the conceptual artist, whose work consists of calling our attention to existing relationships rather than making any artifice at all, an approach to art that would have been inconceivable to the Victorian. It was probably this outlook that replaced urban renewal with restoration between 1960 and 1970, and led to the saving and preserving of Victorian architecture that previously had been perceived as monstrosity.

Again, tolerance is implied in this outlook, a capacity to see other views, a willingness to look for harmony in what had been perceived as ugly. Far from being an outlook that foreshadows the decline and fall of everything, it can be seen as an outlook that is reconciliatory, benevolent, healing.

ORGANIZATIONAL STRUCTURE

Our time is one of organizational structure. Our regulatory, productive and distributive institutions are organized in a complex manner that has a profound effect on the actions of individuals.

Organizational structure is characterized by a muddling of political and economic functions and an increasing perception of the need for planning, regulating, coordinating and measuring complex interactions, and the frustrations of this planning by the limiting and protecting as well as creative activities of semiautonomous subsections and departments.

The interactions of the autonomous subsections in the general complexity of the organizational structure tend to dampen the effect of hierarchy and the impact of organizational leadership, with the result that the controlling factors in the process of decision making become increasingly difficult to ascertain. All of this becomes embedded in an atmosphere of blandness, impersonality, and what seem to be irrelevant responses to particular problems or situations.

This organizational structure has been damned for its various characteristics, particularly its irrationality, its slowness, and its impersonality: the organization manager is often seen as uncreative, obedient, responsive either to public opinion or to superiors, lacking a capacity for internal judgment (Sinai 1978, 193–194; Reich 1983).

The muddling of political and economic functions comes about because the educational system produces organization people who can function in one as well as the other. Organization officials are often drawn into governmental positions for which they seem strangely qualified, often being called in to carry out regulatory functions for organizations in which they themselves carried out the activities that needed to be regulated. Automobile officials enter the Department of Defense or oil executives join the Department of Energy. Retiring generals, in turn, become officials in the aerospace industry.

The necessities and difficulties of planning are overwhelming. Designs must be drawn and chosen, funding must be anticipated, the product must be produced and tested and ready for markets that are anticipated. Even the termination of production must be planned to make way for the next product on the design board. The variables are nearly impossible to calculate, and anecdotes about miscalculations abound both in the public and private "spheres" when these can be sorted out.

If the government launches an interstate highway plan, it must calculate the effects on other forms of transportation and weight the value in relation to other possible programs. It must estimate the possibilities of local opposition, it must calculate ecological effects, and it must plan for the world as it is going to be several decades hence. It is hardly surprising that it would fail to see that besides performing the intended interstate functions, such highways would contribute to a population redistribution that would lead to overcrowding and stultification of the suburbs while central cities would suffer from lost tax base, depopulation and general decimation. Or that the decline of the railroads, which might have been anticipated in the building of the highways, might be followed by a return to coal as an important energy source, and a general perception that railroads might be superior to roads as energy conservers.

In normal times, central planning must allow considerable regional autonomy. Differentiated production often has its origins at the local level. When greater leisure and affluence came into existence early in our age, boating, camping, surfboard and transistor markets developed. They then impacted on future plans but could not have been in the original plans. Within each organization there are also competing departments that have not only markets in mind, but also their own perpetuation and expansion. Sometimes it helps the plan reach its objectives. The Soviet system, with its central orientation, has been greatly helped by highly ingenious regional bargaining, involved unauthorized several-way swaps (tires for cement for wiring for bicycles), that could never be carried out within the time span of a plan (Crankshaw 1962).

For better or for worse, large organizations must operate by committee decision. The committee is not an attractive entity but there is no other way in sight to bring together various kinds of knowledge necessary for decisions. Genius is not the province of the members of the committee, though it may be helpful to the systems or organizers who bring the committee together, and perhaps some intuitive flair is helpful here too.

It is very difficult for leadership to compete with the recommendations of committees. Even if the leader enters his job with the desire to bring about change, he must rely upon committees for his information. If he does not like the information provided by the first, but in that case he is likely to get another committee report that won't be too much different. If he wants to overrule, he destroys the effectiveness of the committee and he does so on the basis of a hunch. But even if he does overrule, he must meanwhile accept the information and recommendation of most other committees because he simply doesn't have time to investigate all their data himself or to appoint verification committees to check on existing committees (Galbraith 1967).

Politically we know the effect of this is to maintain a continuity despite changes of philosophy in leadership. We know that leaders campaign and get elected vowing to bring about changes, but that after they are in office their actual power to do so is limited by the committee system. This is also the case, though we do not have such dramatic examples, in the organization world. But this is also why young executives are having an effect on policy even while old men are digging in to resist. These young executives are committee members long before they come in to the "positions of power." But those who hold these positions, who can verify or block their decisions, must rely on the information provided by the younger executives. In a few cases they can block, but every block costs them several verifications. No one of the young people in the committee can do very much, but when they carry a prevailing general philosophy, there is not much the men at the top of the hierarchy can do to resist.

Thus committee decisions tend to have a conservative effect in that the leader cannot quickly bring about change. But on the other hand, when the underlying philosophy changes, the leader cannot resist it, he can only contain it.

The committee method works, given the nature of the organizational system. It is the only way ordinary people can function within a complex system. In a normal society, there is a tendency toward a consistent relationship between the social system, the enterprises it encompasses and the individual. In the final shaking down, the goals of the technostructure will be modified to conform with those acceptable to the younger generation, because the younger generation will dominate the middle echelons of the technostructure about the time that it becomes a majority of the politically active and economically responsible population.

William Whyte (1957) worried that the committee approach is not very innovational. He pointed out that some major innovations have come about entirely outside the organization framework and that organization men themselves admit that they could not easily accommodate an Einstein. This is probably true. But given the nature of a normal period, there is not going to be a crying need for major innovation. The organization is going to be concerned with perpetuation and developing a system whose outlines are already delineated. When innovation takes place, it is likely to be of a secondary, homeostatic, storing nature. If the need is seen to be relevant, the innovation will be adopted by the organization after it has been invented by an outside genius, even if it is too far out for the organization. If the relevance is not seen, the work of the genius is likely to go unappreciated, a frequent misfortune for geniuses.

Does the postwar increase in the percentage of women in organizations (Lauer 1986, 275) have a significant impact? It is hard to see that it does. For one thing, women have been striving to prove that they can perform as well or better as men within the organization structure. They have modified the rules with regard to flextime and leaves, but they have chosen to play the organizational game according to men's rules, particularly with reference to stressing instrumental over affective behavior within the committee. Relational behavior, however, may be more emotionally interactive, but that would apply to men as well as women.

The way in which the organization works tends to have a dampening effect on organizational leadership. The top leadership is flooded with reports and recommendations concerning particular problems or objectives from its middle management or its civil service. The leader must make yes or no decisions. If he says no, the problem still must be dealt with, some middle management or civil service committee must reconsider and come up with new recommendations. The process is slow and cumbersome, the most radical proposals will disappear in the compromises within the system, the committee report will be bland, cautious. Saying no wastes time, and the revised proposal may not be that much different or better.

These characteristics of organizational structure lead to the perception that no one is in charge, that they have their own rationale. Is there a technological imperative, as Jacques Ellul (1967) argues? The automobile and aerospace industries will make weapons on platforms that roll or sail or fly (Kaldor 1981). Since that is what they can do, that is what they will propose, each in response to possible other weapons systems that possible opponents could create. If it is possible to get to Saturn, man must get to Saturn. If anything is possible, reasons can always be found for doing it. The leader, by contrast, cannot pose problems that are out of the system.

The image becomes more disconcerting when you add to the picture of cumbersomeness and inexorability the rapidity of modern technology.

Rockets travel halfway around the world in half an hour. The computer communicates from anyplace to anyplace else instantly. When radar is combined with the computer, we get images of very quick decisions having to be made with hair-triggered implements by an organizational structure that is characterized by slow and cumbersome decision making, and irrational decision making at that. No wonder we have an image of a balance of terror.

But there is an alternative possible interpretation. Instead of straining to conceive of possibilities that might occur, we can consider what exists. In the developed world there are two cumbersome bureaucracies with fearful power but an organizational conservativism that causes them to decide against action, if they have to make a decision about anything. The governmental structures are not very different from the organizational structure in which they are embedded. They do not have the capacity to act deliberately with great speed. Their technology permits the possibility of accident, but they are also aware of that. It is the very cumbersomeness of the bureaucracy that insures that they will respond slowly to crisis; that in the event of a nuclear episode, accident will be presumed. And given the structure, accident it will turn out to be. A first strike capacity may be technologically possible, but its bureaucratic implementation, during our time, is on the improbable side of a continuum.

DECENTRALIZATION, DIVERSIFICATION, DIFFERENTIATION

The dominance of the organizational structure does not mean that our age is characterized by a tendency toward bland uniformity, of relatively few choices between similar offerings. The tendency toward reduction that might be offered by the organizational structure is countered by other tendencies leading toward decentralization in the organizational structure, diversification in the interests of the organization, and differentiated production by the organization or in its interstice.

Against the constraining authority of the organization, there are varieties of life-styles: not just choices to experiment with premarital living or group condominiums, but the possibility of fixing up an old house in a small town rather than buying a new one in a suburban development, or moving back to the city in the controversial phenomenon sociologists call gentrification. Middle-aged people abandon remunerative careers in order to seek out other kinds of work, requiring more creativity, or more social contact.

International problems are greatly concerned with maintaining diversity. African and Asian nations are seeking modernization, but attempting to carry it out within a framework that maintains their own cultures. Within developed counties, the process of assimilation from immigrant to citizen is reversed by later generations. Once full citizenship is established, ethnic differences are accentuated as grandmother's old recipes are recovered along with a few words from the old language. In Ireland and Israel ancient languages were resurrected, while after World War II, Warsaw was reconstructed in a Baroque style. Toynbee (1939) has seen this sort of thing as "archaism," a loss of creative impulse, but it could also be an attempt to maintain distinctive characteristics against the bland threat of world technology and international art. The Poles, for instance, have been active in theatre and film, and even in political style, despite despotic limitations, and the Irish continue to produce important writers.

The same kind of spirit is leading corporations to move into other areas of production that relate only marginally to their original enterprise. Producers of media may also buy book companies, other kinds of communication enterprises, or even baseball teams. In America, as Jane Jacobs (1969) points out, differentiation of production is such in the clothing industry that no one in a large crowd is likely to be dressed exactly like anyone else. As large newspapers merge or fold, new suburban papers replace them, along with hundreds of specialist publications, directed at players of one game, practitioners of one hobby.

Within the interstices of the organizational structure small firms are constantly springing up that can produce a particular product better than a large firm. Perhaps it requires special precision, perhaps it fulfills a unique need, perhaps the requirements promise short-term markets that long-term planning can't meet. Often the skills of these small firms have been learned within the corporations and often their lives are short, either because they misjudge their fourth or fifth market and don't have the capital to cover the mistake, or because they are so successful that they are bought out by a diversifying corporation.

Decentralization, diversification and differentiation are products both of the relational outlook—which seeks new combinations of relationships—and normal times, which allow for decentralization as problems and opportunities can be subdivided and solutions do not require unification or mass effort.

WHERE IS THE LEADERSHIP?

There has been concern expressed that the United States, having been so committed to mass production and large corporations, will be undersold by European, Japanese and Third World firms that are more flexible, can meet the needs of short-term markets and move on to new areas of production more quickly (Reich 1983). Either the United States will adjust to changing competition as the younger generation becomes dominant, or like Britain it will cease to be the world's greatest power, much to the relief of the rest of the world. It is not necessary that the United States be the world leader. Most Englishmen seem to survive without that responsibility. Most Belgians do not lose sleep over never having been in such a position.

Still, if America is not going to provide the leadership that will take the world triumphantly into the next century, who is? Who is going to prevent nuclear war, solve the energy crisis and bring us back to a period of steady growth and prosperity without inflation or unemployment? Where are the Roosevelts and Trumans, the Churchills and De Gaulles, the Adenauers and Khrushchevs? By contrast, our leaders of the 1980s, the Thatchers and Mitterrands, the Kohls and Nakosones, have not inspired confidence.

In normal periods, however, leaders generally have not been charismatic. They have been boardroom types, team players chosen because of abilities to work with others, and perhaps favored because they could not become men on horseback. Even in earlier, normal periods the leader has been an organization man, selected partly because he had worked well in the system, often by a monarch who kept a low profile. Extraordinary men are called forth to lead in times of crisis. But in normal times they remain on back benches, or they are sent on difficult and dangerous tasks that will keep them out of the way, perhaps permanently.

The good leaders of the Baroque and Victorian Ages do not provide exciting models for undergraduates: Walpole and Fleury, Palmerston and Guizot, or monarchs like Maria Theresa, Louis Philippe and Victoria herself. Those who were more colorful were dealing with national crises: Peter the Great and Bismarck, for instance; or out of touch with the system, notably Joseph II of the Habsburg Empire. Outstanding leaders who did stay in power, like William of Orange and Frederick the Great, knew how to trim their sails.

In normal times, the leaders cannot make the situation. The situation shapes the leaders.

But then, what a tragedy that there should not be more innovative leaders to cope with the incredible changes through which people are living. "The status quo is change," declared the charismatic Khrushchev, during the course of drubbing Walter Lippmann in a game of badminton (Lippmann 1961).

At all organizational levels, the cooperative, dependable, sociable personality is emerging. This is true even in areas that once were respectable for adventurers. The 1983 film *The Right Stuff* is a reminder that heroes, such as the astronauts, who do dangerous and complicated work, are typical organization men. John Glenn, the first astronaut hero, was so interchangeable that he ran for political office. His friend, Scott Carpenter, the only astronaut to exhibit a maverick personality, was safely (and symbolically) transferred to deep-sea diving. Creative but temperamental explorers like Columbus and Lindbergh would have had no chance of being accepted for training as astronauts.

When talented charismatic personalities do appear, they are regarded as something of a problem. The mechanism for insulating charisma is becoming so well organized that William Whyte (1957) can describe handbooks for dealing with the man who speaks too frequently at committee meetings and Amatai Etzioni (1971) can list "preventive" and "post factum" controls that are recurrently employed. Some charismatics are weeded out in selection by personnel departments and employment agencies. Some are observed in training, which is one of the reasons for on-the-job education. Once established, some are sidetracked into positions where their talents may be used but in which they cannot do much harm. Sometimes they are kicked upstairs, to higher sounding but less powerful positions, or given challenging trouble shooting jobs, with the trouble that is to be shot located an excitingly long distance from the home office. If all else fails, the charismatic must be discharged from the organization, excommunicated, or read out of the party. But the days of character assassination have passed, and such events are usually accompanied by expressions of regret, ambiguous letters of recommendation, generous praise for past contributions, and vague references to new challenges and opportunities.

Two leaders of the 1980s may not seem to fit the description of the leader in normal times. What about Ronald Reagan? What about Mikhail Gorbachev? Are they not charismatic?

Reagan has impressed most observers as a likable person. But because of that he would fit very well into the bureaucratic structure. He is hardly a follow-me-as-I-lead-the-charge kind of leader. His 1989 successor seems likely to be abnormally normal.

As for Gorbachev, Russian reformers hoped he would lead a fundamental shift toward decentralized management, which they felt essential to economic problems. The decentralization had been delayed, perhaps, partly by the Byzantine structure of the Soviet Union and partly by the unusually high age of the leadership. Even when Gorbachev—born around 1930 in the transitional period between the older and younger generations—became the youngest full member of the Politburo, the median age of the membership was over 70. Four years later, at the death of Andropov, the leadership was divided equally between Stalinist and post-Stalinist generations (Cohen 1985, 79–80). So Gorbachev, able and competent though he may be, was making way for a process that had been considerably delayed, not leading the way toward a bold solution to a crisis (Tucker 1988).

There is still some use for charisma within the organization, particularly in positions involving the coordination of different groups. But what is wanted is a radiant personality that is closely attached to the objectives of the organization, whatever they may be, however they may change. There are also charismatic writers, journalists and teachers as well as founders and operators of numerous small businesses. But charismatic leaders are out of place in normal times.

Leadership in normal times comes from the social elites. These are not so different from the elites of the past, except perhaps in their greater interaction and interchangeability. Elites are formed from the business management, government and academic worlds. Individuals often move freely from one of these sectors to another, and there are similarities in the way the members of this elite think and make decisions. Therefore the determination of decision making becomes blurred between top and second echelons and between the public and private sectors of society.

This gloss ignores the military, which is generally regarded either as vaguely sinister or as a pillar of authority. But military men are government officials who operate within another bureaucracy. They move out of their area and into the others as easily as anyone else. One of the most famous followed his military career by becoming president first of a university, then of a country. Many others retire to business directorships. The outlook of some military men is that of the older generation, while others have that of the younger generation. Military institutions, like church institutions, tend to be conservative, but many of its members may be innovative.

This interaction of elites also reduces the importance of the old question of whether business follows the lead of government or whether government serves the needs of business. After World War I, this was still a meaningful question because the armaments makers were entrepreneurs, with objectives that differed from those of government. But today the men in the upper levels easily become policymakers in government. Their objectives and ways of thinking are similar. Therefore, if government is devoting a great deal of its budget to military expenditures, this probably represents a consensus among the elite. Industry is not controlling government, but government is managed by men and women who have been and will be again either business or academic administrators.

Will women and minorities make a difference in leadership? It doesn't seem likely. The outstanding female leader of the 1980s has been Margaret Thatcher, who has been dubbed "The Iron Lady." The nickname is an unconscious tribute to her ability to play a man's game, to play her role as a man would play it, with a particular emphasis on firmness.

How about Jesse Jackson? But Jackson did not win, he only opened the way for other minority candidates. What candidates come to mind? Someone like Tom Bradley, who has been through the orthodox political process, who would have ideas more like those of other leaders. As for Jackson, he becomes increasingly effective, the more he becomes like everyone else. If he could get a congressional seat or some other government position, he might by 1996 become sufficiently "normal" to win a nomination.

Most contemporary institutions that are run on the basis of information and advice garnered from the middle echelons are normal institutions. They have acquired a form and they are working toward the solution of problems. A society dominated by such institutions is a normal society. This is most clearly seen in Chinese history, where empire after empire went through decades of strong leadership followed by centuries of bureaucratic domination that finally ended in disintegration, anarchy, and a new period of strong leadership. The centuries in which bureaucracy ran the empire were the normal periods.

In normal periods, leadership is provided by a complex and mobile elite, not an oligarchy or single individual. In most societies, access to this elite is limited by birth, wealth and education. This is still true in the Relational Age, but given the power of egalitarian attitudes and the large number of positions that do influence leadership, it is probably also true that in most developed countries a much larger percentage of those who do not have advantages of birth or wealth nevertheless receive the education necessary to enable them to achieve such influential positions.

MOTIVATION BEHIND DECISION

So we have a mediocre leadership arising out of a relatively fluid elite. The decisions of this elite are greatly affected by a broad middle echelon of information gatherers who, sorted by the system, are likely to have a range of agreement among them, a perspective that is colored, however, by the increasing power of the relational outlook. What will influence, is already influencing, the decisions of leadership out of such a mixture?

First, the decisions are likely to be conservative in the sense that they will be made within the system. If problems arise that cannot be solved by the system, they will not be met until they must be, and the meeting is likely to be part of the crisis that marks the end of our time and with it, the likelihood of preserving peace.

Within that framework, they may be more holistic, more cautious, slower, less energetic. The older generation is likely to attack the symptom, to take action of some sort, even though the action may prove to be superficial. The younger generation may look at the problem more completely and have more insight into how the problem involves the system itself. Having that insight, however, will make the problem much more difficult to solve, and may lead to inactivity. The building of Connector Route 675 was blocked for a number of years in Ohio because it was perceived that it would take traffic out of the city of Dayton and hurt downtown business and real estate values. No other action was taken, because no action was better than any action. On the macrolevel, no action over the Iranian hostages was probably the best approach the government could take.

Decisions may be less influenced by monetary incentive. The organization man will get his promotions and will have moderate comfort if he makes no mistakes, so there are likely to be fewer risks. The same caution is likely to bring the prestige of arcane middle echelon titles: assistant director in charge of quality control; vice-president of the emulsion division; development coordinator.

Beyond prestige, however, is another possibly more satisfying motivation, the imposing of one's own personality on people, structures and events. This is seen by students of political science like Bertrand Russell (1969) or Hans Morgenthau (1973) as "the will to power," the desire to influence or control the minds and actions of men. To a student of organizational structure like Galbraith (1967), however, it appears as a less sinister "adaptation motivation," the desire to persuade the organization to accommodate to your objectives. In a transitional period such a desire is likely to emerge as rather raw and ugly, with a single man shaping an industry or a government to fit the needs of his (sometimes emotionally inadequate) personality. But in a normal period men have to act more within the framework of the organization: the prime minister must persuade his cabinet, the member of the Politburo must accept a *quid pro quo,* the junior member of the technostructure must phrase his suggestions so that he does not threaten his colleagues or his superiors. The charismatic personality, who in a transitional period might have shaped an industry or a state, now can hardly function in an organization at all. He may find compensations bullying his family or playing the demagogue in the espousal of losing causes. Or else he may see his psychiatrist and try to find out if he can modify his neuroses or exchange them for others more suitable to the era in which he lives. On a more positive note, he may find a role as Steve Jobs appears to have done, starting new innovative companies and losing control as they reach an organizational level, or selling out to a larger company and starting over again.

The organization provides ample opportunity for play. Winning is fun and losing is painful. It is obvious that men try just as hard on the golf course as they do in committee. But one plays games in committees too: there are rules, strategies, victories and defeats. The game itself is intriguing—"fun" doesn't seem to be quite the word for it. Other things being equal, winning is more satisfying than losing. It is difficult to say whether there is more satisfaction in winning a personal combat or a group combat, and it doesn't seem to make much difference whether the participation is physical or vicarious. Once identification is established, the emotional effect is similar. In times of crisis it is easy to identify with large institutions over a long period of time. So most people in the developed world identified with their nation in World War II. In normal periods, in which ideological factors are reduced, the focus of identification tends to become decentralized. One plays the game within the business or government in which one finds oneself. But the complex organization lends itself to many games, and one can lose one's life winning them.

Play is an essential element in creativity. In a normal period there is plenty of opportunity for creativity, although as Kuhn (1962) and Kroeber (1944) have shown, it tends to be channeled perhaps, as Kavolis (1972) suggests, by a collective attempt to reestablish reality (e.g., this book). Writers, artists and craftsmen are apt to be prolific, but there is also plenty of opportunity for creativity within the organizational structure. The process of establishing procedures for summer school—coordinating the dean's office with that of the advisors, registrar, finance office and public relations office the drafting and redrafting of charts, the testing against performance, the redrafting, the sudden inspiration—all these activities involve processes not unlike designing a car, a sandal, an abstract sculpture, a triptych, a novel.

In considering various motives, we have ignored money. Certainly profit continues to be a factor, particularly as a measure of success and a source of capital in small and new businesses. But even where money is personally desired, it still is convertible into prestige, security and comfort. And as security and comfort become marginal, and as the younger generation depreciates material accumulation, the profit motive seems certain to play a subordinate role.

Since the relational outlook takes all sorts of social relationships seriously, there is a tendency to regard play as good, money as bad, and the combination as an indication of degradation. Thus Christopher Lasch writes of "the anguished cry" of the "true" sports fan who "brings to sports a proper sense of awe" only to find them corrupted by the "entertainment ethic" (1978). What is novel here is the sociology of analyzing the effect of communication or money on a peripheral aspect of our society. The "entertainment ethic" is introduced as if sports were not entertainment. Play, then, is understood to be a valid motivation. Entertainment, however, smacks of passivity and hierarchy. The entertained ought to participate, not just imbibe. Money, which was meaningful in itself to the Victorian, should only be a means to the relationally oriented. Hence there is a feeling that play ought not to be associated with money or entertainment.

Finally, but most significantly, considering the transformations of other motivations and the outlook of the younger generation, we ought to consider altruism. There is hardly a better way to find satisfaction than to act in ways that clearly bring satisfaction to others. Whatever other motives men have, they receive greater image reenforcement if they can also see their actions as altruistic. Certainly self-deception is necessary in many cases in which the action is actually selfish or worse, frivolous. But people will also set priorities by what seems to be the better, grander, nobler thing to do. In crisis periods, what is good is often fairly obvious. In normal periods the possibilities become diversified, and it is easy to underestimate the importance of altruism as a motive.

It is almost superfluous to add that altruism is consonant with the relational outlook. From the relational viewpoint the question of the growth of the firm is important only as it related to society. The real question is whether the organization is creating a more healthy environment and making a better life for everyone.

Put another way, what is good for society is good for the organization.

So at all levels within the organizational structure, both in government and in business, we have a general framework in which action can be taken, but a range of reasons for taking such action. While it may be that decisions come from within the heart of the organizational structure rather than from the leadership, it does not follow that such decisions are irrational or random or value-free.

A tendency not to act, or to act slowly, may be advantageous in normal times. There are likely to be fewer interventions in situations that intervention cannot change. There is no reason why there could not be responses to ecological problems that would fit in with the collective security, prestige and altruistic goals of the organization. There is no reason why decisions could not be made that would move production from arms proliferation to other areas that were perceived to be more valuable, not necessarily in terms of profits or growth. It would be consistent with the structure of organizations to include external costs in bookkeeping procedures, which might considerably alter priorities within the organizational structure.

PEACE AND PROSPERITY

The postwar period coincided with the dominance of Keynesian economics. By the middle 1950s we had absorbed the idea that government fiscal policies, alterations in taxation or government spending, could stimulate the economy permanently, controlling inflation, maintain high employment levels, and protecting the economies of Europe and the United States against a recurrence of the Great Depression.

By the 1970s, it became evident that something was wrong. Inflation and unemployment were occurring at the same time, contrary to Keynesian logic. Cooling off the economy, preventing full employment, did not stop inflation. Government investment and military spending did not solve the problem of unemployment. In the 1980s Keynesian normality returned to the United States, with high unemployment and low inflation. But the world economy seemed unstable, with stock market upheavals, currency imbalances, unpayable Third World debts.

In retrospect, it appears once again that our time is neither a utopia of endless growth and full employment, nor an inferno of catastrophic depression and pervasive hardship. It is a normal period of sporadic growth and periodic episodes of unemployment, inflation or high interest rates. The organizational, industrial system is not likely to be replaced by anything else in the next several decades. That does not mean that problems cannot be addressed by other means, with small enterprises developing frequently in the interstices, perhaps to be acquired by the oligopolistic establishment when they are successful. That does not mean that the government will not be intervening here and there, altering taxes or focusing investments to influence certain sectors. But these interventions are likely to have side effects, with an improvement in one area leading to dysfunctional developments in others. Choices may be made, and some choices may be more beneficial to economies than others.

Whatever the failures of Keynesian economics, they do seem to have had some effect in eliminating the destabilizing effects of the business cycle. For about 90 years, from the European revolutions of 1848 through the Great Depression of the 1930s, the cycles consisted of alternate bursts of prosperity and depression. These alterations were a product of the industrial revolution and the rise of industrial capitalism, and their increasing impact may have contributed significantly to the World Wars crisis. The cycle problem has been presented in various ways, but basically depressions seem to have been caused by fluctuations in capital investment.

If industrial firms collectively reduce the amount of earnings they devote to the creation of new capital, a chain of consequences can develop that brings about depression. The firms fail to make anticipated increases in orders for the construction of new buildings or the addition of equipment with a surplus of inventory. They must curtail production and when they do so, their demand for labor falls and unemployment increases. The increase in unemployment means a decline in purchasing power, a fall in consumption, a reduction in sales, and less incentive for further construction or even replacement of depreciated equipment. There is still some debate about why firms should fail to make the anticipated increases. It may be that their inventories build up because of a fall in consumption. The fall in consumption in turn may arise because of the natural ending or a spurt of business activity relating to a basic invention. Thus the first depression in 1848 was attributed to the completion of basic construction of railroads.

Whatever side effects and problems may exist, it would appear that the expectation that the government will increase investment when it declines sharply among corporations has had some effect in eliminating the business cycles of the Victorian and World Wars periods. Cycles have been much milder in the Present Age, and this is certainly a factor in economic stability as well as the anticipation of future stability.

The disappointing performance of Keynesian economics has frustrated the hopes of those who, in the 1960s, expected that by steadily increasing production and growth, we would be able to reduce and finally eliminate poverty while at the same time providing economic support for the increasing percentage of retired elderly. This dream has gone awry as the percentage of people living below official poverty levels has leveled off after two decades of impressive decline, and now may again be rising. Meanwhile, demographic changes and medical costs together are indicating to economists in most developed countries that it is going to be more difficult to provide for the elderly. Since the baby boom of the early part of our time will be producing a demographic bulge in our elderly population in the first two decades of the twenty-first century, we can look for a problem in that area in what we can expect will continue to be a normal period. If these problems are solved by a greater transfer of wealth, it could be that our standard of living will be declining as we reach the new century. By some measures, the standard has been declining for some time (Kohr 1977, 25–46). If production does not recover to levels of increase of the 1950s and 1960s, considerable segments of the population will undergo hardship. There is time to anticipate the problem of the elderly, at least, and it may be hoped that an increase in relational attitudes will contribute to a sharing rather than a shrugging solution to the problem.

These economic problems doubtless will receive constant attention because they hit, for example, those who are in the business of writing articles about our society. They are members of the middle class, and as such are underpaid in comparison with others they know in industry. Their mortgages are difficult to pay, their children go to expensive colleges and prep schools (because of the "crisis" in public education) and they don't have lamb or veal on the table anymore. Economic problems are really painful because they are continuous, they involve endless comparisons, and they are most painful where the range of comparisons is widespread and upward mobility is possible for some, but ultimately limited for most. Some of us are threatened with unemployment if government contracts are not forthcoming, or if demand fails to keep expanding. All of us are threatened by inflation, which upsets our calculations and is imponderable in the future.

But it is probable that if we are considering real income, our lives are better at any class level than they were in any previous period, normal or crisis. The middle class is harried. But to be middle class is to be harried, as Victorian novels of Dostoevsky, Zola, Hardy and Howells make clear. To speak of an oppressed proletariat as constituting the entire working class puts considerable strain on the term "oppression" if it means that drinking beer and watching the Mets is not as enriching as selecting wine and attending the ballet.

The thrust of this section has been to indicate that the economic problems we are encountering are those of a normal period. The economy is not prospering to the degree that most of us would like, but neither has it reached levels of disaster that were characteristic of the Great Depression. The studies of peaceful societies that I have worked on (Melko 1973; Melko & Weigel 1981; Melko & Hord 1984) all seem to indicate that there is only a weak relationship between peace and the economy. More peaceful societies have been relatively prosperous than relatively impoverished, but there are a number of examples of economic change or highly unsatisfactory economic conditions within peaceful societies, so that it cannot be said that either prosperity, poverty, or change from one to the other is likely to be closely related to peace. If the economic situation in our time, therefore, were to get much better or much worse, to change suddenly or gradually, that would probably have relatively little effect on the continuation or the termination of peace.

PEACE AND MORALITY

The relation between peace and morality is probably worth a book in itself. There already are books on war and morality, particularly on the concept of the "just war," or on war atrocities as opposed to war niceties. If war brings out the moral best in man, causes him to put aside his petty differences and give everything to the "just cause," then one must suppose that peace does the opposite—causes him to resume his petty concerns and give as little as possible. In that case, the more immorality we can find, the safer we would be.

If that is the case, this society would appear to be in pretty good shape. There seems to be a great deal of cynicism about the moral climate of our time. Among the more salient perceptions seems to be that our leadership is normally corrupt; that we are a godless people; that our younger generation, in any event, has lost the conception of the morality of work; that the world is a jungle in which any may be the victim of any.

But what age has been morally adequate? When can we find a period for comparison? The older generation must be referring to the 1920s and 1930s, when life was simpler, when you could leave your door unlocked, when you could hitchhike in safety. But this was also the period of the Teapot Dome scandal, of greed and get-rich-quick schemes, of the rise of fascism and anti-Semitism in Europe, racial prejudice and segregation in America. It wasn't even a safe period: violent crime in relation to population reached a peak that was not to be matched until the late 1970s.

Managers operating in the organizational system have tremendous reliance on their reputations. If they are going to be effective in committee operations, they must have respect, and to have respect they must seem to be above reproach. Even to be attacked when you are innocent is damaging to your reputation, and it is therefore better not to get into a situation in which you might be attacked. This leads to excessive caution, it is true, but that is a different problem.

If the building of one's image is a major motivation, private dishonesty is surely a problem unless one is a master of rationalization. But it is certainly more difficult to build up an image of oneself as powerful, benevolent and selfless if you are accepting or offering bribes.

Watergate and Iran-Contra suggested a pattern of political immorality, but that hasn't been proven as compared to other patterns. Both cases were characterized by men and women who were loyal to a subsystem that contravened the laws of the overall system. They were dedicated pursuers of what, from the system's viewpoint, would seem to be irrational ends by immoral means. But, for the most part, they were not seeking personal economic enrichment. Organizational corruption is complicated, and often involves a conflict of system loyalties measured against complicated and changing laws. By contrast, the immoral bosses of Lincoln Steffens's (1931) day are refreshing in the candor of their immorality. But they too were operating under subsystem norms, except that those norms are easy to expose by standards of another period.

Corruption is a normal problem, one familiar throughout history, a problem that can cause some individuals to be cheated and others to be disgraced, that can cause governments to fall. It makes good journalistic copy, it titillates. The many business or government officials who were again honest this year do not make interesting news.

Another perception of immorality lies in the older generation's view of the younger generation, that it is indulgent, lacking in backbone, lazy, without self-motivation. Members of the younger generation lack the work ethic, and indulge themselves with drugs and sex.

Well, of course, there has been a developing ethos, at least in the middle class, that life is about more than work, that an individual with a holistic frame of reference ought to balance his life, not become overly involved in work. The term workaholic has been coined to characterize the man who becomes excessively involved in work to the detriment of his family. It follows that insofar as these ideas have impact, they are going to undercut total devotion to work. They are supposed to. And if this sort of idea is taught, it would not be surprising to find college graduates less willing to sacrifice their families to their work and therefore, from the point of view of many managers, less dedicated to the work. This does not, of course, mean that those who take such a view are less moral than those who put their work first. From some points of view, they may be more moral.

If the outlook is different, it is more likely to be in the person who has been raised in the middle class and has some latitude to experiment, to remain free of commitment. Peter and Brigitte Berger (1971) pointed out that the first-generation child of a blue-collar family may be quite willing to move into the spot that is vacated by the child of the middle-class family. It may also be that a higher percentage of the middle-class jobs today are organizational, they can be set in a framework of predictable hours and do not require the long hours of dedication that new businesses often do. And such new businesses, if they succeed, usually involve people who are prepared to sacrifice many hours, but not necessarily forever.

As far as drugs are concerned, the use of harmful drugs is not peculiar to our age. It appears that the use of drugs such as opium and morphine was much greater among the middle class in the years before World War I, and that, if statistics were available, alcoholism must have been greater in this country in the early nineteenth century than it is now, was greater in eighteenth-century Britain of Hogarth's day, and probably is greater in contemporary Japan than in America, except that many Japanese may not be aware of alcoholism or even think that drinking is a vice.

On the sexual question, it depends on whom you are reading whether we have sexual liberation going on or sexual degeneration. And there is even some question whether anything more is going on than was in the past. It is difficult to compare the overt to the covert over time.

An easier example of increased vice, already discussed in another context, is child abuse. The term child abuse was invented only in the 1960s, prior to that date the maxim "spare the rod and spoil the child" was thought to be a statement of knowledge and virtue, and growing awareness of child abuse can be perceived as growing sensitivity, a process of civilization. Also mentioned was the process described by Robert Lane (1969) who showed that the people of Boston throughout the nineteenth century perceived the growth of violent crime, whereas city statistics indicated that violent crime was declining. What was happening, Lane thinks, is that Boston was transforming from a frontier to a central city, and that saloon brawls at the beginning of the century became assaults by the time the century ended. The result was that the citizenry insisted on more and more police protection, and more and more arrests were made.

So today, in a shorter period, more and more child abuse is reported, as levels of acceptability have changed. Since we live in a period of growing sensitivity to human relations, we should not be surprised at a growing awareness of flaws in these relations.

So it seems doubtful that we live in a time of exceptional immorality and possible that in some respects ours is a period of uncommon moral sensitivity.

FREEDOM

Our time seems to be one of at least moderate freedom. The extent of freedom one has varies by capacity, luck and cultural situation. It can be extended or repressed by particular forms of government and the impact of technology.

I consider freedom to be an awareness of the possibilities of one's own situation. A man who has the choice between death or slavery is more free if he is aware of the choice, than the man who believes he is free to do whatever he wants, but never questions what he wants. This definition of freedom may be somewhat unusual, perhaps relational. Others may prefer to consider that what is being discussed here would better be called by another term, such as awareness of situation.

In any event, given the definition used here, normal periods open up possibilities for freedom. But as they progress, these possibilities narrow somewhat, as the younger generation loses the contrast of perspective that is evident in the conflict of generations. Crisis periods narrow freedom further by binding people to responding to the central threat. But the process is complicated, and there are other factors of outlook and technology that serve to increase or decrease the possibilities of freedom.

The relational outlook tends to increase freedom in that it provides considerable awareness. We are aware, in the first place, that our position is relative and that there are rational alternatives to almost any position chosen. There is access to a great deal of data from other cultures and from the history of our own. The contemporary social situation is one in which people have the capacity to change their own lives considerably.

Threats to this freedom are seen from many directions. Some are concerned with the threat of despotic government that will deprive people of their chance to vote for alternative political candidates or worse, will create an atmosphere in which one may not speak freely. It certainly must be unpleasant to live under such a government, but the very fact that one must be careful about what one says indicates he has considerable freedom. Most of the people in world history have been peasants, and for the most part they have not lived under such constraints because they could not say anything that would threaten the system under which they lived.

They were less free than the man in the despotic state who must be constantly alert. If anything, such a situation forces a man to be free.

Such states, in any event, are short-lived and becoming extremely rare in the contemporary period. Of more concern is the limiting of individual freedom through planning. Some states utilize advertising, others simply limit information, but in either case they attempt to mold the citizen-customer to their designs. Many irrational wants are thereby created while other more rational wants are probably suppressed. But these same societies must create a vast educational apparatus in order to operate, and education must teach people to think, to use the empirical method in various possible situations. When people are so taught, it is impossible to prevent them from using the method to criticize the system itself.

It is perfectly true that the majority of people are greatly inhibited in their freedom not only by the information provided by the state and the corporations, but also by the culture patterns that surround them. They do and think whatever is acceptable to do and think and they have no way of attaining a standpoint from which to reflect upon the limitations of the situation in which they find themselves (Thompson 1985, 3–12). But this has been true of most people in most cultures most of the time, and for all people in all cultures some of the time. One of the things that freedom teaches us is how limited our freedom is. Another is that every free choice we make closes off the possibility of making a number of other free choices. Freedom, therefore, is limited by the exercise of freedom.

If relational orientation increases freedom by increasing awareness, this freedom is declining somewhat with the development of the age. There is more freedom after a crisis than later phases. After the crisis there are more basic alternatives, more awareness of contrasts between the past and present. But as a normal phase progresses, the insight of the crisis is lost, and freedom is circumscribed.

So there is more freedom in the Relational Age than there was in the Victorian Age because of the differences in outlook. But while the progression of the age in time increases the dominance of the relational outlook, and therefore perceptions supporting freedom, at the same time the insights of comparison with the previous phase are gradually lost, and to that extent freedom diminishes.

Freedom is increased as ideological intensity declines. Whatever became of the Communist Menace? In these days of waning ideology there is less concern that people around us will suddenly rise up and overthrow the government or become converted to an idea of communal ownership of property. The developed world is too fat and satisfied to give much credence to this, and younger people can't remember the idealistic days of the 1920s and 1930s that bred so much good and so much evil.

The connection between democracy and freedom is not automatic. Most governments in history have been despotic. Athens was an exception limited in size, duration and franchise. In modern times, as the industrial revolution has brought forth a dominant middle class and destroyed the nobility, electoral franchise has indeed widened. But power ultimately resides with an elite. Governments are responsive to the electorate, but to an extent governments always have been responsive enough, at least to the demands of the more influential members of society, to stay in power.

Does despotism prevent freedom? The man who reads *Pravda* knowing that certain catch phrases indicate certain developments may be more aware of the political situation than the man whose Sunday *Times* "Week in Review" tells him the answers to the key questions, but asks the wrong questions. If freedom involves an awareness of one's situation, this may be easier to come by in a situation in which you believe the news you are receiving is slanted than if you believe it is in fact "the news."

Political freedom is not essential to a productive life. The world promises much. If it is unwise to exercise political freedom, there are theaters, food, sports, babies and vacations. If a man does have political freedom, he is likely to find himself restricted in some other way: he cannot freely express himself within the business organization or to his wife.

Does a person need freedom? For many, equality is more important than political freedom. We measure ourselves against our neighbors and our community and we are anxious that we get our share of whatever there is to be had. Comfort is more important than freedom. In all states the citizen and his government are somewhat at odds. It makes him pay taxes and fines him for infractions of the law. But if it plays a relatively small part in his life, if it does not obtrude on him continuously and if it does not terrorize him, he can be relatively comfortable.

Government, then, continues to be what it has been. Its leaders are politically oriented men, men who desire power. In some countries voters will have more power than in others, but this will depend more on internal patterns and atmosphere than on a particularly identifiable executive or legislative structure.

Wide participation in the electoral process is one of the characteristics of the Relational Age. Each man has a vote equal to that of every other man, many women do too, and of late even children are being considered. It is widely believed that the final achievement of government will be to provide free elections everywhere. When this happens good government will follow, for if candidates fail to achieve what they promise, they will be voted out and replaced. When such freedom is completely achieved, it will never be necessary for one power to intervene in the affairs of another, for the people at home will be able to handle their own problems when the next election comes around.

So goes the dream. Yet we all know that in the freest of situations, you have no political choice. I lived for a number of years in a district dominated by one party. In that district, the candidate of the majority party always won, by a four to one majority if he were popular, by a three to one majority if he were not. This is a very common situation in any two-party system.

Citizens of multiparty countries would appear to have more influence on choice of parties. They can create quite a change in a given district by replacing, say, a conservative with a communist. And because there are many parties, their district is less likely to be dominated by any one party. But when they have had their say and the new legislature meets, a new coalition is formed that is almost like the old one, with one more minor party included and another excluded, with half the cabinet members of the old administration returning to the new one. The communist will surely find himself on the opposition benches.

But this is not to say that governments do not represent the electorate. They do, whether there are many parties, or only two, or even one. A democratic election will produce minor changes because only minor changes are wanted by the majority. Leaders of despotic governments will also respond to desire for minor changes, through reading letters in local or national papers (or petitions in earlier times), through listening to the opinions of representatives to the one-party legislature, or through traveling through the hustings as Khrushchev did. If governments fail to respond they risk rebellion, coups, revolution, guerrilla warfare, and these make a strong impression. But such events have not been happening in the developed world.

Major changes do not come from changing the electoral system. The electorate will get through to the government no matter what system exists. But change will come only when the electorate really wants change. And this is likely to happen only when there is a major change in outlook in both electorate and government.

Such a change is in process now. More candidates with relational outlooks are running for office, and even when they are defeated they are causing modifications in the views of victorious candidates with essentially developmental outlooks.

In the 1980s, legislatures in most of the developed countries were coming to be dominated by the relational outlook, but so were the cabinets, the men appointed to high office, the civil services, industrial management, educational administrations and military leadership. And this was as true of one-party systems as it was of multiparty systems. The changes that were taking place were not due to structural changes, though these may happen along the way, but to the basic transformation of outlook.

Freedom of speech and freedom of the press are associated with democracy. But not everyone has something unique to say. And those who do may not be heard.

Until quite recently, it was possible for anyone to express himself publicly through available media. It was possible to start a small newspaper or journal. It was possible for a Leonard Woolf to start his own press and print the works of his friends, if they were not accepted by mainstream publishers. It was possible for impressionist artists to get shows outside establishment institutions. It was possible for actors to express themselves "off Broadway."

But this has become more difficult, not because of any conspiracy against freedom, but because of the changing nature of the industrial system. Costs of publication have skyrocketed, and, as in many other industries, expenses can be met only by big business. Woolf (1975) and Alfred Knopf (1965) have both written that they could not do in the 1960s and 1970s what they were able to do earlier: start a small press on a small budget. They couldn't pay editorial salaries, and if they did succeed in putting something together, they couldn't afford to advertise.

Ted Solotaroff (1987), editor for a major publisher, is concerned that most of the old commercial publishing houses are being taken over by diversifying, management-oriented conglomerates. The result, he thinks, is that attention is being focused on what will make a profit, and money is being spent in bidding for established popular authors rather than in seeking new talent. Even if a new author's manuscript is accepted, there is not enough budget money left to give her sufficient exposure.

The same is true of newspapers. There used to be many in each big city, but gradually costs have forced mergers, and the efficient production of large papers has resulted in the elimination of small papers. America's largest city has two morning dailies and one evening daily, where once it had 10 or 20.

It is possible, of course, for the individual to attempt to cope with the situation as it is. If he wants to express himself, he can publish through existing media. But this is where planning comes in. When a producer produces, he must know ahead of time that there will be a market. To some extent this can be shaped by advertising, but it is always safer to produce for markets that are known to exist. The result is that publishers must judge material in accordance with the market they believe to exist, not in accordance with its intrinsic value or its originality. Originality, if anything, is a handicap, because it will not be understood and certainly is not in demand. C.P. Snow remarked a few years ago that a book of his (1959) received wide attention precisely because it was not original, because it articulated what everyone knew. He had said one or two original things in his life, he added, ruefully, but no one noticed them.

It is not novel that a man who is really original does not receive a hearing. A man who is ahead of his time can expect this. When Giambattista Vico brought out his *New Science* in Naples in 1725 and sent copies to his friends, they would greet him on the street without even having acknowledged receiving the copies. What is novel is that the absorption of publication by big business had made it extremely difficult for authors to publish at all. The same is true of painters trying to find galleries and playwrights trying to get plays performed: off Broadway has become too expensive also.

It is also worth noting that the problem is not much different regardless of whether you are living in a democracy or a despotism. In both cases, one of the requirements for getting a hearing is writing on acceptable subjects in an acceptable manner. In both cases there is a market to be considered.

What has been said here about publishing applies more strongly to more expensive media like television and movies. It does not make a great deal of difference whether media are privately controlled or government controlled. This is particularly true in normal periods because of the nature of the establishment, the nature of leadership, and the limitations of freedom by culture.

Suppose an independent television network desires to present opposition viewpoints, how does it find proponents? It takes a really original mind to escape the mind-sets of a culture, and such a person is not likely to take kindly to the atmosphere of a television setting nor is he likely to make an effective presentation to a lay audience. This type of person will want to define his terminology and establish a frame of reference, his footnotes taking the form of parenthetical asides, his personality projection nil, his sentences rather like this one, more or less. So the network must seek instead interpreters of the original thinker, and in particular interpreters who can make the new ideas sound sufficiently like the old ideas so that they will be recognizable to a moderately attentive audience. Some of these interpreters prove to have attractive personalities, and they are repeatedly called back to represent types of views on all sorts of subjects: one for the conservative view, another for the Catholic view, and others for the liberal view, the libertarian view, the artistic view, the sociological view. The contexts are inevitably stereotyped, narrowed, and simplified.

Suppose, on the other hand, that a government wants to control viewpoints, how does it do that? If a single, adulatory, everything-is-wonderful tone is adopted, if all presentations are carefully censored, the programs will become sodden and terrible things will happen. People will read books instead, or drink at taverns and have discussions; they will feel impulses to act or to live lives outside the reach of the government. If an attempt is made to make the programs interesting, the government runs the risk of creating a really shrewd audience that knows a "friendly" discussion means the Bulgarians are toeing the party line, but a "frank" discussion means that someone in the Bulgarian delegation dumped his bowl of goulash over the bald pate of the minister of communications.

It isn't that the medium is the message; it's that the medium is limited in the message it can deliver. If television does not lend itself to profundity, neither does it lend itself to demagoguery. The message givers do not have much of a message to give because not much of a message is all that can be given. This is perhaps unfortunate for educators, but it is equally unfortunate for aspiring despots.

Still, when all these limitations to freedom have been acknowledged, it is nevertheless possible to reach an audience from a soapbox on the public green. Anyone can do that. If there is a public green, if the speaker isn't violating a local ordinance, and if he can find a soapbox that isn't made of cardboard.

Yet there are factors in the Relational Age that are dissolving this complex set of problems. There is the tendency toward decentralization that tends to break mass society into locally-intelligible areas. The big-city press is being supplemented by the local press, off Broadway by local theaters. It is more fun to act or paint scenery than to go to the city to watch someone else. If you can't publish nationally, you can offset, stencil or word process. It is possible at low cost to reach specialized audiences interested in tapeworms, labeling theory or the comparative study of civilizations. The "proliferation of journals"—over 40,000 of them in the United States alone—is often viewed as an indication of the decline in quality (Bracey 1987). This phenomenon can also be seen, however, as a manifestation of a wide variety of interests being explored in our normal society and of continuing vitality and increasing creativity.

The relational outlook is more accepting of the idea that each person should do what he wants and what he can. It lacks critical capacity, so that good work and bad work are likely to be given equal encouragement, but it encourages participation rather than the passive acceptance of the mass audience.

The suppression of freedom envisioned by George Orwell does not seem to be a problem. Freedom is likely to decline in coming decades, not because of despotic suppression, but because of loss of perspective on the preceding age, common to any normal period after several decades, and because of a lack of historical perspective particularly characteristic of the relational outlook. For all that, the opportunities for expression are likely to continue on a regional and local basis. The question is whether these regional and local sources can make themselves felt in terms of providing solutions for the maintenance and extension of the present peace and, if so, whether they have the creative power to produce such solutions.

6

PROBLEMS TO BE RESOLVED

THE DECLINE OF THE WEST

If we grant the possibility that we live in a period of relative peace, a peace that is comparable to the *Pax Britannica,* and that this peace should last another six to ten decades, what then? How does this possibility affect the ways in which we should approach the immediate future?

Speaking on this subject at Swarthmore College, to an audience that was probably sprinkled with Quakers and peace activists, I made the case I have had more leisure to make here, probably without convincing very many. But I was asked, finally, if my interpretation of the present situation were accepted, what then should be our course of action? I replied that I had been working on the problem analytically, and had found members of the audience several decades of peace they didn't know they had. Surely it was up to them to do something with that time. I can't do everything.

With more time to reflect, that answer seems a little flippant. Just as the Victorians had to address a number of problems, such as slavery, franchise, and the protection of the poor from the ravages of the industrial revolution, so there are problems today that must be addressed. While solutions to any of these problems remain beyond this analysis, perhaps some can be singled out that seem to be most important along with some of the approaches and resources available to meet them.

Two of the problems are ominous and obvious: the nuclear dilemma and the impending energy crisis. Two others are equally obvious, though they do not seem to directly threaten the peace: inequality and the waning prospects for world development. A third pair are vaguely ominous but hardly a matter of general concern at the end of the twentieth century. One of these is the possibility that peace itself can be a cause of war. The *Pax Britannica* may have contributed to World War I and the subsequent world crisis and the present peace could contribute to the next. The other problem is even more obscure to all but a few hundred students of comparative civilizations: the idea that general, devastating wars are less products of technology than they are of the developmental phase of a civilization. Since the notion of phases of development played an important role in this analysis of our present situation, it may be well to begin this general chapter on the problems to be resolved with a consideration of this question, because there is nothing that can be done about problems of nuclear war and energy if the real problem is the irreversible and inevitable "decline of the West."

The World Wars period was certainly a major crisis in world history. The immense number of casualties; the spread of conflict around the world; the advent of machine guns, tanks, gas, air warfare and the atomic bomb; the mobilization of civilians; the extremist ideologies; the prison camps; the economic depression—no one could live through this series of horrors without being impressed with the feeling of a general, all-pervading crisis.

One explanation for the crisis was that Western civilization, which had spread its influence around the world, was undergoing a major transformation that had been experienced before in other civilizations. The primary exponents of this theory were Oswald Spengler (1932), a German philosopher who wrote during World War I, Arnold Toynbee (1934–1961), an English historian, and Pitirim Sorokin (1957), a Russian sociologist, all of whom wrote their major works in the years of the World Wars crisis. They varied tremendously in their approaches, but all agreed that the crisis would be resolved and a calmer period would ensue. Spengler and Toynbee noted that in preceding crises of this kind, various international systems had been incorporated into empires under a single government. All three stressed a corresponding change in atmosphere, which would be calmer, but perhaps less vital. Sorokin also expected that it would be less materialistic, more concerned with ideas. Spengler and Toynbee received particular attention because they agreed that this calmer period would also be the twilight of Western civilization, and that if it followed past experience, it would eventually dissolve in chaos and anarchy, to be succeeded by a new dark age. Such had been the fate of Greco-Roman, Mesopotamian, Minoan, Egyptian, Indian, Chinese, Mexican, Andean and perhaps other civilizations.

These civilizationists were very much affected by the new scientific paradigm. They employed relational methods in treating tremendous historical units such as civilizations as comparable social systems. They responded to the drive for syntheses by combining information from a large number of fields such as science, anthropology and aesthetics into a unified theory. They took advantage of the technology of the time, which supplied new information on the ancient civilizations. And they exerted their Faustian propensities to project themselves out of their own world and into others.

How relevant has their analysis proved to be for our own times? In many respects it has proved to be quite accurate. The crisis has been resolved. We are living once again in a calmer period. Materialism may be on the decline. There is no single empire, but there may be special reasons for that. Perhaps the Relational Age is more vital than the comparative historians anticipated, but it is nevertheless a period of working out, not of innovation.

But is the Relational Age a twilight period? Is this a last calm before the "decline of the West?" Considering the number of problems that are being stashed away for resolution in the future—the population expansion; the problem of economic growth in a period of declining materialism; the harrowing difficulties facing underdeveloped countries; the normal tendency for bureaucratic institutionalization and the availability of nuclear weapons for the next crisis period—the "decline of the West" seems to be a distinct long-run possibility.

In the past civilizationists have observed an interesting transformation between the development of war and civilization. For much of the period of development, war is not harmful to a civilization and is sometimes helpful, in that it encourages economic development and provides national unity. But when civilizations are really in decline, war is overwhelming, ubiquitous and disastrous. All hell breaks loose and there is no recovery. There is a correlation, also, between the quantity of war and the size of a civilization. For a very large civilization like the Western, even World War II was a stimulant. Though it was a ghastly war and deaths numbered in the tens of millions, it led to economic recovery from the Depression and a resolution of the problems that had brought on the crisis. The civilization of the succeeding period has never been richer, nor more successful. A major nuclear war, however, would clearly have a different effect. It would have sufficient magnitude to terminate Western civilization.

Most civilizationists, however, do not agree with Spengler that the course of a civilization is inevitable. Many do agree that there is a tendency for interstate systems to terminate as empires. An interstate system is a system of autonomous political entities that relate to one another, as do the nation-states of the world today. Eventually a challenging state emerges, defeats all the others, and forms an empire that incorporates the previously autonomous states. Thus the Ch'in state conquered all others in China's period of contending states and created what became the Han Empire; thus Rome challenged the states of the ancient world and formed the Roman Empire (Wesson 1978; Wilkinson 1985, 1986).

In arguing for the possibility of peace in our time, I have noted that there have been several challenges to the Western interstate system, each of which constituted a crisis and each of which resulted in the defeat of the challenger by coalitions of other states. Other histories also show such challenges, such as the challenge of Carthage in the third century B.C. or of Macedonia in the fourth. When we are concerned with the formation of empires, however, we tend to focus only on the successful challenges, without noting that the preponderance of such challenges are unsuccessful. Thus the argument that the present peace will last 10 to 15 decades is based on the assumption that previous patterns will be repeated and that there will then be some new challenge, and with the challenge the next crisis. Since such challenges have involved war, and since the stakes are higher in such periods and emotionalism more likely to dominate, it follows that war would involve nuclear weapons. If Napolean or Hitler had won, there would have been an empire. Nuclear weapons, however, may undercut the process and prevent the victor from completing the unification, the destruction being so great that the whole civilization rather than the individual state system is terminated, prematurely from the civilizationist's viewpoint, and doubtless from the viewpoint of survivors as well.

Whether the empire could be formed or not, what is important with relation to peace is that the civilizationists observe that the termination of an interstate system has always been accomplished by conquest, never by federation or any other kind of agreement. So, if their analysis is valid, it is not likely that some sort of federation leading to world government could be peacefully accomplished.

In fact, from the viewpoint of Spengler, the general desire for world federation would be a sign of an approaching civilizational conquest. The conquest is made, not so much because of the formidability of the conqueror as because of a general readiness to accept government from any source that promises to bring peace. Thus very capable leaders like Napoleon and Alexander failed, Napoleon strikingly because of the vigor of his opposition, particularly Britain and Russia. But when there is a desire for peace at any price, then there will be peace—after a bloody conquest.

The alternative possibility suggested by a R. S. Scanlan (1985) should be recalled. In considering past transitions to empire, Scanlan says, we have assumed that the conquerors dominated the world. The Achaemenids dominated the Mesopotamian world, but the classical world was beyond their realm. Darius's unsuccessful ventures against the Greeks were much like the Romans' unsuccessful efforts to conquer the Parthians—an annoying but peripheral problem. In the same sense, Scanlan says, there is more than one "world" today, and we have admitted as much with our use of the term "Third World." The first and second worlds, therefore, are the West and the Soviet bloc, each separate civilizations. The Russians, despite their interactions with the West, are the heirs of Byzantine civilization and, in fact, represent the latest phase of the Byzantine Empire. The earlier empire of that name, was for most of its history one of several states in an interstate system.

The West, it follows, is a separate civilization, either in an interstate system phase or, possibly, already in an imperial phase with the United

States as the conquering power. The war in which the conquest occurred was World War II, and the Carthage of the period was Germany. The Americans, like Napoleon, leave their client states limited autonomy and the illusion that they run their own affairs, just as their Russian counterparts do in Eastern Europe, except that the Americans are more relaxed and less boorish in their domination.

Scanlan's version provides a way out. Instead of worrying about the Russians, we would need to worry only about the management of the American "Empire," allowing as much autonomy as possible, and preventing the rise of any other power that could threaten American hegemony. Let Russia manage her own, however boorishly. Nor need America worry about Japan; let China worry about Japan if there is to be a coming struggle for dominance in East Asia.

If Scanlan's analysis were to prove valid, the problem of peace would be simplified. Instead of several decades of peace, there might be a couple of centuries. Empires have other problems, including a loss of vitality and economic stagnation. The appearance of the latter in both the United States and Russia provides a modicum of support for Scanlan's theory.

If, on the other hand, the viewpoint of the majority of civilizationists is correct, then Russia and the West are still sharing an interstate system, and if it behaves as its predecessors have, we are in a period of calm that is likely to end in a crisis, probably in the latter half of the twenty-first century, which has been the basis of the analysis of this essay. In that case, given the probability of a growing chance of crisis as the twenty-first century progresses, the question is whether anything can be done in the meantime to deal with those factors that, left untended, would be likely to exacerbate the crisis or render it unresolvable.

THE NUCLEAR DILEMMA

Recently residents of a small midwestern community were asked about their expectations for the community in the next ten years. Some people thought it would stay pretty much the same, others were worried about urban encroachment. The worst thing they could think of was the possibility of condominiums being built in nearby cornfields.

Not one person suggested that the community might be destroyed by a nuclear war (Koebernick and Orenstein 1989).

In a 1988 class on "The Nuclear Threat," 28 students were asked about their three greatest concerns and what they expected to be doing in 1998. No one expressed a concern about nuclear war, and all but one expected to be engaged in peaceful and prosperous employment ten years hence.

To test this, members of that class designed a survey in which they first asked general questions, then nuclear questions. Table 6.1 shows some of the answers they got.

TABLE 6.1
FEAR OF NUCLEAR WAR
1988 SURVEY

1. What is your major concern today?

Possibly Nuclear		Other than Nuclear	
n	%	n	%
2	2	130	98

2. What do you think you'll be doing ten years from today?

Nuclear Affected?		Nuclear Free	
n	%	n	%
2	2	129	97

3. How do you feel about the future?

Optimistic		Pessimistic	
n	%	n	%
103	73	12	9

4. Do you think a nuclear war is probable?

Yes, within 20 years		Not in my lifetime or ever	
n	%	n	%
29	21	94	68

5. Are you concerned about nuclear war as a threat to children?

No or moderate concern		Strong concern or wouldn't have children for fear of	
n	%	n	%
94	67	46	33

6. Are you afraid there could be a nuclear war at any time?

Yes		No	
n	%	n	%
32	23	107	76

7. Do you consider nuclear war a threat to your life?

A major threat		One among many		Generally do not	
n	%	n	%	n	%
7	5	53	38	81	58

Only people in the 18–29 age category were surveyed. Within this category, only 2% expressed anything remotely concerned with possible nuclear war when asked an open question, and only 9% were pessimistic about the future.

But when asked about nuclear war, 21% thought one was probable in 20 years, 23% were afraid there could be one at any time, and 33% were strongly concerned about nuclear war as a threat to their children.

If you ask people, even children, if they are worried about nuclear war, they will say yes. Responsible people are supposed to be concerned about nuclear war. But if you ask them open questions about their own future, mushroom clouds are simply not on the horizon.

It could be that people are just irresponsible. Not having experienced even the memory of a nuclear war, they just don't worry about it. Or it could be that they are repressing the worry. Or it could be that they genuinely are not concerned because they sense the contexts of the situation.

Our time may be one of anxiety, but it does not seem to be one of overwhelming fear. People are worried about mortgages and college expenses. They are concerned about being stuck in a dead-end job. They do fear dying of AIDS or Alzheimer's Disease. They jog and watch their diets to prevent heart attacks. They give up smoking to prevent cancer. But they don't worry much about what they can't do much about.

Is this realistic? Is it responsible? When we buy insurance we protect ourselves against the more likely catastrophes: death, fire, automobile accidents. We hesitate on more specific kinds of insurance, such as insurance against tornadoes. And we are not inclined to insure against nuclear destruction, not because we think it couldn't happen, but because we doubt the ability of our insurance company either to protect or compensate us. These are realistic and responsible choices.

If everyone were to be worried about nuclear war, to make that the first priority in their life's work, the social consequences would be severe. It is probably just as well that only a few devote their lives to the cause of peace. They may have some successes, but if they don't other things will still get done. And one can understand what C. P. Snow means when he says that after the war, J. D. Bernal rather wasted the remainder of his life on world peace, when he might have done something really useful (Halperin 1983).

If people are not preoccupied with nuclear war, it may be that there is a general perception that we are no longer in a crisis situation. While long-run disaster is possible, it is not likely to interfere with next Saturday's wedding, party or ballgame. It has been suggested earlier that our present situation may be compared to the Victorian Age, when there were problems to be solved, and they were indeed solved, or at least ameliorated. If the argument that we are in a period of lower risk is granted, and if there were time to resolve the problems, what is resolvable, and what is not?

Over the next several decades, for instance, countries may reduce arms expenditure as a percentage of gross national product. By the middle of the twenty-first century, the arms race might be over and with it, some of the economic problems to which the arms race contributes.

If confidence is retained in second strike capacity, something also might be done to reduce the chance of accident. Either computers would be made more accurate, or there might be less reliance on computers if there were reasonable certainty that there would be time to assess data before a response was needed.

The very factors that could bring about a reduction in the arms race and a general relaxation can also increase the danger of war in another way. Some historians have perceived the *Pax Britannica* as contributing to World War I. The statesmen of that period had no memory of any previous general war except some of them remembered the Franco-Prussian War, which had been resolved in six weeks. This may have made them more receptive to war as a possibility in the summer of 1914. The general populace, moreover, was likely to accede because war was interesting, a kind of summer sport that one might follow vicariously in the daily papers, rooting for the home team.

On the other hand, there have been states that have had long periods of peace that have been reenforced by positive valuation of peace. The Swiss seem always to be aware of the value of peace in their precarious situation among great powers. In quite a different situation, the Chinese have welcomed unification of the country as the normal situation, and its preservation as something desirable. This has allowed the country to remain peaceful for decades or even centuries after the government has lost its effectiveness, and the situation would seem to be open for revolution and usurpation.

In our time there has been considerable awareness of peace as a value. There have been active proposals and experiments including peace studies, which are highly value-oriented and normative in content, in the school curriculum. Middle-class social action groups have been strongly peace-oriented. While their proposals, from nuclear freeze to arms reduction discussions, may not be realizable or even contribute much to peace if they were realized, the attitudes inculcated could be important. If valuing peace were genuinely assimilated by governments, they would be more inclined to look for alternatives, to regard war as an undesirable choice in their range of options.

So the experience of peace could either increase or decrease the desire for peace. At present there seems to be a reasonable chance that peace will continue to be valued and that war will be considered a relatively undesirable alternative.

But, again if the argument presented here is accepted, there will come a time, probably well into the twenty-first century, when relationships are no longer easing, and tensions begin to build because the next crisis is approaching. The balance of power will become less stable as new powers arise, the leaders and people of which feel excluded from full participation in the world system. The relational outlook will be challenged by a different outlook, perhaps one less favorable to peace. Irrationality, emotion, and ideology will begin to play a large part in world affairs. A situation will develop that is analogous to the Edwardian period, or the last days of the ancien regime. What would need to be resolved to prevent nuclear war from occuring as the crisis approaches?

The existence of usable nuclear weapons itself would become a problem in such a period. There is no way to get rid of them. If they were to be eliminated, the knowledge of how to reconstruct them would still be present, and in such a crisis period they would be reconstructed. So the weapons would be available in a period when their use is less inconceivable, in a period in which destruction may be perceived to be preferable to surrender of a particular way of life or a principle. Whereas in the present the odds against nuclear war may lengthen each decade, with the approach of crisis, each year they would shorten.

Figure 6.1 illustrates the problem. Let's suppose in 1950, the days of the Cold War and Korea, there was a 3.5% chance of nuclear war. By 1960 things had not improved much, with an aggressive Khrushchev in power, and an equally macho John F. Kennedy about to become the American president, and with the Berlin Wall and Cuban Missile Crises soon to follow. Suppose the chances were 3% in 1960, good odds when you consider that Kennedy himself felt they were between 33 and 50% during the Cuban Missile Crisis.

But then things begin to get better. By 1970 there is Vietnam, with no threat in that, Nixon and Brezhnev in power, and the Yom Kippur War still to come. Say a 2.5%?

The situation further improves. Suppose the chances drop to 1% in 1980, 0.5% in 1990 and a bottom of 0.3% in 2000 and 2010. Then the Relational Age begins to shift from "latency" to a new phase, with a gradual but modest increase in danger, say 0.5% in 2020, rising to less than 2% by 2050, after that accelerating to around 3.5% in 2070, about what the Cold War chances were in 1950.

If all of this sounds plausible and illustrative of the thesis, it is disconcerting to learn that if there is even an average of 1% chance of nuclear war in a given year, over a 64-year period there would be almost an even chance of a nuclear war. During the safest period, from 1980 to 2040, by this hypothetical estimate, there would be a 36% chance of nuclear war. This provides a basis of logic to the reasoning of people, described in the survey (table 6.1), who thought there would be a nuclear war in 20 or 40

Figure 6.1
Chances of Nuclear War in a Given Year

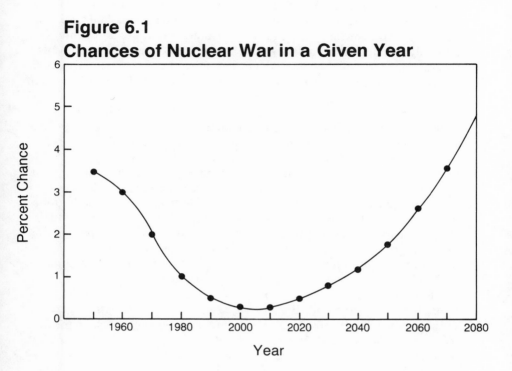

years, but weren't worried about it today. As Kenneth Boulding says, an event for which there is a small chance in a given year becomes a probability over time. If there is such a curve, then, even at lower figures, an eventual nuclear war would be probable unless something happens to change the situation radically.

What nation is to challenge the system? A recent view is that both the United States and the Soviet Union have become centralized bureaucracies incapable of the flexible development necessary for the employment of high technologies. They have the resources for basic research, however, with the result that they are producing innovations that are being developed by the Japanese system, which seems designed for implementation. If this continues, will not Japan become the dominant economic country and, if so, can political dominance be far behind (Desai; Goldman; Reich: all 1987)?

Well, it does not follow that economic development leads to political dominance. Germany and the United States had fantastic economic booms between 1860 and 1900; Germany became a dominant military power, the United States did not. On the other hand, a vital economy is certainly important for military development, and Japan, over the next several decades, could become the new dominant power. If so, this would be following the pattern of modern history, and could lead to another crisis.

The emergence of the challenging power is not inevitable. It has been characteristic in history and unless changes take place, it is likely that such a power will again emerge. It is likely, but not inevitable.

There is no obvious solution to this problem. All that can be said is that there have been other periods in which no one had a solution, yet a solution later emerged. Population booms were threatening Europe with permanent decline when the opening of a world frontier completely transformed the situation and started the burst of development now regarded as modern history. Many people think in those terms, with outer space as one desperate resolution. But it is a very unconvincing resolution and moreover, rather conservative. It is simply a hope that what happened unexpectedly 500 years ago will somehow happen again.

If history has shown that problems are resolved by unexpected solutions, it may do so again. But in that case, it is not likely that someone writing before the solution becomes apparent would perceive it. In the first place, "worldview" is against it. The solution, if it comes, would come out of a changing worldview, and this is not yet possessed. If, by some exercise in lateral thinking, one were to hit upon the solution, it would be implausible by today's standards. One could list a dozen implausible solutions, and one of them might prove to be close to the mark, especially if it is sufficiently vague, but there doesn't seem to be much use in that.

The alternative would be that the problem will not be solved, the weapons will be present, irrationality will increase, the crisis will explode, and the large-scale nuclear war will occur. Exercises concerning response to that are already plentiful. In any case, the war itself would certainly represent the end of peace in our time.

From the present perspective, this seems to be the more likely outcome.

Are there any visible reasons to hope that nuclear war could be avoided? Perhaps. One hopeful possibility would be the reduction of defense budgets as a percentage of gross national product. This might happen by a series of decisions not to produce particular weapons systems or, since we think of defense in relation to GNP, it might actually involve a bill to relate both defense and national debt to GNP. This might be followed by reductions in other countries, though it would be some time before there would be an awareness of that. Once there was awareness, there might be a move to reduce the defense budget in some systematic way, again with reciprocation following in other nations. Such a gradual reduction in military contracts would also reduce domestic hardship that would be felt by employees of weapons producers (Welty 1984), which would also make such an approach politically more acceptable. Arms reduction in this way seems more likely to take place and more likely to be effective than would arms control agreements. The latter, in fact, are likely to be manifestations of the former, if they have any meaning at all.

It is also more likely that unilateral reductions will be gradual than spectacular. Since the nuclear dilemma is so dramatic, it has seemed to even our wisest analysts (e.g., Kennan 1981) that some kind of dramatic gesture is necessary, such as a unilateral declaration of a 50% reduction, or a proposal that both major protagonists reduce armaments by 50%. This is not likely to happen in normal times, and if it did, would be greeted with alarm or disbelief, and would be very difficult to implement. A reduction over time, by a combination of votes against new proposals and the gradual obsolescence of what exists is politically much more feasible in either a despotic or a democratic country.

Another possibility would be an expansion of representative government in fact as well as form. The form is pretty general now. The fact could follow to a limited extent. Indeed, it is limited in democratic nations now. It need not involve a multiparty system. Japan has had a de facto one-party government, but most would consider Japan a democracy. All that is needed is a system in which alternative views can be represented within a one-party system. As noted previously, there has been research (Babst 1964, Melko and Hord 1984) that indicates that representative governments are less likely to fight one another and, in the past two centuries, more likely to produce long periods of internal peace. The research has been less than satisfactory in terms of explanation. It does not, for instance, suggest whether the existence of despotic governments contributes to interdemocratic peace. But few of us think that Britain, France and the United States are likely to fight one another. Why not? Would the situation be different if Russia became a modified republic? Russia aside, would we feel more secure if Britain, France and the United States were the only nuclear powers, or would that change the outlooks of those three countries? I'm not sure about the answers to these questions, but if there is a possibility that representative democracies are less likely to fight one another, then that could be a factor in perpetuating peace in the twenty-first century. If there is a relationship between authoritarianism, sexual repression, and war (Eckhardt 1975), then sexual and political liberation may contribute to breaking that combination.

A possible third factor would be the problem to be discussed later in the chapter. If the problem of disappearing fossil fuel proves to be real, and if the many difficulties around the development of nuclear power prove to be too recalcitrant to solve, then a growing nuclear energy problem could contribute to the stagnation, so to speak, of the nuclear war dilemma. The search for solutions to the energy problem could provide a world problem of sufficient magnitude to lead to cooperative ventures rather than conflict. If there were enough success to warrant continued research, and enough decline in living standard to focus attention on this search, perhaps that would reduce interest in the problem of rising nations not having their share of world power. If brownouts, power shortages, television hour regulations, fuel coupons and the like interfere enough with daily lives, there might be more attention to these problems, and less concern about territorial sovereignty. It would not be the first time a problem was resolved because another problem proved to be more interesting.

From our present perspective, no one of these possible factors would solve the nuclear dilemma. If there are unresolvable differences of great importance, countries will fight at their current level of armaments, and race to make more, as the Americans did during World War II. If representative democracies have been less inclined to fight, is there something in their governmental processes that enabled them to resolve differences, or did they just not have irreconcilable differences? If there is a compelling resource shortage, might that not be a cause of war rather than a distractor? If all these factors are taken together, however, they could produce different results. Nations armed only defensively, accustomed to working together to resolve problems, encounter a major long-term problem that commands their attention and calls upon them to use with greater intensity the methods of operation that have been working to resolve lesser problems. It is possible, but not compelling. It is suggested as one of a number of possibilities that can be foreseen from our present situation. But again, it is unlikely that any future resolution would be foreseen in the present.

None of these possibilities would solve permanently the nuclear dilemma. The know-how will always be there and the dilemma could always reemerge. But so can totalitarianism, slavery and feudalism. It is best to take life one century at a time.

THE ECOLOGICAL CLOUD

The principles of economics have been based on the factors of production: land, labor and capital. Much of the debate has been on the combination of labor and capital acting on land. It has been presumed that the capacity of the land was infinite.

While it is difficult to evaluate the seriousness of ecological problems, particularly the availability of energy, there seems to be some agreement among participants in the debate about the situation in our time. We may run out of fossil fuels to the extent that we cannot depend on them as the primary source of energy for more than several decades. Then they will have to be replaced by nuclear energy, or by solar power, or by some combination of solar, nuclear and other sources of power, or by something we have not yet perceived. The period of grace may be extended by reversion to coal, which could give us several more decades, unless greater use of coal creates a CO_2 problem that would cause a mild rise in temperature and an unacceptable level of ocean flooding. If the problems that prevent the development of nuclear energy have not been solved by then, there may have to begin a process of decentralization involving an increase in local production, a switch from service to agriculturally based production, and other changes that may be ecologically healthy and relationally appealing, but which have the look of a reversion to agrarian society (Rifkin 1981; Henslin and Light 1983).

There appear to be hopeful aspects to this problem. If a shortage of energy could lead to reduction in the construction of unnecessary roads, the manufacture of big cars, the desiccating heat of public buildings and ostentatious outdoor advertising, so much the better. If it means less travel and more local enterprise, the replacement of agribusiness by the organic family farm, that could have beneficial effects on the moral quality of our society and on our regional creativity. The relational outlook seems to have prepared the way for such a transformation, with its greater emphasis on social relationships, and its capacity to find value in nonmaterial aspects of our culture. One could almost look forward to this prospect as a kind of gigantic monastic retreat, a cleansing of the collective cultural soul, a return to some of the old values while maintaining some of the new. With such a transformation, might there not be a return to some of the better aspects of medieval times, the just price instead of the market price, the commending of one's being to one's God rather than the arrogance of individualism, but all of that tempered by our hard-won knowledge, our more humanistic perspectives? We might live in harmony with nature, rather than dominating it, and that would include a sense of maintaining a stable population rather than assuming perpetual increase (Rifkin 1981). All of this has a healthy sound in terms of what we hear about our stressful lives. It also seems to go with a decline in pollution from high energy, fossil fuel sources and the development of a conservation ethos. All healthy, good for our bodies, good for our characters.

This quiet, gradual, healthy resolution, however, seems unlikely to occur. Though it may appeal to the relational outlook, it won't appeal to the organizational structure, nor to our propensity for technological solutions. Even if those problems were surmounted, it hardly seems possible that reversion to agrarian society could be accomplished with less political turmoil than accompanied the onset of the industrial revolution. Moreover, such an agrarian society could again develop the characteristics of most such societies: great inequality, despotism, slavery perhaps, a loss of technological capacities including medical capacities preventing childbirth deaths and a decline in health systems leaving a population particularly vulnerable to contagious diseases. Knowledge does not determine social and political institutions. The knowledge of the Weimar Republic does not bring democracy to East Germany. A transformation to an agrarian society would not necessarily mean a transformation to a better society.

The ecological cloud seems likely to grow rather than diminish, to loom over our society rather than to dissolve. But as the analogy of the Lily Pad on the twenty-ninth day makes clear, the cloud is still small and distant, and though it grows rapidly, it will remain small for some time. By the time it is widely observed to loom, it will be too late. Adjustment to the diminution of energy sources, on the other hand, is likely to be catastrophic and violent.

The time before the looming becomes ominous is likely to be several decades. As with the nuclear dilemma, there may be several decades in which to solve the problem. If new insights are had within that period, well and good. If not, and the nuclear dilemma is not solved either, it is not unlikely that the two problems will catalyze each other. The growing ecological crisis will exacerbate the rising nuclear crisis, and vice versa. In that case, the ending of our time, the ending of our peace, is likely to be dramatic and decisive.

HUMAN NATURE

To say that both the nuclear dilemma and the energy problem pose problems that *may not* be solved is not the same as saying that they *cannot* be solved. Interesting and popular books in recent years (e.g., Lorenz 1966; Ardrey 1961) have been interpreted to mean that humankind is by nature aggressive and that no social structure nor technological solution can prevent this from manifesting itself in violence.

The implications of this assumption have been vividly summed up in a baleful "credo" that S. N. Goudsmit rightly believed would never be delivered by a television panelist:

> I believe that most people want war because I observe that pacifists are considered odd and misguided and are not to be taken seriously.
> I believe that wartime is the most unforgettable period in our life, the only time when we feel that we are doing our best, that our life is worth living and that our cause is worth dying for.
> I believe that the wave of anxiety which occurred, for example, during the Cuban Missile Crisis was mixed with a sense of excitement.
> I believe that an urge for self-destruction is part of man's animal nature and that the threat of over-population will be regulated only by an atomic suicide, similar to the periodic drownings of lemmings in northern Europe (Goudsmit 1963).

If it were in the nature of humanity to erupt in violence periodically, then there would not be much that could be done. No matter what laws and agreements there are, periodically there would be major eruptions of violence for species reasons, and when this collective instinct peaked, whatever instruments of violence were at hand would be used. Deterrence would be ineffective since destruction would be the purpose of our activity.

Indeed, the whole thesis of this book could be interpreted in these terms. The lemminglike cycles are described; we happen to be in a period of remission now, but it is certain that the violence will reemerge in the next crisis period. There is nothing to do but take advantage of the remission, and all long-term plans should be provisional. There is a good chance, as already observed in the previous sections, that this is how it will turn out.

Or else, perhaps, it may be argued that the bread and circus treatment is exactly the thing to prolong the remission. If man gets enough violence on television—boxing, football, violent crime, war films—he will be able to sublimate. Even increases in homicide and family abuse are not an unmixed disaster, since they can be interpreted as comparatively mild social substitutes for war.

Again, it could be argued that since it is the nature of *man* that is the problem, the emergence of *women* in the political arena is a source of hope, since women are more nurturing and protective of the lives they have been at such pains to deliver.

Human nature has also been used to explain the ecological devastation that seems to be occurring. Revisionists are saying that human society has always exploited its environment, even the American Indians who have sometimes been revered as "ecological saints" (Steinhart 1984). It is just that we have never before had the technological capacity to do such permanent damage. But this exploitative instinct, like the aggressive instinct, is innate in the species, and no rational action can overcome it.

Whatever happens, this human nature explanation seems unsatisfactory. Goudsmit's credo is an honest expression of the feelings of the older generation. The crisis period *is* exciting, and for some, ordinary times never provide the same opportunities.

Vicarious observations of violence do seem to be titillating for many people, but the vast majority do not practice violence themselves: they do not rape, murder or physically abuse members of their own family. Attempts to link television violence with violence in the world seem unconvincing, but if such a link were established, violence on television could be reduced without threatening an increase in war and revolution, or even homicide and family violence. Periods of peace of more than two centuries have been attained a number of times without the need of circuses and without any notable psychological dysfunctions. Some cultures—notably the Chinese, and probably the ancient Egyptian—seemed to have been so organized that people did not get on one another's nerves (Melko 1973).

As for women, the examples of Maria Theresa, Catherine the Great, Indira Gandhi or Margaret Thatcher do not suggest that women in power are more likely to be oriented toward peace than male leaders. After all, in the contemporary sense we are really discussing the nature of humans, and while women should be welcomed to the political arena, and their availability widens the pool from which political leaders may be chosen, other concerns besides gender alone dictate their actions and attitudes. They may make a substantial contribution to the resolution of what appear to be insoluble problems, but that will be on the basis of individual merit combined with cultural advantage, not gender alone. The requirements for leadership, even in normal times, are likely to appeal only to certain temperaments, regardless of gender.

The instinct to exploit is even less convincing than the aggression instinct. For most of history, people have not been facing the problem of overwhelming ecological catastrophe. They were confronting ecological pressure in the fifteenth century when the discovery of the New World took them off the hook. They have confronted ecological limitations in various regions, and shown themselves capable of living within harsh limitations of climate and resources. When last the problem was confronted on a worldwide scale, in several different places over a couple of millennia, the solution appears to have been the invention of civilization (Coulborn 1959; Edwards 1985).

Either the nuclear or the ecological dilemma may prove to be insoluble, but if that is the case, the failure will not lie in human nature.

FAMILY RELATIONSHIPS

The literature on contemporary social relationships is vast, and there is certainly a great deal in it that could lead one to believe that the world is on the abyss of a great social collapse, with the family system terminating in either divorce or violence, or else ceasing to exist because our never-married population grows to 100%. Much has been written about contemporary alienation and apathy, about the decline of the city, the general breaking down of the social bond.

My view is that if our central problem were the social bond, and perhaps it is, there is no danger whatsoever of its self-destruction. Changes have taken place since Victorian times, but they have not been devastating, and the case has been made that social relationships in the Present Age compare favorably with those of the past, e.g., the Victorian Age, the Age of the Baroque, or almost any other age.

It is probably an older generational approach to attempt to organize social relationships. The relational approach would probably be to write about whatever occurs and let that lead to whatever else until enough had been said and the system had been presented. But for the sake of coherence, I am going to mention just a few social relationships that are often perceived as symptomatic of breakdown: the breakdown of the family; cosmopolitanism; the loss of geographical roots; alienation of the individual from work and friends; and social inequality.

The decline of the family is reflected in the increasing divorce rate, the increasing percentage of singles in the total population, the increasing concern about family violence, changes in relations between men and women, the stresses of the prolonging of youthful dependence and the period of dependence of the aged, and the stress of work-related nomadism. The cumulative picture could be the impending dissolution of the family. But this death seems to be exaggerated.

Between 1960 and 1975 there was a marked change in the composition of population between marrieds and singles. The singles population over 14 in the United States rose from 32% to 37%. It seemed as if not only the extended family, but the family itself, was being challenged as a viable way of life. During the same period, the percentage of divorced population increased by 130%.

This was, however, a reversal of a long-term trend in the other direction that had persisted through the crisis period from 1900 to 1960, when the percent of the singles population had decreased from 44 to 32%, and of course the percent of married population had increased from 56 to a high of 68%. Much of that reversal is attributable to the population boom of the late 1940s and 1950s. Of the 19 million increase in singles population, 13½ million were never-married young people, people under 24 (Cargan and Melko 1982). To a considerable extent, therefore, the increased visibility of singles and that of the youth subculture are part of the same phenomenon—not a product of the relational outlook at all, but of the return to normal times. That progeny of normal times, however, is much more likely to possess a relational outlook.

The terrifying percentage of increase in divorce is greatly reduced in effect when translated to numbers. About 3½ of the 19 million can be accounted for by the increase in the number of divorced people in the country. That does probably represent the effects of a change in outlook. It is now a more acceptable alternative to seek divorce and to reject or defer remarriage.

But still, the increase in the percentage of singles has already peaked, and as the young marry, that percentage began to decline regardless of the trend in divorce. The percentage of married people in the United States, during the earlier decades of the Relational Age, is likely to remain several points above its level in the later decades of the Victorian Age (Cargan and Melko 1982).

Concern about family violence is not in itself a sign of an increase in family violence. On the contrary, it represents an increase in sensitivity to family relations. The first child abuse conference was held about 1960, and since then child abuse has been followed by concern for battered wives, battered elderly and finally all kinds of violence occurring within the family. The phrase "spare the rod and spoil the child" is an older generation celebration of what the younger generation would call domestic violence. Strapping children, swaddling clothes, child labor—there is no end to the list of family behavior that would today be considered violent, immoral, or even illegal (Shorter 1975). The very perception of family violence is a phenomenon of the relational outlook.

The development of women with careers, as distinguished from working women who work before and after child raising, does not seem to pose a crisis for the family. Studies of the families of career women do not seem to indicate a marked deterioration when compared to children of women who stay at home (Baruch & Barnet 1983).

The combination of the youth subculture with the plight of the aged probably represents social values in the normal period. A decade ago one would have had to explain the youth subculture, its independence, its turning against the older generation and the family, particularly on the issue of the Vietnam War, but on many domestic issues as well, in Europe as well as in the United States. But the decade has passed, the generation gap is disappearing as a subject of interest for reasons already explained (chapter one), and the generation that is now receiving more attention is another semidependent generation, the elderly. They are filling the nursing homes and gobbling up social security money at an alarming rate. Where they congregate in large numbers, as in Florida, they come to be perceived as a problem very similar to that of a society with an unusually high percentage of young people (Gustaitis 1982). Both of these age groups are demographic problems, the one fading as the other grows, though the generation gap had been compounded by the difference in outlook. The gap may reappear as increasing numbers of elderly have the older generation outlook, while their middle-aged children hold to relational views. This is leading to a good deal of conflict, as it did in the 1960s and 1970s. It is the last conflict the older generation will be able to make, and the relational younger generation is likely to be more indulgent than the action-oriented, instrumental older generation was about the foibles of the younger generation. The earlier conflict was solved by the growing power of the relational outlook in organizational society, by holders of the outlook growing up and taking power. The second conflict between the same two generations will be resolved, less happily, by the death of the older generation.

Organizational nomadism would seem to pose a threat to the family. If the percentage of men involved in organization work is increasing, it is likely that their families will live in several places as their careers develop.

What happens to families when children live in different states, and relationships must be maintained, if at all, by letter, phone and occasional visits? What happens to children who make friends at school, then are moved to a different school in a different state, not just once but several times? How can adults make friends if they move every few years and have to start over again? And what about the development of multinationals? Are there an increasing number of young people whose children are likely to grow up in Tanzania, Australia or Thailand as their fathers are promoted and move on?

Well, this is not a problem unique to our time. It has been American to move. When pioneers and homesteaders moved, they left their families behind for many years, if not forever. First generation Americans made a long sea voyage to another continent, had to learn a different language and the ways of another culture. A corporate move from Portland to Portland, on the other hand, would require very little change in style of living.

Europeans say of Americans that they are more immediately friendly, but it is difficult to form deep friendships with them. That would be what one would expect of a more mobile people. But it does not mean that the mobile people suffer more greatly in terms of mental health. Moreover, the children who were nomads growing up would naturally assume that nomadism is part of life, as have all nomads. And if they do live in other countries, they may learn something about deeper relationships, perhaps seek and find them on their own, perhaps maintain them by mail and visits. And, of course, organizational nomads form only a part of the population. A majority of people in Europe and America tend to live in the region in which they grew up. And if fuel shortages make travel more expensive, more regionalization may take place, and travel may play a lesser rather than a greater role as the age progresses.

Nomadism can be a problem for family relationships. But it is not that much greater a problem than it has been in the past, it does not apply to a majority of the population, generations growing up under it may not have greater mental health problems, and ecological considerations may reduce the amount that occurs in the future. It also appears that the extended family remains in touch with visiting, phoning and writing connections (Orenstein 1985).

It seems improbable, then, that the breakup of the family, or even a great increase in family stress, is likely in our time any more than in normal periods of the past.

THE BREAKDOWN OF SOCIAL RELATIONSHIPS

The other social relationships mentioned in the previous section that seemed possibly indicative of crisis were: cosmopolitanism; the loss of geographical roots; alienation of the individual from work and friends; and social inequality. The problem might be cut in other ways, but this list includes many of the kinds of social relations problems that are perceived to be critical. As you add more, you find you are discussing the same kind of things, and after some point you begin to perceive diminishing returns. Cosmopolitanism and alienation will be considered in this section; inequality will be reserved for the next.

In discussing cosmopolitanism some of the ground covered earlier when family nomadism was discussed, will be retraveled. Spengler (1932) saw the cosmopolitan as a recurrent phenomenon in civilizational history, the man who is at home in any big city, but out of place in any province. The city was draining the lifeblood of the civilization, bringing its most creative spirits to the megalopolis, where their creative impulses were merged and diluted. From the city there spread a sort of entropic universality, leaving the culture barren of creative impulse.

It was noted before that the rootless organization nomad may move from city to city, and his family from suburb to suburb. If he encounters similar people everywhere, is he cut off from creativity? The truly rural person is not easy to find in an age of mass communication and supermarkets. He is usually not a farmer, who is likely to be a businessman dealing with urban markets, technology and concepts. He might be found in tourist areas, making a living outsmarting complacent slicks. But will he find heirs if his children go to urban regional schools? The rural village still exists, though Vidich and Bensman (1968) have shown us that it is controlled by the urban-educated superintendent-of-schools, borough attorney and clergyman.

We are, of course, aware of the decline of rural society and we make considerable effort to preserve what is left. Paths and parks are maintained all over the world, city parks, English footpaths from village to village, American state parks, wild commons, wildernesses, wildlife societies, re-created historic villages, organized birdwalks, Scout achievements, family camping trips, bird feeders, farm vacations, river canoe trips, mountain climbs. It is certainly possible to maintain bucolic contacts. That these facilities are widely used does not prove that there may not be a substantial proportion of urban populations who never use them, and it may be that they are thereby culturally or aesthetically or nutritionally deprived. The local and associational efforts to reserve such areas, however, are very much alive. They are available if a need is perceived, probably to a greater extent than they were in any other age.

Whether cosmopolitanism is also harmful to a sense of family history is difficult to determine. Interest in family roots may be a source of pride and confidence, just as a family name may be a source of reenforcement. But insofar as it is weakened, it also means that others who lacked such support are less at a disadvantage.

Nor does the expansion of the city mean the destruction of the community. The existence of associations, particularly in America, provide communities of interest. The relational outlook, combined with the fact of cosmopolitanism, may contribute to the phenomenon of these associations, though de Tocqueville indicates they long have been at least an American phenomenon. In any event, people seem to regard it as no inconvenience to travel a number of miles to meet at someone's home for Marriage Encounters, candle dippings, book club meetings, recorder practices, woodcock watches, peace marches, minimarathons, or even prayer (Naisbitt 1982). Small societies are formed that combine networks of interest that may be worldwide, even though physical meetings may be infrequent.

The large, cosmopolitan city seems itself to be a symbol of crisis. Cities are dangerous places, and their centers seem to be widening in patterns of sprawl and blight that are disheartening to experience. When encountering a blighted area along a strip-zoned road, it does seem as if some kind of decline and fall must be at hand.

But it is not easy to compare the present with the past. We can measure poverty, which has gone up and down in some sort of relative scale, and it figures that poverty and unpleasant living conditions will go together. If these occur in the central city, they will be visible. If they are in rural areas, or away from the central city, they will not. Violent crime has been up, but it peaked in the late 1970s and has been declining, as it did in the United States in the 1930s and before that in the 1860s. The causes are complex. City slums are no novelty, nor is city crime. The descriptions of Lewis Mumford (1961) indicate that cities were worse places to live in the nineteenth century than they are now. And Robert Lane (1969) has shown how violent crime declined for a whole century in Boston while people in the city perceived it to be increasing. What was really increasing, therefore, was awareness. In the same sense it is not easy to ascertain for the developed world over a period of time whether the city is or is not a worse place to live than it has been at various times in the past, and if it is, whether there are suburban or rural compensations.

But the persistence of slums and violent crime, while part of life in all periods of modern and medieval history, do not in themselves tell us much about normality of social relationships. Many slums continue because their populations are transitory. They are cheap places to live while people are hoping to improve their lot. Many do. Even if they fail to rise socially, the poor often experience a vital social life within what the middle class perceives to be a slum. If the city becomes more attractive as a workplace, more will be attracted from the rural areas and slums may expand. If rising mortgage rates, gentrification, urban renewal, "white flight," tax base withdrawal, failure of cities to maintain import replacement mechanisms, and other factors reduce the availability of cheap urban housing, the poor will have to either remain impoverished in rural areas or become part of the visible urban homeless population of the 1980s and 1990s (Forester 1969; Jacobs 1969; Banfield 1970; Gans 1962; "We Will Not be Moved" 1980).

The continued existence of the city will mean the continued existence of city problems. Cities will always be disorderly, dangerous and unpleasant as well as compelling centers of excitement and vitality. They are always in a process of disintegration and renewal, and what is regarded as an urban crisis is really a normal process to be found wherever cities are found.

Charles Silberman (1978) warns against complacency in this kind of analysis. He thinks the viciousness of American crime in the 1970s was particularly great, and that to dismiss it as a recurrent process of ethnic assimilation is to overlook the particular pattern of discrimination suffered by the American Negro. That may be so, and the pattern of exceptionally angry violence of this period may be attributable to the opening of possibilities through school integration and affirmative action, the reducing of support groups as black middle classes were able to move out of cities, and the difficulties city schools have experienced in preparing black children, particularly black males, for higher education. All of this may be so, but still the extent of violence, most of it black on black, would seem to be part of the price paid for the decades of repression that ensued from the 1890s to the 1950s. This is precisely the working out of a normal problem from a relational standpoint after a long delay that was brought on by a crisis period particularly loaded with racial intolerance throughout the Western world, for it was the concept of racial purity that led to the reclassifying of a religion as a race preceding the European genocide against Jews of 1939–1945.

Organizational mobility and cosmopolitanism imply social alienation. If individuals move frequently, they cannot maintain deep social relationships. If they are cut off from their roots, their relationships acquire nomadic aspects, perhaps assuming new acquaintances are like the old, using them as props, or for special purposes such as bridge or tennis partners, but failing to see them as people, as a whole. Yet certainly there would be a longing for deeper relationships, unarticulated though this desire might be.

Added to this there is the idea, deeply reenforced in organizational psychology, that the individual is alienated from work, either because he does manual work that is repetitive and meaningless, or because he does organizational work in which he sees only a small part of the whole, e.g., the processing of company insurance forms (Savells 1972).

This double alienation, from work and from family and friends, leaves a large percentage of our population in the developed world in a damaged psychological condition, with the result that desperate efforts are made to compensate through spectator activities, such as watching television or mass spectator sports, or through various kinds of social groups or work-shops on interrelationships, such as Marriage Encounter or EST. The younger generation tried to cope by dropping out of the work situation, or by living in experimental situations such as communes, or with drugs.

On the other hand, alienation is not a novel theme in the twentieth century. Marx made the idea central in his appraisal of the nineteenth century situation, and we certainly find it in the Victorian novel, in which so many characters are fighting to find a place, from the middle-class women of Trollope's *Phineas Finn* (1869) to the working class of Bennett's *Clayhanger* (1910). Writers, of course, are people who think about the society they live in, which is automatically alienating.

It may be, also, that normal times are more alienating than crisis times. The crisis unifies people, fighting against the enemy or the economic spectre, with peace as the goal. Once peace is obtained, however, each individual must find his own way. He has choices, and there is no longer unanimity about what is to be achieved. No activity is automatically validated. If what is being done is, in addition, not particularly interesting in itself, alienation is understandable, especially in contrast with the crisis.

The growth of democracy may be a factor here, encouraging people to think for themselves, to develop as individuals. Rimland countries like the United States, Canada and Australia may be particularly susceptible here. The very groups that represent a response to alienation often stress that it is all right to be concerned about oneself, particularly women who have long been socialized to sacrifice their own well-being to men. On the whole the development of individualism and self-sufficiency can be seen as a gain, but an increase in alienation may be one of the consequences.

Searching for relationships, on the other hand, need not be compensa-tion for the alienating nature of society. If there is a relational outlook, we may expect those who share in it to develop it in different ways. The various counseling and relational workshops would appeal to people who want to spend more of their time in relational activities, not necessarily because they are alienated. In fact, such groups may create a greater desire for relationship, a greater awareness of its absence, so that participants in such activities would be more aware of the difference between reality and possibility. They would not be more alienated, but more aware.

Marriage Encounter, for instance, portrays contemporary marriages between "married singles." The husband goes to work and the wife stays home or goes to her own work. When they are home, they are often preoccupied with activities involving the children, or they bring their work home. They go to bed tired and sleep back to back. They may have had many human interactions in such a relationship, but not with each other. The desire to deepen the marital relationship doesn't prove they were alienated before or are alienated now. Certainly the married singles con-cept would fit most of the arranged marriages of past periods, the marriages in which the woman stood behind the husband when he ate, and in which sexual relations for her meant meeting his needs and pregnancy. The attempt to add something more to such a relationship is risky. It may succeed, or it may open up unrealizable possibilities that lead to a perception of alienation and sometimes to divorce. But the attempt to add something is not in itself a disaster for society.

Nor is alienation from work an invention of our time. Factory work was just as dull in Victorian times and involved women and children to a greater extent for longer periods. Crafts were highly specialized and divided. Textile manufacture was usually not intrinsically interesting. The fuller, who did nothing but subject the fabric to a tightening process by mauling it in mud and water and then cleaning it off again, was not involved in an intrinsically interesting activity, nor did he have a feel for the total process. Much of our work in any period is hard and boring, but that does not end the peace or even the possibility of living a meaningful life.

POVERTY AND INEQUALITY

In looking at an imperfect world from the point of view of probabilities of relative peace, one is recurrently in danger of seeming inordinately callous by concluding that there is sufficient freedom in the world, or sufficient family interaction, to make conflict on this or that particular issue seem unlikely. This danger seems particularly manifest in the area of inequality, since it is the very progress in this area that makes anyone seem insensitive who seems to say that there has been "enough."

Through all of civilized history, men have been unequal. And even here, perhaps, I ought to explain that I mean men in the generic sense, a qualification that would not have occurred to a writer of any other age. In agrarian periods, class was related to landholding, and the possibility for vertical movement in normal times were limited. Today the possibilities for vertical mobility are greater, but they are still limited by education, and education is limited by income, wealth and family connections. Mobility will be defined in certain ranges. An automobile worker may become a foreman or a railway worker may become a stationmaster, but they are not likely to rise to the ranks of middle management.

When Sjoberg (1960) studied the preindustrial city, he found only two classes: upper and lower. But as he described the lower, it broke into further subdivisions consisting of higher status workers such as shopkeepers and artisans, as distinguished from lower status laborers, peasants and outcasts.

The same distinctions still exist. The higher status middle class in effect becomes an upper class that controls the upper echelons of the technostructure. The shopkeepers and artisans have been replaced by white-collar workers and skilled laborers, while the working class constitutes a lower stratum. Social mobility consists mostly, as always, of a movement from working to middle class. And there continues to be a supply of outcasts drawn from minority groups, immigrants and those who fail to fit into the educational system.

It does not matter how strong egalitarian ideals may be, people separate because any civilized system provides a wide variety of experiences. Man is a small group animal, and he associates with people with whom he can communicate. Even if discrimination because of appearance declines, people will discriminate in favor of congenial associates.

Even if a de facto class structure persists, it might be supposed that public education, open college admissions, the decline of nepotism and a wider acceptance of egalitarian attitudes would combine to provide greater mobility within the social structure. But it seems doubtful that this is really the case. For one thing, even in the preindustrial city there was a fair amount of mobility within the classes below the nobility. The children of peasants became workers and the children of workers were apprenticed to craftsmen. Moreover, the daughters of merchants married into nobility and upper-class rank could be achieved. More recently there have been self-made men who could rise quite rapidly in their own lifetime if they had luck and skill and became entrepreneurs in their own areas.

Today it is possible for the children of outcasts to get jobs and for the children of the working class to become skilled or to become members of the middle class through state college educations. But it is more difficult for an entrepreneur to rise on his own than it would have been two generations ago. On the balance, the amount of mobility does not seem to be radically greater than it was in the Victorian or Baroque Ages.

Nor does status seem more secure. Great men can still fall through unlucky investments. And middle-echelon organization men can still be reduced in status, as physicists, electronic engineers, teachers and merger victims have been, when the kind of skill they had spent years developing becomes obsolescent.

Stratification persists in this age, and so does mobility, both upward and downward. The contexts are different from those of the past, but the contours are familiar.

Within middle ranks, salary differentiation may become less important for stratification. Insofar as the relational outlook or an ecological orientation leads to reservations about material goods, sometimes not owning can improve one's social standing. Insofar as the organizational structure is full of arcane titles, where a person is in that structure may not have much social impact.

There is no question that social inequality persists where income is a factor. What is debatable is the extent to which poverty has declined, the distribution of income among various segments of population and the opportunities for minorities and people in other subordinated categories. Poverty has declined in our time. Real income in Europe is up ten times over what it was in the 1950s. Standards of living are up four times. Poverty in the United States, by measures that take inflation into consideration, is decisively down between the 1950s and 1980s; but the decline had ceased in the 1970s and the rate had started to rise again in the 1980s (Lauer 1983). Poverty in the world as a whole is probably up, a function of the rise of population and the failure of pesticides, new agricultural methods and technology to keep up with it. But this is a problem of the rest of the world, whether or not caused by a failure of invention, production or distribution in the developed world.

It is also true that the decline in poverty came to a halt, and probably went into reverse, in the 1970s and 1980s in many developed countries. It seemed in the 1960s, when growth rates were high, that government-defined poverty, in any event, could be eliminated. The failure to do so is disappointing, but it is a problem that can be addressed further. Skewed distribution of income, in which some people are absurdly wealthy and others incredibly poor, is a socially unpleasant fact to many (though not all). It may be that a higher percentage of people in our time agree that it is a social problem. But that we have failed so far to solve what no one else has solved is not likely to end the peace in itself.

In minority relations there has been a great improvement in the United States. A great change took place in the beginning of our period, in 1945–1955, which was supposed to be the height of the "Cold War." Integration of the armed forces, the advent of Jackie Robinson, the Montgomery Bus Boycott and *Brown vs. the Topeka Board of Education* all took place within this period. This was not only part of the atmosphere, it contributed to peace. The subsequent Civil Rights Movement was essentially peaceful. Even the riots of the 1960s produced very few casualties compared to war or almost any other kind of violence. It is hard to say whether similar patterns were occurring in Europe, but the British withdrawal from empire in this period may have been part of a changed perception, as was the failure of more determined nations to hang onto their colonies.

Today, whatever inequities still exist—and they do—there is no comparison to the 1950s, to the days of segregated buses and restaurants and public facilities and colleges.

And it isn't just racial minorities. Women, the handicapped, and those with minority sexual preferences have vastly improved life possibilities. Women also take more risks. They can be divorced and left to support children on an income lower than that of men. But it is hard to think of any period when women, except for the upper classes, have had such opportunities. Equality of opportunity has not been obtained, but the awareness of the inequality has been greatly increased.

The handicapped never were perceived as a minority until the Present

Age. They had been scarcely perceived at all. Young men and women maimed in limb, blind, deaf, speechless, are attending college and living in the world. They are immensely discriminated against, and resented for intruding by the able-bodied (the handicapped's term for honky), but at least the discrimination is perceived.

More is possible. More is always possible. But compared with most periods in civilized history, ours is a period of relative tolerance, relative accessibility, relative openness to upward mobility. This does not seem to be an age in which peace would be destroyed because channels were blocked.

THE PRICE OF PEACE

One area of major discomfort in our time is inflation. Countries all over the world have had periods of sharply rising prices that have been worrying to most of the working and middle classes. How can one be sure of the future if inflation exceeds wage increases over a period of time? Instead of an anticipated gradual increase in affluence, people have been finding that they have had to cut back, to sell the boat they had saved for, to send their children to state instead of private colleges, to remain in the house they have instead of moving to the more affluent section of town. There is a fear that it may get worse, and that retirement will be an experience in poverty rather than a reward. Most spend much more time worrying about this kind of problem than we do about the possibility of nuclear war.

We have already considered armament from the standpoint of its influence on peace. Even with challenges to Keynesian economics, it seems probable that armament is inflationary, since that which is produced cannot be consumed, and therefore those involved in armament are paid wages and salaries to be used in purchasing consumer items, but contribute nothing to the inventory of consumer goods. If armament remains constant in relation to gross national product, as it has been doing, it will continue its contribution to inflation.

Inflation has both positive and negative effects. It stimulates production and encourages new business enterprises. It benefits debtors. It can be stimulating to labor unions, which are needed to support the wage earner against the employer. On the other hand, it works against the creditor, the salaried employee, the retired. Insofar as it encourages hedging against inflation and planning for inflation, it is self-perpetuating. Insofar as governments combat it by making money more expensive, that is, by encouraging or allowing interest rates to rise, they can discourage investment and act against inflation's initial impetus for expansion. These are certainly complicated relationships involving delicate and tenuous balances, but in our time, in the developed world, they are not proving to be totally unmanageable. The horror of the German inflation of the 1920s, cited in every introductory textbook as an example of what can happen, has not happened, is not likely to happen again.

So far society has not had 20% inflation as a steady diet in the developed world, but that level has been reached in some countries for some years, often for more than one year in a row. People have come to expect inflation and have explicitly or implicitly endorsed wage indexing as a compensation. The concept of compensatory wage increases to keep up with inflation that are in addition to wage increases that raise real income have become common. If wage payers failed to do that, unions or associations would not fail to make clear that real incomes were falling, even though income figures may be rising. Since inflation reflects a relationship between quantity of money and available goods, it seems clear that indexing, which increases quantity of money without increasing production, is itself inflationary, and the more it is practiced, the more it will have to be practiced.

Indexing should do no harm to the individual. If he has an income of $15,000 when he buys an $8,000 car, and 6 years later has an income of $45,000 when he buys a $24,000 car, he is in approximately the same situation as if he had gotten no increase and the price of the car had remained constant. But certainly the psychology of the situation is different. In the inflationary situation, one might have the feeling of receiving spectacular wage increases and some frustration that one's standard of living does not change. In the stable price situation, one might have a depressed feeling of going nowhere. So the choice is between manic-depression and chronic depression.

In fact, though 20% inflation figures have been reached in some developed countries, prices have been comparatively stable in the first decades of our time. The United States may have an exaggerated response to a relatively low rate of inflation because it had a period of steady growth with little inflation between 1950 and 1970. From 1970 until quite recently, however, the U.S. had a spectacular price increase, at least as spectacular as drawn in Figure 6.2. In the comparable period of the Victorian Age, France, by comparison, experienced generally falling prices from 1815 until 1850, with a price rise taking place only after the establishment of the Second Empire. Thereafter prices fluctuated more, but wound up lower in the early twentieth century than they had been in 1850. It seems likely that the problem in our time will be maintaining a price ceiling; the Victorian problem was supporting a price floor.

The ability of government to control inflation by monetary policies may, in any event, be dampened by the organizational structure. To the extent that organizations invest out of retained earnings rather than borrowing from banks, they cannot be influenced by monetary policies. In fact, a long-term increase in monetary approaches to controlling inflation could lead to large corporations building their retained earnings and

FIGURE 6.2
Price Index: Victorian France and Contemporary U.S.A.

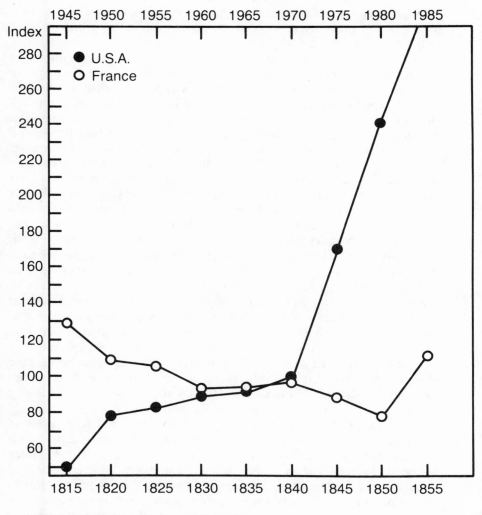

Wholesale Prices 1837, 1967 = 100
Sources: Mitchell, 1975, *Statistical Abstracts*, 1986

relying less on financial institutions. If a crisis were to arise, it might be a crisis of financial institutions, not of the corporate structure or the economy of the developed world.

The attempt to use monetary policies to curb inflation seems to have raised interest rates and created a housing shortage by making it more difficult to procure mortgages, and more difficult for the small contractors who build houses to borrow for new construction. Insofar as it has discouraged other small businesses, which have had greater difficulty borrowing, it has probably reenforced the organizational structure, whether or not that is more efficient.

Fiscal policy is conducted by manipulation of taxes as well as by government expenditure. Government expenditure provides immediate investment; the lowering of taxes provides additional income, much of which will go for consumption, which will stimulate investment. Figure 6.3 shows that after the first decade of the respective ages, taxes in Victorian England and the relational United States are comparable, even though the Victorians never heard of fiscal policy. A combination of income and property taxes were used for both periods, though property taxes were more important in the Victorian period and income taxes more important in the present period. The percentages taken were of what is being called national product, though the figures given for Britain were for national income, which may be comparatively a somewhat lower figure than the gross national product used today. If there is any error in this comparison, it is likely to represent the British taxes as being somewhat higher than they were, while U.S. figures would be about 2% higher if corporate taxes had been included. In any event, as Figure 6.3 shows, taxes as a percentage of the national product seem to have been fairly stable beginning from ten to fifteen years after the termination of the crisis. If they were higher in the United States, that could be a function of the graduated income tax. Incomes are probably higher per person in the United States than they were in the United Kingdom, and higher incomes pay a higher percentage of taxes. Whether that is a valid factor or not, there is no denying the steadiness of the taxation since 1960. It does not seem that overwhelming taxation would be a factor in upsetting the peace.

But what if taxes are too low, so low that they lead to a series of unbalanced budgets and, in the United States, a climbing national debt that has passed three trillion dollars? The recent debt of the United States has been alarming, and probably it could not continue to increase for long at the rate the Reagan administration had allowed. But even in this alarming period, the American debt is not overwhelming, in terms of percentage of budget used to pay off interest on debt, or in relation to gross national product, in comparison to earlier administrations of the Relational Age. But, in contrast to taxes, the debt as a percentage of national product is far

Figure 6.3
Income and Property Taxes as a Percentage
of National Product
Victorian England and Contemporary U.S.A.

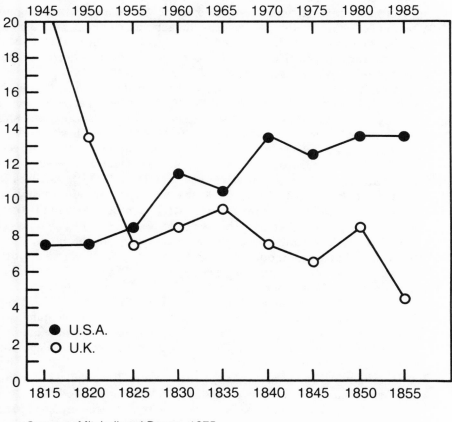

Sources: Mitchell and Deane, 1975
Statistical Abstracts, 1984

higher than comparable debts in Victorian times (see Figure 6.4). The American national debt fell as a percentage of gross national product through the 1950s and 1960s. In the 1970s, in the Nixon-Ford-Carter years, it leveled. In Reagan's first term it jumped back to the level of the Johnson administration during the Vietnam War. The British had no corresponding climb, despite the Crimean War. Some economists forecast severe consequences if the American debt continues to go unchecked (Rake 1986). Is the rise in the American debt a symptom of the beginning of the next world crisis, or just an idiosyncratic consequence of the policies of a government that happened to be oriented toward sharply increasing military expenditures without a corresponding increase in taxes? On the basis of information available, I would be inclined to believe that it is the idiosyncrasy of a particular government, and that the long-term decline of debt in relation to national product will resume in the 1990s.

One reason for believing the 1980 policy to be idiosyncratic is that Ronald Reagan, born before World War I, would be expected to have an older generational viewpoint. His successor, born in 1924, may still share this outlook. It may be 1996 before the United States has a president representing the viewpoint of the younger generation. (In fact, all recent presidents have been born in the hypothesized older generation period: Johnson in 1908, Reagan 1911, Nixon and Ford 1913, Kennedy 1917, Carter and Bush, 1924). Meanwhile the Soviet Union, after a series of older generation leaders, now has a General Secretary born in the transitional 1925–35 period (1931). This is not to argue that older people can't have younger generation outlooks and vice versa, but the probability of the younger generation outlook, with an expectation of normality rather than crisis, is more likely with a person born in the 1925–35 period, and much more likely in a person born after 1935.

An interesting footnote comes out of Figures 6.3 and 6.4. The British had a very high tax rate at the end of the Napoleonic Wars that quickly fell to a "normal" rate. The Americans seem to have had a similar experience with national debt. It would appear that taxes financed the Napoleonic Wars, while debt financed the World Wars.

International economics is a mysterious realm. It would take an economist of great sophistication to assess what is happening there. But a couple of observations may be possible. Free trade, once perceived to be a panacea, has never been achieved and isn't a panacea anyway. But this is a period of relatively low tariffs, and trade has developed in greater volume than in any preceding period, though perhaps not if measured of some sort of per capita basis, if such data were available. If trade isn't free, in any event, the volume is still high. There is a greater amount of trade, however, between the developed countries than between developed and underdeveloped. The developed countries are not buying the goods of the underdeveloped in sufficient volume to transform the latter's economies.

FIGURE 6.4
Public Debt as a Percentage of National Product
Victorian Britain and Contemporary U.S.A.

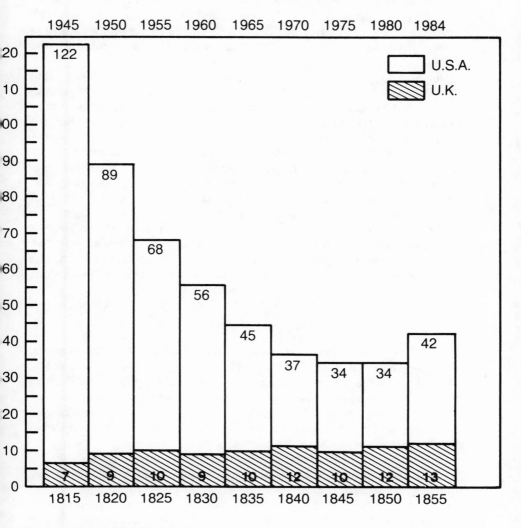

Sources: Mitchell and Deane, 1975
Statistical Abstracts, 1984

The floating gold standard may be a factor in the increase in trade, or maybe it isn't. But the idea of a floating gold standard is delightfully relational, since nothing is the basis of anything; even gold has a relative price, and since it has been an inflationary period, that price generally has been going up. When a nation runs short of currency, it can acquire more by buying gold, but buying gold bids it up, and makes the currency worth less. That, however, encourages imports and discourages exports, which bring in currency. Whether it works or not, the idea of floating gold, a gold that is never seen, just conceptualized, is a marvelous symbol for the Relational Age.

Is inflation to be permanent in our time? Not necessarily. Prices fell in the Victorian Age after the American Civil War. The great spurt of production in that period must have outdistanced the capacities for monetary expansion of the time. It is hard to see that occurring again. But the decline in belief in war could lead to a decline in military expenditure. Serious concern about ecological problems could lead to decentralization, more small-scale local production, a decline in trade. Perhaps the relational outlook will carry with it a decline in the work ethic, a willingness to accept less income and more leisure, and with a decline in demand for all these reasons, a decline in prices might follow.

Though rising prices have been a consistent phenomenon so far, it is not essential to the peace that prices continue to rise. It is probable that an absence of wild fluctuations would tend to support peace, but again, it is not clear that there is a close relationship between economic fluctuations and peace.

GOVERNMENT POLICY: IF . . . THEN . . .?

There is a charming convention among social and political analysts. After they have made some sort of analysis based on the way the world is, an analysis that is likely to be either controversial or ignored, they follow with a set of policy recommendations for the government of their country. It is hard to say whether they expect these pages to be copied and rushed to the appropriate ministers, or whether they are simply indicating what will happen when philosophers become kings.

In any event, the desire for an opinion from the analyst on what should be done seems strong. There is certain to be a question from the audience that goes something like this: "If the world is as you say it is, which I don't for a moment believe, then what should the government be doing about it?" You respond hesitatingly, because you know little about legislation or administration, and the questioner sits there shaking his head negatively (the government would never do that) or positively (he's just as looney as I thought).

Out of such questions, the following hesitant responses have been formed. If the government of a developed country were to assume that nuclear war is unlikely for the next several decades and that further accumulation of armaments would have little effect on national security, what kind of policy might it follow?

It might stress the facts of recent history. Spokesmen for the government might make the point that there has been less warfare in the developed world in the past several decades than there has been in any comparable period in the past quarter of a millennium. Instead of attributing this to the numbing accumulation of armaments by Russia and the United States, they may ask if it is not attributable to some extent to other factors and whether there are not diminishing returns to further armament. Such questions lead to a consideration of whether government funds might not be employed more usefully in other ways. If not, should taxes be reduced? At any rise, such questions and such alternative considerations would seem to be politically feasible in many countries. They may find greater sympathy among colleagues and be well received among the general public. A candidate may be able to win nomination and election by taking such an approach. The example of Japan suggests that a developed country may do very well without spending seven to fourteen percent of its gross national product on armaments.

In all discussions of weaponry, we are at the mercy of the speculations of experts whose hypotheses cannot be tested. It does not matter if some experts believe there is a "missile gap" or a "window of vulnerability." What matters is whether political considerations are such that a leader of either great power could believe his counterpart had decided to launch a nuclear war that would destroy his headquarters (not to mention him) and with it any plan for a counterattack. The emphasis of government policy, therefore, rather than being focused on the necessity of constructing any particular weapons system, should be focused instead on defusing confrontational situations and avoiding rhetoric that could contribute to fear of war (Schwartz and Derber 1986, 40–41).

If government and public attitudes were so reoriented, it might not be difficult to go a step further and reappraise relationships with Third World countries. Does the Third World pose any danger to the West? Why is there such a high rate of violence in the Third World, and can anything be done to reduce it? Are there indigenous causes beyond human control, or is the West itself a major contributor?

If a government can ask that much, it could then follow with questions about the economies of the Third World. Why are these economies developing so slowly? Why is there starvation and malnutrition in so many of these countries? Is it because they are not willing to adopt sensible population policies, or does it have something to do with our own policies? Do we encourage them to overdevelop their cash-crop exports at the cost of subsistence farming? Are multinationals based in our country imposing terms that Third World governments are unable to resist, even at the cost of the lives of their citizens? Should our policies toward these countries be based on their military or their economic responses (George 1977; Berger 1974; Lappe and Collins 1977)? If Third World hunger is related to arrested demographic transition, what are the alternatives? Is a combination of cash-crop and subsistence farming possible, so that farmers can produce for themselves, perhaps accumulate some cash-crop wealth of their own, and at the same time contribute to the capital growth of their nation? In other words, is there some middle route that would lead to continued development without causing great hardship on rural or displaced urban populations? And if there is, who needs to be persuaded: multinational companies or Third World governments? If such a solution were worked out, would that lead to further population explosion, and if so, how could that be managed? These are questions of tremendous urgency, difficulty and delicacy. But they might find a higher place on the agendas of developed countries if the danger of nuclear war occupied a lower priority and the development of the Third World were perceived to be of paramount importance.

The Soviet Union may be seen as a great rival by the United States, but it need not be seen as a dangerous threat. This perception goes back to the Cuban Missile Crisis, when the greatest concern was that the missiles might fall under the control of the Cubans, who could not be trusted. The implication, even then, was that the Russians could be trusted to look out for their own interests to avoid nuclear war. The Soviet Union, then, has a rational leadership with rather conservative objectives. The United States should entertain no great hopes of change. The Soviet Union has little to offer the United States politically, beyond spheres of influence agreements that have already been reached, and arms reduction in areas that are of diminishing concern to both nations. As adversaries go, the United States could do worse. No Hitler or Napoleon has sprung from the soil of Russia, not even a Gustavus Adolphus.

Disarmament negotiations should never be turned down, of course, but not much should be promised or expected. We would do better to point to a declining use of resources for defense by all developed countries, if such a decline can be achieved, and it should be measured that way rather than in actual currency or frightening lists of numbers and deployment of weapons.

Discussions should be held on the reduction of chance of nuclear accident, perhaps beginning with nuclear power accidents, then expanding to the danger of accidental missile release. It would be reassuring to all countries to know that the great powers are working on the problem, and this is an area in which secrets might be shared. If the Americans discover a way to reduce computer malfunctions and increase the Russians' safety, would it not be to their advantage if the Russians were able to introduce the same improvements, and increase the Americans' safety? (At the urging of Sam Nunn and John Warner of the U.S. Senate Armed Services Committee, a high-level Soviet-American discussion on preventing accidental nuclear war was held in 1986 (Gordon 1986).)

As an economic market, the Soviet Union could have a great deal to offer all developed countries, providing its government could be persuaded to produce goods and services that would be worth trading for. Perhaps such markets can be opened; perhaps a country can only wait and be supportive to its own industries while inquiries are raised. Certainly Manichaean "Evil Empire" rhetoric belongs to the older generation outlook and can no longer be of much use (Kavoloski 1986). If economic exchange with the Soviet Union were increased, this would probably have very little political effect. The benefits of greater economic exchange with the Soviet Union would have to be economic.

The Soviet viewpoint should also be considered. On the one hand, despite demographic changes, the Soviet Union remains distinctly Russian, with a certain top-heaviness of administrative apparatus and a deeply ingrained suspicion of the West. This suspicion is hardly paranoid, considering that there have been seven (Polish, Swedish, French, two joint great power and two German) invasions from the West in the past four centuries. On the other hand, the Soviets too are now becoming dominated by the younger generation, and fear of the West has to compete with desire for domestic development. Indeed, suspicion has often been accompanied by envy, and envy could now support policies encouraging greater emphasis on the development of consumer products. Inducements to the West to reduce arms production and a change in the tone of rhetoric, both characteristic of the Gorbachev administration, would possibly ease such a transformation (Sestanovich 1987).

That Gorbachev might be more in tune with the younger generation while Ronald Reagan is of the older generation could be a factor in the difference in their rhetoric. In the 1990s younger generation perceptions are likely to dominate most governments, which could lead to the gradual emergence of policies of the sort described in this section. The perception exists, however, that with Gorbachev an opportune moment for reapproachment has arisen (Kavaloski 1986). It could be, however, if Russia and the U.S. are entering the middle phase of a "normal age," that decades rather than a passing moment are available for working out problems that can be resolved. Having such a time framework in mind could contribute to making such negotiations more fruitful.

THE ROLE OF THE ACTIVIST

If it is almost amusing to play the role of advisor to governments, it is another matter for an aging professor to communicate with a continually replenished group of activists, many young, idealistic, intelligent, passionate. They exist in considerable numbers all over the world, and despite observations here about the experiential quality of the younger generation, they want to *do* something about peace. Nevertheless, on the same if/then basis that applied to governments, what should activists do?

They could remember that activists are everywhere in the minority. They scare people. Or else, when they forecast the *dies irae* and it doesn't come, they can look comic, like the cartoon Judgment Day people.

So it would seem that the activist might be more successful if he were to assume there is time, and adopt approaches that would go with the tide, effecting changes through mainstream strategies. Instead of supporting nuclear freeze, which looks both threatening and inflexible, he might have greater success supporting those proposals that have to do with reducing arms expenditures or deciding against further commitments. Instead of marching on symbols or going to prison, it would probably be more effective to enter the political process, supporting more acceptable political candidates or becoming a party worker and eventually a candidate himself.

Instead of advocating disarmament conferences, an activist could advocate fiscal responsibility and oppose (to borrow a phrase from the conservative Russian bureaucrats of the 1960s) "hare-brained schemes" that cost billions and do nothing for security. Such advocacy could lead to reduced defense expenditure and eventually disarmament conferences.

Concerned Citizens for the Prevention of Nuclear Accidents might get some response, since this is a fear that affects everyone and resonates throughout society. This would seem to be an area in which there could be mutual cooperation and trust. It would be much easier for private groups to encourage such conferences, since there would be little need for confrontational activities and great opportunity to support government initiatives in this direction.

In general, it would appear that activists would probably be most effective if they concentrated their activities on trying to bring about those developments that might contribute toward the reduction of reasons for future encounters, encounters that otherwise would be likely to take place several decades hence, and they would be more effective if they tried to achieve these ends by mainstream methods.

The tide that is beginning to flow in this direction comes from the perception that mounting arms expenditures bring little security and much discomfort, and that perception in turn comes about because we are well into a normal period and a generation is coming to power that has never known anything else.

It would be well if the peace researcher and peace activist were to talk to one another, a goal William Eckhardt tries to achieve at annual American and Canadian peace meetings. The researcher should take the activist seriously, and try to be helpful; the activist might consider, from time to time, whether his worldview is in need of modification.

Again, it may not be appropriate for the researcher to try to suggest action to the activist. The very general suggestions made here may seem inappropriate to the analysis. But at the very least I can concur with Derber and Schwartz (1986, 42) that the seeking of technological solutions is inadequate to the deeper social problem of war and peace.

THE NEW ERA

A number of contemporary writers and thinkers have suggested in various ways the possibility that the world is at the dawn of a "New Era," a period of history that is qualitatively as different from past civilizations as these civilizations were from primitive societies. This theme emerges independently, from men pursuing all sorts of fields. Kenneth Boulding suggests that this period ought to be called "Post-Civilization," since it cannot at this stage have a generally accepted name (1964). One would have to wait a millennium or so for that.

Lewis Mumford (1956), despite his reservations about the modern world, sees the basic change as already setting in with the advent of modern European civilization, as early as the time of the Reformation, and he thinks that from this time on there have been two kinds of men: Old World men and New World men. The latter are gradually supplanting the former. Downing Bowler (1981) thinks that our full commitment to the empirical method, combined with an immense increase in our understanding of the basic nature of humankind, has put us on the threshhold of a period in which a much larger percentage of people might live vastly more fulfilling lives. David Richardson thinks we are experiencing a new civilizational worldview (1988).

There is another possibility, even more hopeful, but less likely. Rushton Coulborn (1959), looking at civilized societies from the other end, thought that volatile civilizations might just be a transitional phase between the long-lived, slow-changing primitive societies and some other equally stable social form. Could it be that in the Relational Age an understanding of social processes will be achieved that will enable man to alter social cycles during the World Wars crisis? By planned obsolescence, by manipulation of social patterns analogous to the medical manipulation of physical patterns, by correlating accurate quantitative analysis with sophisticated social hypotheses, could Faustian man succeed in prolonging the Relational Age and creating a "New Era" in which the 6,000-year history of civilizations will be seen as a brief transition from a long period of primitive culture to a long period of something else that is yet too obscure to have a name?

Boulding, reading a draft of this book, returns to another possibility and reenforces Coulborn's suggestion in another way. To argue, as I have done, that the role of weaponry has been exaggerated may overstate the case in the opposite direction:

> In social systems, especially in regard to war and peace, technical changes in weaponry and organization played this role: the invention of the mobile army, which created empires; the development of the effective cannon, which destroyed the feudal system and created the national state. Now, of course, the nuclear weapon, which I think you underestimate, which has now made national defense inviable and will lead us either to total destruction or to a world system of stable peace, which I don't think necessarily involves world government, though it probably does require world political institutions.

So if the problem is resolved, the resolution may be long lasting and permanent on a new level, just as the modern interstate system replaced the feudal system as the result of the development of the cannon.

This is both plausible and possible. But historians describing the origins of the modern Western state usually argue that the castle-destroying cannon was one of a number of factors interacting. And interstate systems have emerged where no such cannons existed (Wesson 1978; Wilkinson 1985), while feudal systems have fallen under different systems of weaponry (Coulborn 1956). Still, Boulding and I arrive at similar conclusions. The next phase would be either total destruction, or at least, destruction sufficient to usher in a new feudal system, or some sort of resolution well short of world government that would provide a period of stability Boulding hopes would be long lasting. How long? Ten or fifteen decades, as suggested here, or a few centuries, as has been the case for several historical empires?

The present obviously is different from the past in many ways. The technology of modern Western civilization dwarfs that of all other civilizations, including the West in its earlier phases. The amount of knowledge is far greater and continues to grow at some kind of frightening, geometrical rate. Our knowledge of the unconscious motivation for human behavior is rapidly growing, and this is also true of our understanding of irrational cultural influences. Commitment to the empirical method means much more emphasis on testing rational hypotheses. And now the relational outlook adds a new dimension.

On the other hand, there are many elements of continuity between the present and the past. The culture patterns that have such a strongly determining influence on the actions of individuals continue to exert this influence and we can, by studying patterns of social change and institutionalization, learn a good deal about how the behavior of man is irrationally channeled despite his knowledge and his technology capacity. Technology, however complex, is incorporated into group operations that are familiar. The amount of knowledge that exists is shared by a larger civilization, but that does not prove that individual capacities have been vastly expanded. Empiricism and relational outlook may be unique, but each civilization has had its unique aspects and has still functioned as a civilization. The Greeks were uniquely contained and secular. The Chinese have been unique in their use of a scholarly elite, in the intellectual and religious capacities of their gentry, and in their ability to create substantial, peaceful, political entities; the Indians were unique in the degree of their ideational orientation. The relatively slow-changing, well-integrated, consolidating nature of a crystallized period is also familiar and comparable to many other such periods sustained by civilizations.

Another factor that may give an exaggerated appearance of newness to the age in which we live is the expansive nature of Faustian man. It is his unique characteristic that he is moved to limitless extension, and this takes many forms, some of them—world exploration, space exploration, urban expansion—have rather spectacular effects. What Mumford saw as new, Spengler (1932) saw as the peculiar characteristic of a particular culture. But this characteristic is a manifestation of something basic; it is not necessarily basic itself.

The present world has many unique features, and it is important in understanding the period to distinguish the extent to which various phenomena are unique and the extent to which they are recurrences or similar to other variations. But "New Era" concepts are not particularly useful in understanding a period that can be explained with traditional concepts. For the Relational Age can be examined in its historical contexts; it does not require a new set of criteria. It has unique qualities, but so have all other epochs. What really makes the Relational Age unique is simply that we live in it.

THINGS BEING HOW THEY ARE

The analysis of this book has been that we are living in a period of relative peace that should continue for several decades, at least until the middle of the twenty-first century. It is understandable that the reader may want to put that in the subjunctive: if that were the case (because it is contrary to fact). But is there any use in such an elaborate deception?

The ghost of Norman Angell will not rest. Was it useful to people in 1912 or 1913 to read his book and relax their guard because (they thought) the author told them war was impossible? Were they not being lulled at the very time they should have been most vigilant? Is it, then, wise to tempt fate? Is it really not cruel and immoral deception to repeat the folly of Norman Angell, to once again promise peace when war may be imminent, and to compound the hubris by using Chamberlain's infamous phrase for a title?

Well, we have already discovered that Chamberlain never used the infamous phrase. And perhaps the ghost of Norman Angell will not rest because he never wrote that war was impossible. He wrote that it was illogical and unprofitable, but he never wrote and never thought that it was impossible. He was trying to make a case for his own government and others to modify their policies, because he thought they were heading for war, and he was right. Two decades later he wrote somewhat ruefully about how he had been labeled as the man who said war was impossible (Angell 1933) and how impossible it was to destroy the image once it had been established. Indeed it was. Fifty years later I still thought that he had written that war was impossible and it was only in preparing for this section that I discovered otherwise.

Of course, war is not impossible. But there is a good chance that there will be peace for several decades. If this is wrong, it doesn't make much difference. Nuclear war would come, and most people would be killed, whether or not they had prepared for it. Some might have been better prepared spiritually, but they ought to have been anyway, as the parable of the wise and foolish virgins suggests.

If, on the other hand, the analysis proved to be valid, what then? How might this affect our lives and particularly our social responsibilities?

First of all, it seems possible to work within the existing institutions, even for the purpose of disposing of other institutions. There are many useless policies and there are many useless agencies, but the younger generation will call these into question anyway. The policies will be changed even while they are being justified, the agencies will be circumvented, incorporated or even terminated. That is to say, they will be left without function, they will be merged, i.e., submerged under, some other agency, or they will be disbanded with praise and ceremony. The agencies that remain will undertake policies that are consistent with the worldview of the younger generation.

Individuals do not need to leave their positions or overthrow their governments. They may perform some useful services by adding new work to old (Jacobs 1969). They may add social functions to other kinds of production, and if what they add is successful, they may later neglect or subtract what seems less worthwhile. If you assume that time is on your side, that makes a difference.

The nuclear dilemma poses a different kind of problem for the individual. Anything that increases the possibility of accidental war should be opposed, since the odds are low against a nuclear war of policy for several decades. Working toward the reduced production of nuclear weapons won't further reduce the danger, but it may provide resources for other purposes and curb debt and inflation. It is difficult, however, to conceive of any social action that can resolve the nuclear dilemma in the next crisis period.

Action against nuclear energy is more problematical. It is difficult to feel any confidence that nonnuclear solutions can work. Nuclear energy should be pursued, but there is time. The problems of safety should be resolved first.

Within the Present Age, and for the next several decades, individual choices are open. There is no single overwhelming problem. Some may work to attain equality, some to fight poverty, some to preserve ecology, some to foster civilization. Each according to his ability may choose a task he can handle without feeling guilty about not helping to solve all other problems.

But it is possible to do something. It is not necessary to wait for the revolution or to withdraw permanently because of the hopelessness of the system. Possibly to speak of "doing" betrays the essential mentality of the older generation. One may be performing the work of a social worker, a businessman or a student at the same time that he is being in relation to other people with whom he comes in contact. If you can help people feel good about themselves while you are also doing something worth doing, so much the better. If you can influence their outlook, they may act more constructively.

It would be going too far to say that you are what you do, for what you are affects what you do, and what you do affects what you are. And Things Being How They Are, there are many alternatives open for accomplishment and relationship, for doing and being.

REFERENCES

Alexander, Lewis M., 1977, "Regional Arrangements in the Ocean," *American Journal of International Law* (71:84–109).

Allen, Peter, 1982, *The Yom Kippur War*, Scribner's.

Angell, Norman, 1913, *The Great Illusion*, Quaker City.

———, 1933, *The Great Illusion: 1933*, Putnam's.

Annual Abstract of Statistics, 1984, London, Her Majesty's Stationery Office.

Ardrey, Robert, 1961, *The Territorial Imperative*, Dell.

Arkin, William M. and James W. Fieldhouse, 1987, "State of War" in William M. Evan and Stephen Hilgartner, eds., *The Arms Race and Nuclear War*, Prentice-Hall, pp. 5–6.

Arnold, Anthony, 1985, *Afghanistan: The Soviet War*, St. Martin's Press.

Babst, Dean, 1964, "Elective Governments—A Force For Peace," *Wisconsin Sociologist*, 9–14.

Balzer, Richard, 1976, *Clockwork*, Doubleday.

Banfield, Edward, 1970, *The Unheavenly City*, Little, Brown & Co.

Barnet, Richard J., 1983, *The Alliance*, Simon and Schuster.

Beer, Francis, 1981, *War Versus Peace*, Freeman.

Bennett, Arnold, 1910, *Clayhanger*, Ayer Reprint, 1976.

Berger, Peter L. and Brigitte Berger, April 3, 1971, "The Blueing of America," *The New Republic* (164).

Berger, Peter L., 1974, *Pyramids of Sacrifice*, Doubleday.

Bidwell, Shelford, 1978, *World War 3*, Roxby Press.

Boulding, Kenneth, 1964, *The Meaning of the Twentieth Century*, Harper & Row.

———, 1981, *Evolutionary Economics*, Sage.

———, 1985, "Regions of Time," *Papers of the Regional Science Association*, v. 57, pp. 19–32.

Bouthoul, Gaston and René Carrere, 1978, "A List of the 366 Major Armed Conflicts of the Period 1740–1974," *Peace Research* (Compiled and Translated by Gernot Kohler), July (10:3).

————, 1979 "Major Armed Conflicts, 1965–July 1, 1978," *Peace Research* (Compiled and Translated by Gernot Kohler), October (11:4).

Bowler, T. Downing, 1981, *General Systems Thinking*, Elsevier/North Holland.

Bracey, Gerald W., 1987, "The Time Has Come to Abolish Research Journals," *The Chronicle of Higher Education*, March 25, p. 44.

Bradford, Sarah, 1983, *Disraeli*, Stein and Day.

Braudel, Fernand, 1979, *The Structures of Everyday Life*, Harper & Row.

Brown, Harrison, 1978, *The Human Future Revisited*, Norton.

Bureau of the Census, 1975, *Historical Statistics of the United States*, U.S. Government Printing Office.

Caldwell, Dan, 1984, "Introduction to the Transaction Edition," in United States Arms Control and Disarmament Agency, *Arms Control and Disarmament Agreements*, Sixth Edition, Transaction Books.

Camus, Albert, 1946, *The Stranger*, Knopf.

Cargan, Leonard, 1977, *Wei Reninin Fiv Wu*, Wright State University.

Cargan, Leonard and Matthew Melko, 1982, *Singles: Myths and Realities*, Sage.

Cheever, John, 1981, *The Stories of John Cheever*, Random House.

Clayton, Bruce Douglas, 1977, "Planning for the Day After Doomsday," *The Bulletin of the Atomic Scientists*, September.

Clough, Shepard and Charles Cole, 1952, *Economic History of Europe*, 3rd. ed., Heath.

Cohen, Eliot A., 1987, "Computer Combat," *The New Republic*, April 20, pp. 15–17.

Cohen, Stephen F., 1985, *Sovieticus: American Perceptions and Soviet Realities*, Norton.

"Cold Peace," 1984, *New Republic*, Oct. 1.

Coleman, James S. *et al.*, 1966, *Equality of Educational Opportunity*, U.S. Department of Health, Education and Welfare.

Cornish, Blake M., 1984, "A Global Assessment of Problems and Opportunities," *The Futurist*, 18:5 (October), pp. 29–31.

Coudenhove-Kalergi, Richard, 1959. *From War to Peace*, Cape.

Coulborn, Rushton, ed., 1956, *Feudalism in History*, Princeton University Press.

————, 1959, *The Origin of Civilized Societies*, Princeton University Press.

Crankshaw, Edwin, 1962, *Khrushchev's Russia*, Penguin.

Crime in the United States. 1982, 1983, U.S. Department of Justice.

Denton, F. H., 1966, "Some Regularities in International Conflict, 1820–1949," *Background*, 9:4, pp. 283–296.

Drucker, Peter, 1969, *The Age of Discontinuity*, Harper & Row.

Eckhardt, William, 1975, "Primitive Militarism," *Journal of Peace Research*, 12:55–62.

————, 1987, "Cost of Military Intervention, 1817–1986, unpublished.

Edwards, William E., 1985, "The Insular Integration Theory of the Origin of Civilizations," ISCSC Archives.

Ellul, Jacques, 1967, *The Technological Society*, Random House.

————, 1978, *The Betrayal of the West*, Seabury, Tr. by Matthew J. O'Connell.

Epstein, William, 1973, "The Disarmament Hoax," *World* (April 10, 1973), 24–29.

Etzioni, Amitai. 1971, *Active Society*, Free Press.

European Historical Statistics, 1975, Statistical Office of the European Communities, Luxembourg.

Evan, William M. and Stephen Hilgartner, eds., 1987, *The Arms Race and Nuclear War*, Prentice-Hall.

Ferencz, Benjamin G., 1985, *A Common Sense Guide to World Peace,* Oceana Publications.

Feuer, Lewis, 1969, *The Conflict of Generations,* Basic Books.

Forrester, Jay, 1969, *Urban Dynamics,* MIT Press.

Fromm, Erich, 1956, *The Art of Loving,* Harper & Row.

Galbraith, John K. 1967, *The New Industrial State,* Houghton Mifflin.

George, Susan, 1977, *How the Other Half Dies,* Rowman and Allanheld.

Girardet, Edward, 1985, *Afghanistan: The Soviet War,* St. Martin's Press.

Goodspeed, D. J., 1977, *The German Wars: 1914–1945,* Houghton-Mifflin.

Gordon, Michael R., 1986, "Accidental War is Topic," *Dayton Daily News,* May 7, p. 9, *New York Times* News Service.

Goudsmit, S. A., May, 1963, "Credo of an Angry Old Man," *The Bulletin of the Atomic Scientists.*

Graham, Hugh and Ted Gurr, 1979, *Violence in America,* Rev. Ed., Sage.

Gustaitis, Rasa, 1982, "Old vs. Young in Florida: Preview of an Aging America" in Leonard Cargan and Jeanne Ballantine, *Sociological Footprints,* 2nd. ed., Wadsworth, pp. 219–225.

Halperin, John, 1983, *C. P. Snow: An Oral Biography,* St. Martin's Press.

Heilbronner, Robert. 1980, *An Inquiry Into the Human Prospect,* Norton.

Henslin, James M. and Donald W. Light, Jr., 1983, *Social Problems,* McGraw-Hill.

Herz, John. 1959, *International Politics in the Atomic Age,* Columbia University Press.

Horowitz, Irving Louis, 1982, *Beyond Empire and Revolution,* Oxford University Press.

Insight Team, London *Sunday Times,* 1974, *The Yom Kippur War,* Doubleday.

Islam, A. K. M. Aminul, 1978, *Victorious Victims,* Schenkman.

Jacobs, Jane, 1969, *The Economy of the Cities,* Random House.

Jencks, Christopher *et al.,* 1972, *Inequality: A Reassessment of the Effect of Family and Schooling in America,* Basic Books.

Kahn, Herman, 1978, *On Thermonuclear War,* Greenwood (1961 Reprint).

———, 1982, *The Coming Boom: Economic, Political and Social,* Simon and Schuster.

Kaldor, Mary, 1978, *The Disintegrating West,* Hill and Wang.

———, 1981, *The Baroque Arsenal,* Hill and Wang.

Kavaloski, Vincent, 1986, Presentation at meeting of the Consortium on Peace Research, Education and Development, Iowa City.

Kavolis, Vytautas, 1972, *History on Art's Side,* Cornell University Press.

Kennan, George F., 1981, "A Proposal for International Disarmament," Institute for World Order.

Kenny, Anthony, 1986, *The Logic of Deterrence,* University of Chicago Press.

Klein, Ross, 1981, "David Versus Goliath: The Big Power of Small States," American Sociological Association.

Knopf, Alfred, 1965, *Publishing Then and Now: 1912–1964,* New York Public Library.

Koebernick, Thomas E. and David Michael Orenstein, 1990, "Memories of the Past, Fears for the Future, When the City is at the Gates," North Central Sociological Association.

Kohler, Gernot, 1977, Review of Gaston Bouthoul and Rene Carrere, *Le Defi de la Guerre (1740–1974), Peace Research,* 9:4, pp. 189–90.

Kohr, Leopold, 1977, *The Overdeveloped Nations,* Schocken Books.

Krauthammer, Charles, 1987, "Gorbachev's Gambit: Captain Zero Option," *The New Republic,* March 30, pp. 12–14.

Kroeber, A. L., 1944, *The Configurations of Culture Growth*, University of California Press.

Kuhn, Thomas, 1962, *The Structure of Scientific Revolutions*, University of Chicago Press.

Lane, Robert, 1969, "Urbanization and Criminal Violence in the Nineteenth Century" in Hugh Graham and Ted Gurr, *Violence in America*, Praeger.

Lappe, Francis Moore and Joseph Collins, 1977, *Food First: Beyond the Myth of Scarcity*, Houghton Mifflin.

Lasch, Christopher, 1978, *The Culture of Narcissism*, Norton.

Leitenberg, Milton, September 1975, "Obscene Definition," *The Bulletin of the Atomic Scientists* (Vol. 31).

Lifton, Robert Jay, 1967, *Death in Life*, Basic Books.

Lippman, Walter S., 1955, *Essays in the Public Philosophy*, Little Brown.

————, 1961, *The Coming Tests with Russia*, Little Brown.

Lorenz, Konrad, 1966, *On Aggression*, Harcourt, Brace.

Lukacs, John, 1961, *A History of the Cold War*, Doubleday.

————, 1978, *1945: Year Zero*, Doubleday.

Marcuse, Herbert, 1964, *One Dimensional Man*, Beacon Press.

McLuhan, Marshall, *The Gutenberg Galaxy*, University of Toronto Press.

Melko, Matthew, 1969, *The Nature of Civilizations*, Porter Sargent.

————, 1971, *Eight Schools of Thought on the Nuclear Dilemma*, Bradford College Publication.

————, 1973, *52 Peaceful Societies*, Canadian Peace Research Institute.

————, 1984, "State Systems in Harmonious Conflict," ISCSC Archives, Dickinson College.

———— and Ellen Murray, 1984, "The Magnitude of Fatalities," North Central Sociological Association, Indianapolis.

————, and Leighton Scott (editors), 1987, *The Boundaries of Civilizations in Space and Time*, University Press of America.

Miller, Henry, 1961, *Tropic of Cancer*, Grove.

Mitchell, B. R. and Phyllis Deane, 1962, *Abstract of British Historical Statistics*, Cambridge U. Press.

Mitchell, B. R., 1975, *European Historical Statistics*, Columbia U. Press.

Morgenthau, Hans, 1973, *Politics Among Nations*, 5th ed., Knopf.

————, 1975, "Explaining Failures of U.S. Foreign Policy: Three Paradoxes," *The New Republic*, v. 173 n. 15, pp. 16–21.

Mumford, Lewis, 1956, *The Transformation of Man*, Harper.

————, 1961, *The City in History*, Harcourt, Brace and World.

Naisbitt, John, 1983, *Megatrends*, Warner Books.

Naroll, Raoul, Vern Bullough and Frada Naroll, 1974, *Military Deterrence in History*, State University of New York Press.

O'Heffernan, Patrick *et al.*, 1983, *The First Nuclear War*.

Orenstein, David, 1985, *The Sociological Quest*, West.

Orwell, George, 1949, *1984*, New American Library (1981 reprint).

Palmer, Alan and Veronica, 1977, *Quotations in History*, Barnes & Noble.

Postel, Sandra, 1984, "Forests in a Fossil-Fuel World," *The Futurist*, 18:4 (August), pp. 39–46.

Powers, Thomas, 1984, "Nuclear Winter and Nuclear Strategy," *Atlantic Monthly*, November.

Price, Jerome, 1982, *The Antinuclear Movement*, Twayne.

Quigley, Carroll, 1961 (Liberty Press Reprint, 1979), *The Evolution of Civilizations*, Macmillan.

Rake, Launce, 1986, "Economic Problems Balloon," *Wright Stater* (Spring), 18:2, p. 5.

Redfield, Robert, 1953, *The Primitive World and its Transformations,* Cornell University Press.

Reinhold, Robert, 1982, "The Legacy of Woodstock" in Leonard Cargan and Jeanne Ballantine, *Sociological Footprints,* 2nd. ed., Wadsworth.

Reischauer, Edwin R., 1981, *The Japanese,* Harvard University Press.

Richardson, David B., 1977, "Sino-Japanese and Contemporary Architecture: Philosophical Influences and Parallels," *Chinese Culture* (XVIII:4), December.

————, n.d., *The Faustian I World-View,* Edinboro, PA, Unpublished Manuscript.

Richardson, Lewis F., 1960, *Statistics of Deadly Quarrels,* The Boxwood Press.

Rifkin, Jeremy, 1981, *Entropy,* Viking.

Russell, Bertrand, 1969, *Power,* Norton.

Sjoberg, Gideon, 1960, *The Preindustrial City,* The Free Press.

Small, Melvin and J. David Singer, 1979, "Conflict in the International System, 1816–1977: Historical Trends and Policy Futures," in Charles W. Kegley, Jr. and Patrick J. McGowan, eds., *Challenges to America: U.S. Foreign Policy in the 1980's,* Sage.

Snow, C. P., 1959, *The Two Cultures and the Scientific Revolution,* Cambridge University Press.

Solotaroff, Ted, 1987, "The Literary-Industrial Complex," *The New Republic,* June 8, pp. 28–45.

Sorokin, Pitirim A., 1944, *The Crisis of Our Age,* Dutton.

————, 1957, *Social and Cultural Dynamics,* Abridged Edition, Porter Sargent.

Spengler, Oswald, 1932, *The Decline of the West,* Allen & Unwin, Atkinson translation (Knopf reprint, 1980).

Spock, Benjamin, 1976, 3rd. ed., *Baby and Child Care,* Dutton.

Statistical Abstracts of the United States, 1983–1988, U.S. Bureau of the Census.

Stavrianos, L. S., 1976, *The Promise of the Coming Dark Age,* Freeman.

Steffens, Lincoln, 1931, *Autobiography,* Harcourt Brace, reprinted 1968.

Steinhart, Peter, 1984, "Ecological Saints," *Audubon,* July.

Stevenson, Burton, 1967, *The Home Book of Quotations,* Dodd, Mead.

Taubes, Gary, 1987, "Is Anything Left Out There?," *Discover,* April.

Thomlinson, Ralph, 1965, *Population Dynamics,* Random House.

Thompson, E. P., 1985, *The Heavy Dancers,* Pantheon.

Thurber, James, 1945, *The Thurber Carnival,* Harper.

Toffler, Alvin, 1970, *Future Shock,* Random House.

————, 1980, *The Third Wave,* Morrow.

Toynbee, Arnold, 1961, *A Study of History,* 12 vols., Oxford University Press.

Trollope, Anthony, 1869, *Phineas Finn,* Oxford University Press Reprint, 1949.

Tucker, Robert W., 1986, *The Nuclear Debate: Deterrence and the Lapse of Faith,* Holmes and Meier.

United States Arms Control and Disarmament Agency, 1984, *Arms Control and Disarmament Agreements,* Sixth Edition, Transaction Books.

Viccica, Antoinette D., 1980, "World Crime Trends," *International Journal of Offender Therapy and Comparative Criminology* (Vol. 24:3).

Sartre, Jean Paul, 1956, *Being and Nothingness,* Philosophical Library.

Scanlan, R. S., 1985, "The Western Empire," ISCSC Archives, Dickinson College.

Schumaker, E. F., 1975, *Small is Beautiful,* Harper and Row.

Schwartz, William A. and Charles Derber, 1986, "Arms Control: Misplaced Focus, *The Bulletin of the Atomic Scientists*, March, pp. 39–44.

———, Charles Derber, Gordon Fellman, William Gamson, Morris Schwartz, Patrick Withen, 1989, *The Nuclear Seduction: Why the Arms Race Doesn't Matter—and What Does*, University of California Press.

Sestanovich, Stephen, 1987, "What Gorbachev Wants," *The New Republic*, May 25, pp. 20–23.

Sheed, Wilfrid, 1965, *Square's Progress*, Farrar, Straus and Giroux.

Shorter, Edward, 1975, *The Making of the Modern Family*, Basic Books.

Sinai, I. Robert, 1978, *The Decadence of the Modern World*, Schenkman.

Singer, J. David, 1977, "The Historical Experiment as a Research Strategy in the Study of World Politics," *Social Science History*, 2:1 (Fall), pp. 1–22.

———, and David and Melvin Small, 1972, *The Wages of War: 1816–1965*, Wiley.

Sivard, Ruth Leger, 1985, *World Military and Social Expenditures*, World Policy Institute.

Vidich, Arthur J. and Bensman, Joseph, 1968 (Original 1958), *Small Town in Mass Society*, Rev. edition, Princeton University Press.

Vital Statistics of the United States, 1978, Vol. II, *Morality*, Public Health Services, Washington, D.C.

Wagar, Warren, 1977, *World Views: A Study of Comparative History*, Holt, Rinehart & Winston.

Warnke, Paul C., 1978, "Arms Control: A Global Imperative," *The Bulletin of the Atomic Scientists*, June.

Watson, Russell, *et al.*, 1987, "Arms Control: 'The Fix is In,'" *Newsweek*, May 4.

Weber, Max, 1961, *The Protestant Ethic and the Spirit of Capitalism*, Tr. by Talcott Parsons, Free Press.

Welty, Gordon, 1984, "Horizontal and Unauthorized Nuclear Proliferation as Impediments to Nuclear Disarmament," University of Dayton.

Wesson, Robert G., 1967, *The Imperial Order*, University of California Press.

———, 1978, *State Systems*, Free Press.

———, 1979, "Wrong Number?" *Natural History*, March, pp. 9–21.

———, 1986, "Superpowers and Their Spheres," Hoover Institution.

Weston, Burns, 1987, Address to Members of the Consortium on Peace Research, Education and Development, University of Iowa.

Wheatcroft, Geoffrey, 1984, "The Anguish of Africa," *The New Republic*, January 9–16, pp. 18–23.

Whyte, William, 1957, *The Organization Man*, Simon and Schuster.

Wilkinson, David, 1980, *Deadly Quarrels: Lewis F. Richardson and the Statistical Study of War*, University of California Press.

———, 1985, "State Systems: Ethos and Pathos," ISCSC Archives.

———, 1985, "General War," *Dialectics and Humanism* (Nos. 3–4), pp. 45–57.

———, 1986, "States Systems: Pathology and Survival," ISCSC Archives.

Willard, Timothy, *et al.*, 1984, "A Worldview Sampler," *The Futurist*, 18:5 (October), pp. 32–39.

Williams, William Appleman, 1980, *Empire as a Way of Life*, Oxford University Press.

Woolf, Leonard, 1975, *Downhill All the Way*, Harcourt, Brace and Jovanovich.

Wright, Quincy, 1942, *A Study of War,* University of Chicago Press.
Zuckerman, Edward, 1984, *The Day After World War III,* Viking.

Papers designated ISCSC Archives may be obtained by inquiry to the ISCSC Archives Librarian, Dickinson College, Carlisle, PA 17013.